Other Books in this Field
by HARRY F. WARD

OUR ECONOMIC MORALITY

THE PROFIT MOTIVE

THE NEW SOCIAL ORDER

IN PLACE OF PROFIT

DK 26
W36

IN PLACE OF PROFIT

SOCIAL INCENTIVES IN THE SOVIET UNION

HARRY F. WARD

WITH DRAWINGS BY LYND WARD

CHARLES SCRIBNER'S SONS
NEW YORK · LONDON · 1933

Copyright, 1933, by
HARRY F. WARD

Printed in the United States of America

All rights reserved. No part of this book may be reproduced in any form without the permission of Charles Scribner's Sons

A

P R E F A C E

Feb. 12

This book comes out of a personal necessity. For some years it has been part of my work to analyse the ethics of capitalist society, particularly at the point of motivation. In the summer of 1924 I went to Moscow to see whether the New Economic Policy meant a return to capitalism. As the Five Year Plan moved to success, it became necessary for me to take the first opportunity to stay long enough in the Soviet Union to satisfy myself whether the building of socialism was developing incentives which promised more for the continuing of human society than those which are manifestly failing in the capitalist world. This opportunity came during 1931–2.

The result is necessarily an analysis of a going concern without its historical background. Within its own field it is not a picture of the whole scene but of the dominant tendencies. That they are dominant is proved by the degree of success they have achieved in laying the foundations of a machine-making industry, a socialized agriculture, and a universal culture. That they will more and more prevail is evident in the attitudes of youth and in the increasing support of the intelligentsia and the peasantry for the objectives of social-economic planning. Current difficulties in food supply and consumers' goods

GIFT 766

were observed in their initial stage and discounted as "infantile diseases" for which the remedy is known and begins to be used.

The data, and the interpretation, have been checked in Leningrad, Moscow, the Central Black Soil Belt, the Volga Region, four out of six of the Trans-Caucasus Soviet Republics, and the Ukraine. We travelled alone and lived, most of the time, not in hotels but with the people, thus seeing things from the inside. Lenin's forecast of the forms of initiative and organisation that would appear in the transition period and Stalin's views on the Party were not read until these things had been seen and judged in operation.

The reader needs to remember continually that forms of organisation are rapidly changing in the Soviet Union, because the present period is definitely viewed and controlled as the transition between capitalism and communism. Therefore there is no such rigidity as we are accustomed to in the social and political structure of capitalist society. What is constant is the general direction and the guiding principles, but even these are regarded as in process of development. Unless this is understood the Soviet scene is inevitably misinterpreted.

The illustrative incidents of the book are selected only in the sense that those which most picturesquely represent the general tendency are naturally always taken by a writer. The amount of such material available is literally legion. An arbitrary line had to be drawn in its accumulation and much had to be ruthlessly omitted. The interested reader will find plenty more in the Moscow publications in English—"Moscow Daily News," the "Soviet Culture Review," and "International Literature."

Statistics I have left out as far as possible, because they change so rapidly and because the quantitative method nowhere reveals its inadequacy with such conclusiveness as in an attempt to interpret the Soviet scene.

I have included an unusual number of quotations; first to avoid the danger of misinterpretation, and next to provide necessary details for the technically interested. Those quoted most frequently are Stalin, who holds no government post but is Secretary of the Central Committee of the Communist Party; Molotov, who is the executive head of the government, being Chairman of the Council of People's Commissars; and Yakoklev, who is People's Commissar for Agriculture, which branch of production is the key to the whole situation. Quotations appear in my text in italic and those taken from sources already translated I have not altered.

I have not inserted any exact source references because to do this for Russian material, unavailable to readers, seemed both pedantic and a needless waste of paper and labor. For the convenience of those who are interested, I have added a list of my sources in English, but many of those cannot now be had.

Instead of a glossary of Russian words and phrases I have explained their meaning the first time they are used, thinking the reader will remember it better in its context than if it were standing by itself. It should also be remembered that many English equivalents have a different meaning in the Soviet environment. For instance the word *government* has a different connotation when the state administers industry and agriculture, but sometimes the old meaning, or part of it, hangs over and confuses the understanding of what is happening.

My obligations to various people and institutions are heavy. To VOKS—the Society for Cultural Relations with Foreign Countries—and particularly to its Anglo-American Section, I am indebted for much assistance in arranging contacts and living conditions; also for permission to reproduce material from its monthly journal. The editors of Literature of the World Revolution, The Co-operative Publishing Society of Foreign Workers in the USSR, and International Publishers, were also kind enough to accord me the same privilege. I am indebted to Professor M. Krivitzky of the section on Economics of Labor in the Communist Academy at Moscow for permission to see material in course of preparation for the press.

To the various interpreters who gave me their efficient aid, to those busy men and women who gave freely of their time and interest to answer my questions and to those workers who, having resided in The United States, Canada or Australia, could take me past the barrier of an alien tongue, I express my grateful acknowledgment.

Very heavy is my debt to J. F. Hecker, who placed at my service so generously and understandingly his exceptional skill as translator, his knowledge of Soviet forces, events and personalities, and the results of his study of Revolutionary Philosophy. When that is published, those who are interested will be able to get a much wider knowledge of the subject.

Heaviest of all is my obligation to Daisy Kendall Ward. Without her companionship, care, and assistance, this material could not have been gathered; without her constructive criticism it would not be in its present form; but for her painstaking revision the manuscript could not have been made ready for the press in the time at my disposal for that purpose.

HARRY F. WARD.

FLINTFORD, SOMERSET,
July, 1932.

CONTENTS

CONTENTS

PART TWO

THE INITIATIVE OF THE MASSES

PART THREE

NEW FORMS OF CONTROL

C O N T E N T S

C O N T E N T S

PART ONE

SHIFTING INCENTIVES

CHAPTER I

THE PASSING OF THE OLD

In the long record of human society—so short beside the story of the stars—the basic fact is always economic activity. Upon that all the other pursuits of man—his loving and fighting, his thinking and dreaming—depend; by it they are conditioned. Hence the power and permanence of any social system are determined by its ability adequately to maintain, and direct to its desired ends, the will to work. The inability of capitalism to do this is now sufficiently demonstrated. At the same time the foundations of a socialist society, in heavy industries, power plants, mechanised agriculture, and cultural equipment, are being laid by the third largest unit of the world's population—embracing more than a hundred and fifty nationalities and occupying one-sixth of the earth's surface—at a rate unparalleled in history.

The essential difference between capitalist and socialist motivation is summarised in the proposal to organise industry for use instead of for profit or, in the language of ethics, to substitute the will to serve for the will to gain. In actual operation the change of course is not so simple. The same forces have moved the children of men to action from the beginning of time, and will continue to move them until the end of days. They have been classified in turn by the ethical philosopher, the economist, the psychologist. What changes, from age to age, is the form and order and proportion in which they are used. Therefore to understand the motive power that is building socialism in the

Soviet Union it is necessary to know which of the capitalist forms of incentive they are doing without, what content they are putting into those they are still using, and what new forms they are developing.

The direct economic incentives upon which capitalism depends—the hope of gain and the fear of loss—socialist thinking has always rejected because of their antisocial consequences and their degradation of human nature. Therefore the basic law of the Soviet Union treats them as evil spirits not to be given a resting place, and in practice the Communists refuse to use them.

ECONOMIC INSECURITY

The defenders of capitalism regard it as essential that both millionaire and day laborer should be driven to work by the possibility and the fear of economic disaster. Communist thinkers regard this as only a rationalisation of the inability or unwillingness to control "the blind forces of the market." So one of the first objectives of the Soviet planned economy is to relieve the worker entirely of that haunting fear of sickness and old age that dogs the footsteps of so many wage earners in other lands. From the risks and hazards of work and life he is protected by a system of social insurance which covers all employed persons, including the vast majority of students. In contrast to less complete systems elsewhere, all costs are borne by the employer. But since the employer is either a governmental agency or a government-controlled co-operative society, and since both are organized by and for the workers, what this means in practice is that a certain part of the common product is withheld from consumption and applied to future personal emergencies by the approved technique of insurance. Thus the risk is lifted from the shoulders of the individual and distributed mutually on the backs of all concerned. Thus the Soviet worker has no worry at all about the expenses of sickness, childbirth, or death.

The payment of unemployment benefits has been abolished because of the confidence of the Soviet authorities that the unemployment problem has been solved forever by the demands of socialist construction under the planning system; also for the practical reason that such payments were keeping alive the tendency of the Russian worker to migrate from place to place, which was seriously menacing industrial efficiency. So instead of the fifty million rubles that were paid out in unemployment benefits in 1930 twice that sum was provided in the 1931 budget for the training of new industrial workers. The cost of this kind of unemployment for purposes of training for jobs which are crying for competent workers is of course a constructive expense. Certainly there is now no unemployment problem in the Soviet Union, and if no disaster in the capitalist world outside prevents them from finishing their industrial plant and attaining efficiency in production, the only factor which could produce one would be mismanagement in the distribution of labor. Collectivisation is substituting for migration from the villages to the cities a controlled exchange of labor between factory and farm. Rationalisation does not throw workers into idleness because the rising standard of living demands more production. The planning system enables control of market crises. As one skilled worker, with years of experience abroad, put it, "with a hundred and sixty million people busy supplying each other's needs there is work for everybody for a hundred years."

The Soviet worker is also relieved from that haunting fear of discharge which so many wage earners in other lands carry with them daily to their places of work. Job ownership—a socialist property right—is guaranteed to him, in so far as that can be done compatibly with industrial efficiency. There is an elaborate section of the Soviet labor code concerning dismissal and advance dismissal pay. Its provisions extend also to domestic workers, home industries, and seasonal workers. It is designed "to protect the interests of the workers and to prohibit unwarranted dismissals." The freedom to discharge, considered so essential for efficiency by many capitalist owners and managers, does not exist in the Soviet Union. The worker can be dismissed only for demonstrated inefficiency or proven anti-social conduct. But the exigencies of the Five Year Plan make labor behavior a matter of general social control rather than of formal rights and duties between employer and employee. In the development of socialist industry that relationship is changed, and the new status brings with it its own forms of control. It is not because of any formal protection in the labor code, but because the nature of industry is changing under the socialist system, that one of the first things American workers in a Soviet plant say when you ask them how they like their new atmosphere is, "Well, I don't have to worry about a job." The next thing they always say is, "Now I don't have to worry about my family in case anything happens to me."

The same economic security is being extended to the former intellectuals who are serving in the new order. Its material benefits and its cultural advantages are now open to them and their children. The younger set are of course to the manor born. Through their membership in the union and Communist organisations, by their training and experience as workers, they have a secured position. In contrast to millions of graduates of high schools and colleges elsewhere they have received their assignment before graduation; indeed many of them have been already working at it as a part of their education. Over against the increasingly limited economic horizon for the professional classes in capitalist society, socialist construction offers an unlimited expansion. On the boat going to Leningrad was an American steel-construction engineer. *Why? Well, for six months now the firm for whom I've worked twenty years has been calling us into the office at the end of the month and telling us they didn't know whether they could keep us after the next pay-day.*

The increasing growth and success of collective farming is also removing the fears born of economic insecurity from the life of the poor and middle peasants. They now produce and sell by contracts covering amount, price, and quality. So their income is determined by a plan, based on cost accounting, instead of a market whose fluctuations may ruin them. Also their risks, like the factory workers, are now shared. When they are asked why they prefer to be in the *kolhoz*—collective farm—they frequently put this fact first. Said one woman, *Before, when our cow died, I was sick. When they buried her out in the field I said "they'll put me there next." Now I don't have to worry if a cow dies. I know there are plenty more.*

An increasing economic efficiency releases these peasants from bondage to their own ignorance and laziness, as they have been released from financial slavery to landlords and *kulaks*—rich farmers. When the speculative market with its blind forces gives way to the scientific organisation of economic activities, economic insecurity is reduced to man's dependence upon nature.

Of course when the responsibility for security is transferred to the collective organisation some individuals will not work so hard. This has to be overcome by education, especially among the peasants. In their first stage, several of the communes had to weed out members who thought that communal living involved the right to share without the obligation to work or that it meant less work. A farm organiser on the Pervaya Pyatiletka Kolhoz says they had not many examples of good organised work *when we started collectivisation in 1930 . . . In most cases it was the middle farmers who were guilty of doing bad work. They failed to take the interests of the collective farm to heart, saying, "This is not my property—it belongs to the collective farm. Why should I work hard?"* Then those with vision start the educational process. When brigade No. 1 on a collective farm fell behind on the weeding plan and turned out only eighty-two out of its two hundred and fifty available workers, the women saying they must have time to bake their bread, the chairman told them: *The first brigade must understand that our fate is in our own hands. If we go on working at that rate and spend our time baking bread, we will soon have no bread to bake, and there is nobody that will give it to us. . . . You can bake your bread early in the morning and come out to work after breakfast. Don't expect anybody to do your work for you. Nowadays those who don't work don't get anything to eat.*

In such manner whatever propulsion for labor there is in economic insecurity is being socialised. Workers and peasants are learning in actual experience what the thinkers have declared, that from the acceptance of mutual dependence comes independence of want and fear.

Also they are finding that the recognition of the right of maintenance for all is one of the strongest bonds for society as it has long been in the family. When this is accepted as a common obligation it increases instead of diminishes personal responsibility. So an educational leader in the Pioneer organisation for children declares in criticising the saving-box plan of the Boy Scouts, that they *call the children into the struggle to destroy that situation in which it is necessary to lay aside pennies in the bank in order to provide for "the evil day." Amongst us the uncertainty about tomorrow is destroyed with the liquidation of unemployment. In our country which is building up socialism everybody knows that his future is provided for since he himself creates this future.*

PROFIT AND PROPERTY

The capitalist world proclaims the profit motive to be its great stimulus. It looks to the spirit of money-making for its chief motive power. Socialists of all schools, on the other hand, believe with the early Christians that the love of money is the root of all evil, at least in so far as society is concerned. Therefore when the Soviet Socialist Republic was organised profit was outlawed, the profit makers were dispossessed and then denied citizenship. So today throughout the length and breadth of the Soviet Union the making of profit is relentlessly punished with religious zeal in what looks to the outside world a terrible and unwarranted persecution of kulaks and petty speculators.

Soviet economists contend that the profit motive cannot develop in their country because the source of profit has been eliminated. This source according to Marx is surplus value. He also traces rent and interest to the same source. The concept of surplus value rests upon an analysis of the economic process in all stages of society which led Marx to decide that all value is created by labor because, he says, in a simple economy, in which the producers are also owners and sellers, the level around which price fluctuates depends in the last resort upon the expenditure of labor. So, he argues, the value of commodities is determined by the amount of socially necessary labor-time expended in their production or necessary to reproduce them. Labor-power also has become a commodity in the capitalist system and is bought by the capitalist on the same basis. But labor is then able to create more than its market value which has been paid in wages. That part of his time in which the worker reproduces the value of his labor-power Marx called necessary time, that in which he creates surplus value for the capitalist he called surplus time. The value created in this time is surplus value. It goes to the capitalist and is the object of the capitalist mode of production. The process of extracting it is what the socialists mean by exploitation, and those who get it they call exploiters.

In their "Outline of Political Economy," including Soviet Economics, Lapidus and Ostrovityanov point out the obvious fact that in the Soviet Union the two main conditions of surplus value, namely the concentration of the means of production in the hands of the capitalist class and the wage market, do not exist. Wages are still paid, but under this form is an entirely different human relationship from that in which the worker sells his labor-power in what is virtually a commodity market. In state enterprises the worker disposes of his labor-power "to the same working class of which he is a component part and which is the owner of all state undertakings." True enough he gives surplus labor but it goes into the further development of socialist industry which he owns and whose advantages he later enjoys, into social services and cultural opportunities for himself and his children, and to the maintenance of the state which is a proletarian dictatorship and so of service to his class. Of profit in any other sense there is no thought. Instead of surplus value the output of socialist surplus labor is called "surplus product," recognising that the term is not quite satisfactory because it presupposes the absence of exchange which still exists. It might be called what in fact it is, "the social surplus," that is the surplus needed above maintenance costs for social purposes. The difference between this and such portion of the net profit as gets used for social purposes in the capitalist economy is first that the amount needed is determined in advance and sought under a definite plan, and next that its making and use are directed by the workers themselves in ways later to be described. They do not get it from the arbitrary bounty of others.

The same reasoning is applied by these writers to the surplus product taken by the state from the peasants who are not yet participating in the socialist economy, whose economic and cultural benefits are open to them: *The appropriation of part of the peasants' income by the workers' state cannot be regarded as exploitation because the proletarian dictatorship guarantees the overwhelming majority of small peasants their development toward socialism through the most simple and easy method—the co-operation and industrialisation of agriculture.*

It is also pointed out that in the present transitional stage of Soviet economy the "law of value" continues to operate. There is still a price system and, as long as they must trade with a capitalist world, it cannot be absolutely controlled by the planners. Nevertheless the contention is that the "law of value" is in process of being transformed into the law of "expenditure of labor," that is, the conscious regulation of productive relations according to measured needs and standards agreed upon. It is argued that when value is used in planned regulation its essence begins to disintegrate. Certainly a planned economy changes its nature. So these Soviet economists, making the wish the father of the thought, expect the form also to be completely changed. They look forward to the abolition of money as well as wages and the development of a system of exchange of goods and services through labor certificates of the amount of time consumed.

However that may be, the practical fact is that the profit motive is on the way to extinction through the lack of opportunities for its exercise. After the old profit seekers were dispossessed, a system was constructed that makes it almost impossible for their successors to be produced. Practically the only opportunity now for individual profits is by speculating in food or clothing. This is a procedure which daily becomes more hazardous; first because, as socialist distribution increases, the shortage of foods and goods available for private trade causes extreme price fluctuations, and next because it is illegal. It will cease in the near future not by more thorough law enforcement but because the emphasis in the second Five Year Plan upon the production of consumers' goods and the improvement of the distributing system will automatically wipe out the speculators' market. When Molotov announced the slogan "learn to trade" at the recent party conference, he meant of course learn to organise distribution efficiently.

For those who are in the Soviet system the principle

of maximum income is in effect, not by decree but through practical conditions. Hence there is no margin for accumulation. Nor is there any need of it since social insurance takes care of financial emergencies and, now that the care and education of children are provided for by community funds, the custom of inheritance naturally disappears save for the passing on of a few personal belongings. There being no opportunity for speculative profits or for the ownership of productive capital, the investment market and its practices do not exist. The fact that the small producer may, in the collective farm and the industrial artel, in some cases draw interest on the capital he has put in or on his membership fee does not constitute an exception. This is no more than supplementary income, making no more than a decent living standard, and cannot possibly become the foundation of capitalist procedure. The same is true of the purchase of government bonds—or "obligations" as they are preferably called—of which several series have been issued, each for a term of ten years. They have been floated by use of the same sort of methods and social pressure that were used in wartime to sell Liberty Bonds, and are regarded purely as a temporary measure to meet present emergencies. The Communists expect them to disappear along with all the measures and habits of a money economy, and they and their sympathisers buy them not for investment, but as a sacrifice to help the Five Year Plan.

In order to stimulate the purchases by that part of the population which is still imbued with the old psychology of financial gain, the authorities revived in connection with these loans the system of premium lotteries which was common under the old regime. The premiums are paid instead of interest, or a part of it.

They distribute it unevenly, by the gambling method. The purchaser can choose whether he takes it at the usual rate or prefers a chance of getting more or less. This is a realistic use of old habits to further the interests of the socialist construction. For the same reason interest is paid to those who put a little money into savings banks to become government capital. The payment of interest on deposits of governmental business organisations is of course a stimulus to business efficiency. At the same time the sphere in which the bourgeois incentives have room temporarily to operate is carefully limited. Maximum premiums have progressively decreased from R. 100,000 to R. 5000. From the winners public pressure usually gets back about sixty per cent of their premiums in subscriptions to public causes, and from Communists the party takes also its share. The development of a group living, in whole or in large part, off interest is practically impossible because incomes are not high enough to permit buying sufficient bonds. Also, what is more important, the whole mind set is developing away from parasitical and toward productive living. It moves toward the view that it is silly to want or to have money. For the able-bodied and able-minded social approval is given only to earned income.

The impossibility of owning productive capital in the Soviet Union cuts the root of the profit motive. The industrial machine is owned by the state, and ninety per cent of the machinery of distribution is in the same hands. As for the land, only the man who cultivates it with his own labor has the right to claim its use, which is all that possession involves. When the Sixth Congress of Soviets in 1931 announced that while *the sovhozes are state enterprises in which the state is the full owner*

. . . *the owners of the kolhozes are the kolhoz members;* the use of the term *owners* was in part a concession to the deep-rooted attachment of the peasant to his own plot of land which Communists regard as one of the greatest obstacles to socialism but which they dare not try to cut too quickly, and was in part due to the necessity of using old words in a time of transition when the facts are changing.

In reality the collective ownership of the kolhoz amounts only to collective use and control for the purpose of getting a living, and of assisting in the nation-wide economic plan. As this plan develops, the local control, like that of the factory, will become more and more merged with the general direction of the planning agencies. This is also true of the communes, to whom as pioneers the government gave the possession of land and usually the buildings of former estates, after the members had subscribed their own money capital, and with whom the sense of local group ownership was therefore stronger. Now the extension of credits makes the government the real owner and tends to transfer the sense as well as the fact of ownership. After sufficient experience in both cases of the disintegrating consequences of permitting members who left to withdraw their funds or land, the capital has now been declared indivisible.

Similar to the kolhoz are the industrial *artels* which are producing co-operatives of those engaged in handicrafts and small machine trades. They have latterly been taken under special government care as an important link in Soviet economy to supply many needed small goods. They are now treated by Gosplan—State Planning Commission—as one unit and are federated under an Industrial Corporation with an elected board which controls their internal business; also educational machinery has been set up to train their members. They must charge the same prices as state business, pay the same taxes according to their turnover, and are subject to similar provisions for the creation of reserve funds. Hence their residual profits, which are divided among the members, are limited. Here too the practice of permitting members to take with them on withdrawal their property or shares paid in is being discontinued. It is therefore certain that the payment of interest on shares will also cease, as it has in the consumers' co-operative.

Another form of collective ownership is in co-operative apartment houses where one may, as in many other parts of the world, own one's own dwelling place. In suburban sections and in the smaller towns an individual can own a small house for his own use on ground leased from the government. It is also possible to rent or to sell half of it in order to meet expenses, just as one may rent a room in an apartment, but that is the limit of the real estate business. To the possession of personal property the limit is set not by law but by conditions, by what is needed for efficient and comfortable living, by what income permits and society approves. While the former conditioning factors tend to increase the amount of personal effects owned above the meager standard of early revolutionary days the latter tends to diminish it. For example the new co-operative apartments are furnished. The occupant pays for its use and the cost is amortised, along with the cost of building, in the rent.

Thus at every possible point the feeding ground for the possessive appetites is being occupied by other forces and they are growing feeble from lack of nourishment. The powerful profit motive that still dominates the capitalist world, driving it toward war against its own judgment and to the repression of liberties against its own professed principles, is here but a pale ghost flitting about in dark places with a lessening company of cringing speculators and bewildered peasants. The Russian Revolution was in aim and fact much more than the seizure of power by Bolsheviks in the name of the proletariat, it was the beginning of a far-reaching change in economic habits and ethical values. It comes now to its climactic struggle in the villages where the roots of capitalism are being torn up.

CHAPTER II

CHANGING FORMS

While the Soviet Union has banished economic insecurity and has cut away profit and property rights as economic stimuli nevertheless it is vigorously using methods that capitalism has employed. Into these forms it is putting a different content and directing them to different ends.

The Communist leaders are well aware that the success of their attempt to create a new social order turns upon the practical question of the productivity of labor. In his speech at the anniversary of the October Revolution in Moscow in 1931 Molotov emphasised this point:

What then is today the most vital factor for our final victory? It lies first and foremost in raising the productivity of labor. . . . (He then reinforced his appeal with a quotation from Lenin's "The Great Beginning," in which Lenin was following a forecast of Marx set forth in his "Criticism of the Gotha Program of the Social Democratic Party.") Productivity of labor, in the first analysis, is the most essential thing necessary for the victory of the new social order. Capitalism has brought about a productivity of labor unknown under feudalism. Capitalism can and will be finally defeated by the fact that socialism will give rise to a new and much higher productivity of labor. This will be very difficult and will take a long time to accomplish. . . .

To increase the productivity of its workers capitalism,

where it is intelligent, relies upon two main factors—improved technique and higher wages with their consequent higher standard of living. It is well known that this combination has enabled the more advanced employers of the more advanced industrial countries to compete successfully with cheap labor elsewhere. Connected with these main factors are various forms of appeal to the workers to increase their output; some psychological, like the "get together" efforts of certain organisations; some technical, like the efficiency movement; some financial, like bonuses, promotions, salary increases, and distribution of stock ownership. All of these forms of personal stimuli to productivity the Communists are using, just as they are employing the mechanical technique of capitalism.

The mechanisation of industry and agriculture gives more than a multiplication of labor-power. It also provides an indirect stimulus for the increase of production by requiring new attitudes and habits from the worker as he adapts himself to the requirements of the machine, and also a new spirit as he attempts to use the machine better than the capitalist world. The results are already manifest in a phenomenal increase of labor productivity in the Soviet Union—it was twenty per cent in 1931.

The authorities of the Gosplan assert that the growth of labor productivity in the USSR *is based primarily on the amount of electrical energy and capital at the service of the workers.* The quantity of energy consumed in industry per worker per annum has risen from 1.12 in thousands of kilowatt-hours in 1926–27 to 2.40 in 1931. But the increased productivity is also due to more direct incentives. For that section of the population which supports the Communist plan and seeks also its goal these incentives operate in new forms of labor unknown to capitalist society. For another, whose mind and life are partly in the old capitalist world and partly in the new, they are contained in a different use of stimuli long employed by the capitalist world. These differences are therefore vital. They answer the question of whether the USSR must swing back into the orbit of capitalism. They determine which way the crowd is moving and whether the inflexible purpose of the Communists to go forward into a new society can in the end succeed.

IMPROVEMENT OF MATERIAL CONDITIONS

It took capitalism some time to learn that to increase the productivity of labor it must raise the standard of living for the workers. The Bolsheviks naturally knew this from the beginning. Being realists and not Utopians they make this one of their first objectives. It is set forth in a phrase that constantly recurs in the speeches and writings of all Party, government, and labor union leaders—*the improvement of the material and cultural conditions of the workers.* The connection of the terms, and their order are vital. They reveal the basis of Communist thinking and practice. The Party instructs its new members that *the beginnings of the new life are being laid on a new material base.*

The necessity of importing an enormous amount of expensive machinery to build up the heavy industries, which has to be paid for by exports, has necessitated the rationing of food and clothing. Knowing the reason the industrial workers have, for the most part, endured the shortage with patience. But there are limits to the tightening of belts for the sake of the future that the Plan promises. It has become clear that no amount of enthusiasm by the elect can overcome a prolonged deficit in living standards. When the Donbas Region was falling behind in its coal production and endangering the whole economic plan, it was found that the basic difficulty was first lack of technical equipment and next unbearable living conditions. Some of the workers malingered in hospitals on pay rather than go back to their inadequate diet. The hard-boiled were deaf to the slogans and appeals of the shock brigaders, who voluntarily set the pace. "Let them kill themselves," they said; "give us more meat, if you want coal." As soon as the food supply and the housing were improved the production went up.

Since technicians were put in Food Category No. 1, it is being remarked in Moscow that even scientists work better than when they were half starved. Unquestionably one factor in the changed attitude of many of the former intelligentsia to the present régime is the increased availability of creature comforts. Indubitably a good deal of such discontent as now remains, certainly in those smaller industrial centres that are not well supplied with food and in those agricultural sections that have been drained for export, lies no deeper than the stomach. In one such region—also formerly very illiterate and ignorant—I have had a party member, an old civil war partisan leader, tell me that the workers were formerly all revolutionists but are now "counter-revolutionary." This phrase is not so meaningful as it sounds for the reasons were merely their inability to purchase a sufficiently varied diet and enough boots and cloth. More than once American specialists in small in-

question. The new collective agreements . . . must lay more obligations on the administration in demanding improved housing, bathrooms, creches, clubs, etc.

Molotov told the Seventeenth Party Conference in January, 1932, that *The party should assure the successful solution in the next five years of the problem of improving the material living conditions of the workers in town and village not less than two or three times.*

The keynote of this policy was struck by Stalin in his epoch-making speech to the Conference of Industrial Managers at Moscow, June 5, 1931.

He (the worker) is no longer a slave but the master of his enterprise. Yet this is not enough. He demands the satisfaction of all his material and cultural needs and we must comply with this demand. . . . The present-day worker is not what he once was . . . (he) wants to live so that all his material and cultural needs are satisfied—his food supplies, his housing conditions, his cultural and all other needs. He has a right to expect it and it is our duty to meet his requirements. . . . Do not forget that we ourselves are now making certain demands of the worker, we demand labor discipline, intensity of effort, socialist competition, shock brigade methods. Do not forget that the majority of the workers have taken up the challenge of the Soviet power with enthusiasm and are carrying it out heroically. Do not be surprised therefore that while carrying out the demands of the Soviet power the worker in his turn demands that the Soviet power shall fulfil its duty and continue to improve the material and cultural position of the workers.

This means that the period of abstinence in order to build the heavy industries that are the foundation of the socialist building is almost over. The Second Five

Year Plan is to concentrate on food supply and housing, on the light industries that produce consumers' goods, and on transport and a better system of distribution.

Meantime the Soviet system has been able, even during its most difficult initial period, to show the workers no inconsiderable improvement in their living conditions beside that phenomenal increase in capital plant from which they are later to reap the benefit. The facts and the figures support Molotov's claim to the Sixth Congress of Soviets in 1931 that *The condition of the masses is steadily improving year by year. Their growing requirements are far from being gratified. Nevertheless the rising level of material conditions for the masses of the workers constitutes the basic and unquestionable feature of the poor and middle peasant masses in the villages. We now witness the manifest diminution of rural destitution and material want among the masses of poor and middle peasants. This diminution of poverty in the village constitutes one of the most essential results of the consolidation of Soviet rule and of the building up of socialism in our country.*

Then he points out the opposite trend for rural life in the United States notwithstanding its advanced agricultural technique.

For industry as a whole the average wage has increased two to three times since 1924. No figures for real wages can be exact, because of differences in the cost of food and clothing for different groups of workers even in the same locality and still more because of the various additions to the income of the workers in the form of cultural and health benefits. These the Soviet economists call "socialised wages." The inexactness however is on the credit side of the ledger. Certainly, in the strategic industrial centres, prices have recently been going down while wages have been going up, contrary to the law of capitalist economics. All the capacities and determination of the planning system, and all the powers of national ownership, are being directed to this end. It is therefore quite safe to say that there has been a steady and considerable gain in real wages. The same is true for the workers' share in production, though here again, and for the same reasons, the figures concerning the relation of wages to productivity are necessarily indeterminate. But despite the enormous amount of production that in this initial period has had to go into capital plant, there is no such disparity between increased productivity and the rise in wages as is shown in the recent records of the other industrial countries. In the Soviet Union the workers of town and country are receiving 33.5 per cent of the national income, and the bourgeoisie only 2 per cent, whereas in other industrial countries the latter class receives 40–50 per cent.

The peasants cannot gain at the same rate as the workers because the margin of profit for agriculture is less and therefore the cost of carrying credit advanced by the government to the collective farms—amounting to about two fifths of their basic capital—is a heavier load to carry. Also at present the key industries are favored in the distribution of goods as a matter of policy. The improvement however is marked. The figures of the Food Research Institute of Stanford University show that the per capita consumption of wheat for Czarist Russia in 1909–10 was 2.9 bushels. In the Soviet Union it is now 4.1 bushels. This means that the peasant as well as the city worker is eating less black rye bread. Also the data of the Central Statistical Board shows that the consumption of meat by the village population in 1925 exceeded the pre-war consumption of the villages by one third. By 1928–29 the peasants were eating 39.6 per cent more meat than in 1925. Then came shortage due to wholesale slaughter of cattle in opposition to hasty and enforced collectivisation. Scientific collective stock raising is gradually overcoming this deficit. Allowing for bread shortage in three local areas due to drought followed by bad administration, a further rise of the rural standard of living is indicated by the report of Yakoklev to the Sixth Congress of Soviets that "all peasants who joined collectives in 1931 increased their income by at least one and a half times." They were able to do this because they could utilize the hours two and a half times better than the individual farmer, eliminate the boundaries of their former strip holdings, and use selected seed, thereby increasing the crop from 10–15 per cent.

This process is made concrete in the story of the "First Five Year Plan" collective farm in Millerovo District, Northern Caucasus, written by a number of its members. The mass meeting of the workers in its signed statement says:

It is two years since we began to plough and sow collectively and this year we have obtained better results with our new-style farming than we or our fathers ever obtained on our individual farms.

Timothy Skorikov, the chairman, states: *The average gross income from grain growing is 400 rubles per family. That greatly exceeds the income previously obtained by poor and middle farmers but it is not enough for the life we expect to lead, so we must make our farming yield much greater profits.*

Gregory Ivanovitch, writing about the farm herd and

mentioning the failure of the board to take any steps to improve the breed, says:

In spite of all these shortcomings, we are making progress. For example my own cow gives seven litres of milk a day and every cow on the farm gives an average of nine and a half litres daily. That is because on individual farms the cows are milked twice a day only, while here they are milked three times. Besides, they are better tended, their litter is kept clean and fresh while the individual farmers let their cows wallow in filth. We wash our cows twice a day. All this keeps them healthy and raises the quality of milk they give.

There is no doubt that the main motive behind the recent growth of collective farming is the conviction of the poor peasants that by the socialist economy they can get up out of their misery; the increasing demonstration of this fact is the main reliance of the party for solving the difficult problem of a socialist agriculture. Next to the economic benefits comes the cultural advantages which are being spread through the villages, making a powerful appeal to the young people and turning them into evangelists for collectivisation. Here and in the Houses of Culture in factory districts is the decisive answer to Balfour's clever gibe that while the Bolsheviks had found an easy way to make the rich poor it was not so easy to make the poor rich. While the new capitalism has been unable to maintain its desired higher wages, while the talk of its social workers about proceeding from the living wage to the comfort and saving and then to the cultural wage has proved vain, throughout the length and breadth of the Soviet Union a cultural standard of living for all is gradually being made universal.

The connection between effort and result, between

material gains and cultural development, is increasingly made clear to the workers and peasants not only by a powerful educational propaganda but also by the regulations that assign a percentage of the profits of every enterprise for the improvement of housing, for clubs, creches, and libraries. Thus the desire to improve life is kept from becoming selfish and socially separative as it has become when pursued by individuals for themselves and their families and then for classes. When it operates through the co-ordination of each for all and all for each it becomes a force making for unity. The productive forces and the rising demands of the masses develop reciprocally when once the supply of needs is organised to meet a measured demand. Also and what is more important, by a frank recognition and social use for social ends of the need for material comforts, the material aspect of life takes on a genuine ethical aspect. At this point practical necessity runs in the direction of ideals.

When comfortable mystics ignore the significance of material gains it is inevitable that they, together with their education and religion, should fall into bondage to the coarser breed whom they despise, because these know quite well how to manipulate the material aspects of life to their own selfish and ambitious purposes. Then the economic side of life is constantly violating the cultural standards and frustrating ethical desires. The same thing happens in the Soviet Union. An acute and prolonged food shortage destroys social solidarity. The worker who demands high wages says, "The government takes from me. I take from the government." The intellectuals who have to buy shoes in the open market at a price which consumes a month's labor are not enthusiastic supporters of the Soviet system. The

more productive individuals in all industries, the purpose is not merely to reward the individual; that is secondary to the fulfilment of the social plan. Back in 1924 the Sixth Labor Union Congress declared, *In order to increase the personal intensity of labor an extensive application of stimulative forms of wages is necessary.* This means piecework and bonuses. More pay goes to those who give more to the common undertaking for the purpose of enabling it more speedily to succeed. The Social Economic Plan adjusts wages and profits to its desired end.

Piecework has always been present to some extent in Soviet economy, both in industry and the state farms. Recently it has received a great stimulus, especially after Stalin's speech of July, 1931, on industrial management. By the end of the year many of the larger plants were working one hundred per cent on piecework, and now it is claimed that eighty to ninety per cent of the workers in the whole socialised economy—agricultural and industrial—are working under it. There are however several important differences from the piecework system in use in capitalist economy. The workers are protected by a minimum income and the speed is not to be allowed to menace the worker's health. In some cases it obviously does but that comes from the intense desire for success of the plan and not from the necessity of individual subsistence. A rate-fixing expert testifies that in his experience "the speed-up system is totally absent." The rates are computed for quality as well as quantity of output and the workers both know and approve the ends for which they are set. They are not allowed to be cut during the job and instead of being lowered with the increased efficiency of the worker because he is making too much, they progressively increase with his output. It is customary to put on huge blackboards the workers' names with quota, rates, amount done, wages and premiums earned. At a large construction I have seen one on a tree by the highway for all the world to see.

This progressive premium system, which provides for increasing pay in relation to the accomplishment of the program of the plan, is rapidly becoming universal. Correspondingly less is paid for labor below the norm —usually only two thirds—and if a man is drunk or sleeps on the job he loses his premium. In the oil industry, for example, the norms are set for a year in the collective agreement, and on the time basis. If a man finishes the job estimated at ten days in eight, he gets ten days' pay and there is another job immediately waiting for him. In agricultural communes and collectives, the rates of pay are based on living costs and in some cases, besides the additional pay for beating the norm, a worker gets a percentage of the profit on his job if cost accounting shows it to reach a certain sum.

The premium system is also followed in the general distribution of goods. The shock workers get special books entitling them to buy goods not available for ordinary workers, sometimes at the factory co-operative and in the larger centres at special stores for their use. Also they do not have to wait in line to get their quota of staples but are served ahead of the crowd. On the collective farms, and in the lumber camps, where there is often a shortage of manufactured goods, the best workers get the first chance at them. Thus one farm worker writes:

This is the way we distribute goods of which there is a shortage: as soon as the goods are received at the co-operative store, the employees inform the board of the collective farm and the chairman of the village Soviet and the goods are fairly distributed among the brigades, in accordance with the work of each.

Another tells in detail how this is done:

On May 15 we received 350 metres of material for our brigade. . . . I called the brigade heads together, we looked through the list and checked the time they had worked and the amount of work each had done. We calculated that each was to get an average of 3.5 metres; the best got more, the idlers got nothing. Shock-brigaders were supplied first. We made up a list and called another conference at which forty people were present, while there had been only ten at the first. The list was checked once more.

The same method is used even with the work of the children. In one small school they were asked for their social work last spring to sort potatoes for planting. Only five stuck to the job until evening. These had their names put on the red board and were given an order on the co-operatives for a pair of shoes. To the shock workers among the wage-earners premiums take the form of a place in a sanitarium for rest and treatment, or a special holiday excursion—last summer a select company of *udarniks*—shock workers—were given a cruise around Europe and the Near East. Also some are given leave for a special course of technical study with full pay and promotion follows its successful completion. Sometimes premiums are paid in cash and their award is an event. The union will take a theatre for the evening and before the play begins, there will be a celebration, with speeches and awards. At one such meeting that we attended sixteen men got from 150–225 rubles each and fifteen received udarnik certificates. Each recipient came up and took his place on the platform while the band played a few bars of the International and the audience patriotically rose. It is becoming a general custom for wage-earners who win these premiums to subscribe them to public enterprises. In the case of technicians they sometimes go as high as 25,000 rubles and are meant to supplement the regular income which cannot provide means of study, travel, or rest. Premiums are also paid for inventions and for rationalisation suggestions. They may be paid to groups working collectively as well as to individuals. An invention problem was assigned to a higher technical school in Leningrad. Seven brigades were formed to work on it, with five or six persons in each. When the problem was solved it was decided that two professors working in the brigades had contributed most to its solution. So to the satisfaction of all they were awarded a premium. A sum of money was given to one brigade for its special work but it decided that the discovery of a professor who was in it had really solved the problem so they decided to give him the largest proportion.

The tendency is to reward in kind rather than in cash and the collective reward in general outweighs the individual. The labor leaders have been complaining that the premiums for rationalisation suggestions are far from sufficient and not in due proportion to the savings effected. So in 1931 the Central Labor Council planned a premium fund of sixty million rubles for this purpose. Also I have heard workers in a meeting called to ratify the annual collective agreement argue that the amount of premium suggested for surpassing the norm was not a sufficient incentive. This represents the type of psychology to which the program of increased monetary rewards is a temporary concession.

The largest portion of the premium fund for better

work is paid out for collective improvements. A typical instance out of hundreds is the award to the Amo Auto Works in 1931 of 750,000 rubles to build workers' dwellings. This was for finishing its year's program sixteen days ahead of time. The combination of collective and individual stimulus is shown by the experience of a woman worker in a collective farm. When the mothers who were working in the weeding brigade wanted to stop to go and see if their babies were being properly cared for in the field nursery, she said to them:

. . . *Remember that if we do not work we will not get a combine* (*harvester and thresher*). *And if we do work right we will get an automobile as a premium and will drive it out to the field.* (*And she adds:*) *I received thirty-one metres of material; three of them were a premium for planting trees. I would have gotten more, but I have not paid up the whole of my co-operative share. I got about sixteen kilos of sugar, so we have plenty of that. Boots and shoes were handed out to those who needed them most. As ours were still good we were given leather to mend them.*

All this emphasis upon payment by results, and especially the deliberate use of the incentive of money rewards, obviously runs counter to the Communist ideal. Arguing that it is only temporary and bound to be overcome, Radek, one of the most skilful of Communist pamphleteers, says: *All children see the inequality which still exists under Soviet rule and the more glowingly a child absorbs the fundamental ideas of Communism, the more sharply he feels the inequality.* So to support the policy of differential payments a vigorous polemic was waged and the "Levellers," like their forbears, soon found themselves to be heretics. Molotov officially proclaimed that, *The levelling policy is out and out "petty bourgeois" having nothing in common with the policy of Leninism.*

All the resources of Soviet educational propaganda were utilized in a campaign against "equalisation" which was proclaimed one of the most dangerous enemies of socialist construction. The attack on the "Levellers" was amply supported by quotations from Marx and Lenin. In his "Criticism of the Gotha Programme," Marx had replied to those who were demanding *the equal right of each to an equal share of the products of labor* by insisting that this like every other *bourgeois right* was in effect inequality. In this case it was because different people are not equal to each other—*one is strong, another is weak, one is married and the other is not, one has more children, the other has less, and so on.* Also Marx pointed out that the Communist principle, which is distribution according to need, could not be put in force in the first stage of Communist society because people would be still imbued with capitalist habits. In that period the distribution of the means of subsistence must depend on the amount of labor which every able-bodied person can contribute to society. In his "The State and Revolution" Lenin elaborates the latter point and shows that, to begin with, *Communist society, which is forced to destroy only the "injustice" consisting in the ownership of the means of production by private individuals . . . is not capable of destroying at once the further injustice which is constituted by the distribution of the articles of consumption according to "work performed" (and not according to need).*

At two points Soviet experience confirmed the analysis of Marx and Lenin. To begin with the small group communes who attempted distribution according to need, all got into trouble. The testimony from the agricultural communes is uniform. They found the poorest workers drawing the most clothes and wasting them. In one case some workers went to state farms to get wages and left dependents for the commune to support. So now they say, *If we had only known earlier about the value of payment by results, we would have succeeded faster. We found out first that equalisation doesn't pay.*

The Komsomol Commune at the Amo Factory in Moscow in which a group of young workers put all their income into a common fund and drew out for personal expenses as needed, found that some were getting too many things at the expense of the others and the skilled workers who were putting more in were discontented. Some became lazy and would not even take their turn in getting food, saying, "Let the committee do it." So after Stalin's speech they decided that equal distribution was interfering with the improvement of qualifications; some would not study, saying, "Why should I advance? I have all I need." So now they are experimenting with a proportionate distribution. Another Komsomol Commune at Selmashtroi Harvester works whose members allowed themselves seven rubles a month for expenses, with clothes distributed by order of the Soviet, after Stalin's speech studied why one member stayed at the wage level of fifty rubles and concluded that he did not care so long as he was provided for. So they changed to the method of each putting into the common fund his share of the living costs and a percentage of his wage for the cultural advantages of the common house.

Similarly the policy of the agricultural communes has changed. Yakoklev reports:

It is possible to cite the cases of dozens of communes, which have increased their income manyfold, and brilliantly set up their husbandry, thanks to this that they concentrated their forces not on the immediate building of a common dwelling, and not on the absolute equality of all the members of the commune, not on the separation of the children from the parents, but on the promotion of dairying, hog-raising, and market gardening, to an extent not only sufficient to satisfy the needs of their members but also to supply the city, while maintaining the principle of dividing the income according to the amount and quality of labor.

We must openly admit that when the commune members ask our advice, what to spend their money on —the building of a common dwelling house or the building of a commonly owned pigpen, we answer: First organise your socialised stockbreeding, your socialised barns, on this basis your resources will begin to grow literally week by week, and in a year or two or three you can build yourselves any kind of dwelling house. If on the other hand you begin with a common dwelling house and equality of distribution—perhaps your business won't go ahead.

The second point at which "equalisation" appeared was more serious. It was the practice in the early days of the kolhoz movement to distribute the product according to the number of souls and not according to work done, and it imperilled the keypoint of the whole Soviet economy—the successful socialisation of agriculture. Yakoklev reported some of the results to the Sixteenth Party Congress:

In 1930 the very worst fault in the work of the kolhozes was the practice, which was very common, of distributing the receipts equally among the members, without taking account of the quantity and the quality of the work done. . . . The question is a vital one because experience has shown that where the income is distributed in this way, per capita, it is impossible to get the kolhozes really interested in the result of their work . . . in every case this resulted in a material loss of interest in production on the part of the kolhozniks, a sharp decline in the productivity of labor and a consequent decrease in the returns. . . . (*He then quotes a report from one farm.*) *This is the way our work was organised. The manager went about in the morning and called every one to work. Some went, others did just as they wished. No records were kept of the work either as to quantity or quality, except on odd scraps of paper very carelessly written merely as routine. And what was the result? The best workers worked themselves half to death and the others did not work at all. But when the time came to divide up the grain they were all right on the spot. Each person got 18 poods. What is more, they even counted in some members who weren't yet born but who the management of the kolhoz apparently thought should have been. Some families got 180 poods of wheat. When it was time for the grain collection it turned out that there was no grain for sale to the government. They calculated it all over again and this time they found that one group had received 2000 rubles more than was coming to them while another group was 3000 rubles short.* (*He concludes.*) *. . . It must be recognised that the Bolshevist conception of collective farming calls for distribution of collective income in real conformity to quantity and quality of labor put in. . . . Without such strict dependence of the share of the products of the collective farm upon the labor invested* *and upon its real productivity there can be no "kolhoz" movement.*

Kuibyshev followed this up by reporting to the Central Committee of the party:

The most serious attention must therefore be devoted to the harvesting of the crop. Here the central question is the stimulus given to labor, and we must accordingly wage most vigorous, decisive warfare against the distribution in the collective farms according to the number of persons per family and not according to the amount of labor performed. It was owing to such an organization of labor . . . that the harvest campaign was carried out so badly last year. The individual collective farmer was not interested in the amount of labor he performed, since he hoped to obtain sufficient out of the general fund of products when it was distributed according to souls.

So the Central Committee decreed:

All labor in the collective farms without exception should be organised on a piecework basis. The forms of piecework should be as simple as possible and understandable by every collective farm member, so that the number of working days performed by him may be written into his time book . . . taking into account not only the work done but also its quality.

The results that followed the adoption of piecework are beyond dispute. Here are some selected from a number in Yakoklev's report:

In the Crimean kolhoz when they were paid by the day it took 180 working days to set out a hectare of tobacco. Under piecework they did it in from 40 to 76 working days . . . a teamster hauled two barrels of water a day on pay-day, on piecework the same team-

given the usual assignment of jobs, and on his return the worker is to have an opportunity to earn his share of the harvest, also his individually owned livestock is exempted from the agricultural tax.

Because it is aimed at securing more skilled labor the Bolsheviks do not regard the policy of payment by results as merely a necessary concession during the transition period to those workers who were not changed by the revolution, who, trained in the capitalist psychology, want a high wage and do not think of giving high labor for it, who lack labor discipline and practise absenteeism. Thus they are using a tendency that runs counter to their ideal. But they claim to be keeping it within bounds. Also they insist that they are making it a means of education to develop the attitude and habits of work which are necessary for the attainment of their goal. Evidently the stimulus of increased monetary rewards, within fixed limits, operates differently in a socialist society where social disapproval falls more heavily upon the "snatcher" than it does in the capitalist world. Therefore the Communists have solid ground for saying, "But remember what we are also doing to improve the conscientiousness of the worker and this will dominate in the end."

On this point a foreman in one factory in Tiflis, who had worked years in the United States, said to me:

In the United States we were always asking for more because we knew the big millionaires had so much. But here if we ask, we are asking from each other. How shall we do it?

Radek in his pamphlet on the differences between labor in the Soviet Union and in the capitalist world says:

In each factory there is a solid nucleus of workers, reaching in some places as much as thirty per cent (it is not our desire to embellish the reality) who consider it a matter of personal honor to raise the productivity of labor to the utmost limit . . . their presence, their example, are already producing a telling effect in the struggle against the morality of personal greed. The latter still persists among the backward workers, among the majority of those coming from rural districts where the old tradition is that of "each one for himself." But the old morality already feels the superiority of the new and it dares not oppose it openly. It can only act on the sly, sabotaging the initiative of the knights of the new socialist morality in which the supreme law is to serve the whole class, to serve the building of socialism. Already with the new factories, there are also springing up the new workers and their new morality.

Meantime one manifest result of high wages for good work is the growth of habits of spending which may easily become anti-social. In the key industries one meets efficient workers with their pockets full of rubles who are puzzled about how to spend it. The authorities have opened a lot of new stores with additional goods at stiff prices to get these surplus wages back again and remedy the situation of the man who said, "My pocket is full of rubles yet look at my trousers." Yet there is a limit to buying what, in the shortage situation, are luxury foods and clothes. Careless expenditure is a characteristic feature of the early period of industrial development when capital plant is building. Later it becomes necessary to give attention to standards of consumption but meantime anti-social habits are developing. When this is called to their attention some Communists dodge the difficulty—and it is pardonable with all the other things they have on hand—by asking, "what difference does it make how the worker spends lic causes. But it is possible for their recipients and for winners in the lotteries to invest in government bonds and receive what is for Soviet society a substantial unearned income. Then comes in the income tax, to take it away progressively. In addition local tax committees have the right to refuse the documentary evidence of the citizen and may estimate a citizen's income above that shown by the data presented. In this manner those groups designed for economic extermination can be, and are, taxed out of existence. From its members the party takes 3 per cent up to 300 rubles, 20 per cent between 300 and 1200 rubles, and 20–40 per cent between 1200 and 2400 rubles and above. From lottery prizes the party takes 25 per cent of the prizes above 1000 rubles but leaves the winner only 5000 rubles of the larger amounts.

Concerning what remains, and especially concerning the awards of premiums, the defense is the same as that urged by persons of tender conscience in capitalist countries—it is needed and used for professional efficiency—for travel, books, apparatus, etc. It sounded quite familiar as we waited for a street car, when an important appointment pressed, to have the interpreter ask "How would we get the business of the government done if Molotov and the others did not have an automobile?" Or to listen to an influential Communist counter a question about the manifest desire among many officials for more comfortable quarters by asking, "Will Magnetostroi get built if a few persons do not have more comfort than those in the barracks?"

There is however one point that is not met by this consideration. One of the basic Communist principles is to concentrate upon helping the weakest, those furthest down. For them—the proletariat in the cities, the poor peasant in the country village—they made the revolution. In their service the strong are harnessed. Now, in the policy of payment by results, the reward goes to the strong and conversely the weak are penalised for their weakness, some of which may be inherited. One Communist answer is that the weak are protected by the minimum wage provision and *more than that we cannot do without endangering productive efficiency.* Then is added: *We cannot stop to think of a few strong or a few weak. It is the general result that we are after.* The better reply says: *Our whole policy is designed to help the weak to be strong. Our wage payments are arranged so to say to him "You may get what the best do if you will work like them and we offer you the means of training." Here again is where we differ from capitalist economy which leaves the weak with no chance to rise.*

The final question is whether the emphasis on payment by results is developing the money mind, whose absence from the Soviet Union so impressed the British economist Keynes that he declared that what made it a new world was the different place of money in life. Granted that there money never can develop the power it has in the capitalist world—which Marx called commodity fetichism—will the result of the present trend away from equalisation be that many people will think more of the reward than of the job? *But we also work for money,* said a realistic young Communist, and again and again in various places young professional students illuminated his meaning by saying frankly, *We want a reasonable living and we want everybody else to have one. That is as far as the desire for money can go in our society. If necessary the pressure of party education and discipline will see to that.*

In the matter of working for rewards there is a rough dividing line between the younger and the older sections of the population. Those raised in the new atmosphere are in general more dominated by the principles of service and sacrifice than the older generation, if there is excluded the little group of Bolshevik revolutionaries. Some even of them are beginning to feel the call of comfort, particularly as they become managers of big industries and sometimes mingle with high-salaried and high-living business men in and from other countries. There is now a tendency to abolish the party maximum salary, which is from two hundred and sixty to three hundred rubles a month, according to sectional living costs. Already men in technical positions can be exempted from it and some are beginning to argue that the party never enforced the principle of maximum income as members could earn additional sums from writing and also—a professor especially—might hold two positions. From these extra earnings however the party takes an extra tax and the best members turn them all in to party and public causes. Also they decline to accept the larger salaries the trusts are entitled to offer them. The tide is turning however in the direction of giving Communist workers and specialists the same privileges that other citizens enjoy. Stalin's six points are to be applied to all. There is to be what may be called a kind of wage NEP all along the line. The NEP—New Economic Policy—it will be remembered restored the private market temporarily and made private profits possible but under control. So it is expected that this wage NEP will last only until the second Five Year Plan is completed. Then a classless society will be achieved and then, or soon thereafter, it is hoped that money and its present significance can be altogether abolished.

Meantime if the maximum is abolished, the party will lose one of its sources of power—that its members took less money and lived a simpler life than others. That example and restraint will be gone. But its spirit lives and its example will be continued by many of the younger generation, who have never known the power of the great God Mammon nor the delights of his worship. The best of them have the same disregard of the softer things of life that led Lenin and his colleagues to live in the Kremlin as simply as they lived in lodgings when exiles in European capitals. Among them one gets the same instances of taking posts with lower pay that are encountered elsewhere in genuine religious service. One man in an agricultural commune who had been commandeered for a year as interpreter for foreign agricultural experts told me he was refusing another year's service and returning to the commune to live on much less income because his work gave him *No moral satisfaction. I haven't the moral courage to go on with it. They would look on me here as a deserter*. That whole commune was eating meat only three days a week that winter because they had decided to give four hundred hogs to help feed the factories and pay for the machinery instead of the two hundred the plan called for. When I asked if they did not need better food for themselves they said, *It was right to give them. The government needed them.*

This younger crowd have a different conception of success than is inculcated in the schools of the capitalist society. They grow up in a different atmosphere at home. When asked about the difference between conditions under the Soviets and in the United States where he had worked for years, one factory foreman said, among other things: *See my girl there. Presently she can go to work in the factory and go to Rabfac* (*courses to prepare workers for higher education*). *After two years' work they will try her and if she can do as good work she will get the same pay as a skilled worker.* Said another, a lathe worker, *Now my boy after he finishes seventh-grade school can go to the technicum. Then he must do practical work. Then he can have more education and go as high as he wants to. And for his education the government pays.* They talk, be it observed, in terms of productive service, not of financial manipulation. Yet when I asked an American technician how it was that a group of young factory workers could solve a problem which he set them, which he said not one in a thousand tool makers in the United States could work out, his answer was: "They are ambitious."

In general the situation in the Soviet Union offers satisfaction to ambition only in terms of social service. It offers creative adventure—which many American engineers say is the reason they stay, the chance to pioneer in the improvement of human organisation, and the wider use of science without any discounts on account of the claims of capitalists. Also youth is offered the satisfaction of its socially justifiable ambitions without having to climb up the ladder trampling upon the less able. The ladder is abolished. All go up together or none go. Success is not bitter in the mouth because others are hurt by it. A report from a pedagogical expert on the staff of the Pioneers to the Ninth Congress of the Komsomol, on "Work among Children" (January, 1931), says under the heading "The Problem of 'How to Get to the Top' is Removed":

Amongst us this problem is removed because everybody knows that he shall find his place in the construction scheme, that in our country every toiler receives every possible opportunity for unfolding his strength, his gifts and talents.

Instead of capitalist competition, instead of the bourgeois law of tooth and claw, the deciding method of education amongst us is socialist competition and shock work.

We are seeking to organise a system of education which would contribute to unfold all the forces in our society, which would vouchsafe the advancement of the best of those who work for society, for their class. Such is the basic morality of our Communist education.

Of course "careerists" appear among the younger generation. The peculiar rewards of the Communist system, and the disabilities operating against those opposing it, invites them. One can meet enough of them in Moscow to say again that the old world is repeating itself. But the party is well aware of the danger, the set of life in the younger crowd is against them, and when their nature is manifest the penalty is swift and sufficient. The dominating fact is that self seeking must take on some aspect of social serving to get anywhere. The path to success lies only in a social machine operating for social ends. Thus the Bolsheviks think they have united personal ambition and social well-being. When they are asked if they have not substituted the love of power for the love of money they answer that the nature and discipline of their organization are such that it is impossible for the ego to become enlarged. They assert, and the evidence is conclusive, that the moment signs of that disease appear a man is disciplined, demoted and if need be expelled. When asked about the power of an organisation for which men will sacrifice their all but through which they may share impersonally in the wielding of vast controls, they reply that the party does not wield power but only leadership. What is involved in that distinction belongs to a later discussion.

SOCIALIST ACCUMULATION

In a much more positive way the first stage of socialist society is using one aspect of the profit motive so as to secure from it the maximum of economic propulsion. Every socialist enterprise and each separate job is now required to show a profit. Every manager is required to keep this in mind, first, last, and all the time. As the workers put it, "We must make a profit for ourselves and for the government." Here is one of the contradictions between form and content that abound in the transition period when some of the old bottles must for a time be made to hold new wine. What is meant of course is that a surplus over the cost of production must be produced and laid aside for reserves, for the extension of capital plant, expenses of government, social insurance, and the development of culture. This was what Marx had to insist upon in the early days of Communist theory when the enthusiasts, led by Lasalle, were talking naïvely about the necessity of the workers receiving the "undiminished" or "full product of their labor."

This fund of social reserves is the social element in private profit which increasingly diminishes as capitalism develops its last stage and becomes financial, rather than productive, but behind which the exploiters often conceal from the public and from themselves the nature and consequence of their activities. It now becomes socialist profit—the surplus over consumptive needs which is used for social purposes. The Soviet economists call this technically "expanded reproduction"; for popular consumption they name it "socialist accumulation." To secure it in sufficient quantity every operation must show a surplus over its production costs, to distribute its burden evenly every plant and every worker must give back to the common fund more than they take out of it. Equally vital to the success of socialist building is the question of how this surplus shall be invested. Hence the Social Economic Congress at Amsterdam, 1931, was informed by the Soviet delegation that *the decisive element in the plan is the plan of capital investments on which depends the direction in which expanded reproduction will take place.*

When Stalin was talking to the industrial managers about the need of a greater rate of socialist accumulation he pointed out that that so far heavy industry had been built up by profits from transport, agriculture, and light industry and by budget accumulations, but that these sources were near their end. Indeed agriculture was now requiring state aid. *There remains heavy industry, particularly the machine-building section. It must provide accumulation.* (*And it must do it by reducing production costs.*) *You know that a reduction of costs by one per cent means an accumulation of from one hundred and fifty million to two hundred million rubles.* Later in the year Molotov seconded this with similar figures before the Sixth Congress of Soviets and added that one per cent reduction in agricultural costs will save one hundred million rubles.

Socialist profit, made for example by the textile syndicate selling to a co-operative the goods made by the textile trust, is thus not simply the transferring of resources from one state pocket to another; it is also the securing of necessary social surplus, and the pressure to get it leads on occasion to some of the practices that socialists properly object to in private profit seeking. On this account the Council of Commissars created a special commission on prices. "Izvestia" for October 24, 1931, reported its decision in the case of Meletev, Chairman of the Milk and Vegetable Trust, who had issued an order, on August 11, instructing the state farms under his supervision to sell their apple crop at the highest prices obtainable and to keep over the unsold apples until the prices reached the highest level. The decision of the Commission was *an unpardonable mistake . . . acted like a capitalist trading concern.* It notes that he admits his mistake and has rescinded the order on October 4, and then severely censures him for his conduct. An official of Kolhoz Centre reports: *Certain collective farms before fulfilling their quota endeavored to put aside inordinately large amounts of grain for cattle feed and reserve funds. This is entirely unjustified.*

Recently, as part of the drive to reduce the cost of living, the Workers' and Peasants' Investigation Commission has been enquiring into the price policies and practices of the co-operatives. In a preliminary report, March, 1932, it announced some cases of arbitrary price fixing beyond legal limits. Some were small, to cover increased overhead due to poor management. But Store 1 of the Leather Corporation had added 3.80 rubles to the legal price of galoshes. Warehouse 1 in Moscow had distributed barley grits at 58 kopecks per kilogram instead of pearl barley grits which should have sold for

25 kopecks. The timber workers co-operative in Belovenski sold sugar at commercial prices.

So the sugar trust was disciplined in 1931 for putting aside reserves unnecessarily and for using a short cut to efficiency and profits by withholding part of its product from state channels of distribution and sending it direct to the industries in exchange for materials it needed, as for instance timber. Thus even within the limits of socialist accumulation, competitive profit seeking, to advance the interests and record of particular enterprises, appears. To check this disruptive disease in its first stages Molotov exhorted the Plenum of the Central Council of Labor Unions in Moscow, December, 1931, to work for interdependence and mutual aid between plants and industries.

An instance of the same stimulus working improperly, but in reverse gear, was observed in a suburban village near Moscow which, in order to make a record, sent its whole potato crop to Moscow as soon as it was harvested. There part of it rotted for lack of storage facilities and the village had later to buy back at higher prices potatoes for its own eating. Meantime the shrewd ones, seeing what was happening, had laid aside theirs, and in the outcome the kulaks were enabled to say: "See, you cannot manage your own affairs. Remember how much better we managed things for you."

The people of the Soviet Union are paying a heavy price for their capital plant. But Soviet workers at least know what they are doing and why. The school children, and increasingly the peasants, will tell you that the building of the heavy industries is the key to defense against intervention, to economic independence of the capitalist nations, and to the foundation of the socialist structure for humanity. It is only because this knowledge of the meaning of what they are doing has sufficiently permeated the working population that they have tightened their belts and exported food products they might have eaten, to pay for their imported machinery. This knowledge is specific as well as general. There is no concealment of profits and capitalisation. The workers are made acquainted with all the accounts of their enterprise. They know just what the profits are and how they are divided. So in the factories they are saying, "We must work for Stalin's fund," that is for the fund for more capital plant whose necessity was popularised by Stalin's speech. But they are not paying for it as did the other industrial nations in depleted vitality from the exhaustion of the workers. And when they get through the plant will belong to those who have built it and to their children. As one youthful interpreter who had grown up in the States said: "Here we work for tomorrow; and I guess the fellow who thinks only of his belly, and can't see the future, doesn't belong."

In this manner communism is taking one section of the inherited profit motive and enlarging it by developing the conscious will to create the funds for necessary social expenses and reserves. Transferred to a higher plane, with more room to grow, it helps to awaken the slumbering social tendencies of the people. How much more powerful and effective a stimulus is this creation of a common pool for future living than individual hoarding, private ownership, and the seeking of the largest possible profit, can be seen in the rate of growth of the industrial plant and cultural capital of the Soviet Union. Both the expansion and the tempo of the national economy under the Five Year Plan are ascribed by the authorities to the extension of the knowledge of the necessity of creating a social surplus. This growth cannot properly be compared with the expansion of plant in capitalist countries in the same period because they were already equipped. But it does not suffer by comparison with their expansion in their initial stages. In presenting the figures of the budget to the Central Executive Committee of the Congress of Soviets in December, 1931, Grinko pointed out that the growth (thirteen–fourteen per cent) of the national income in the past year surpassed that of any capitalistic country in the most prosperous period. Under the Five Year Plan the USSR has leaped from the most backward position to first, second, third, and fourth places respectively in oil, coal, pig iron, and timber.

The demands of the future are inexorable. The present must be sacrificed to it if life is to go forward. But the world which worships Mammon has been sacrificing blindly and unnecessarily. A planned economy can keep capital plant down to the necessary minimum. Because it has the possibility of maximum production power for machines and persons it needs less capital plant than a system which always has a part idle. Because the increase of social capital embodies the increased expenditure of labor energy to raise its own standards of living the socialist economy becomes the instrument of achieving the conscious reproduction of life. Man need no longer work in the dark.

One of the results of the socialist method of providing reserve funds and the cost of culture is the socialising of the economic virtues. When stimulated by the desire for personal financial gains these virtues become anti-social. Better work by the few makes more unemployment for others and so sabotage is defended as an expression of brotherhood. The sight of gains going to others stimulates inefficiency among those who cannot share in them. Industriousness and thrift lead to money lending and, as can be seen in any frontier town, the financial system instead of providing a cash "nexus" creates a cleavage in the community. The modern form of these virtues—the efficiency movement and its wider expression in rationalisation—leads to increasing capitalisation, the multiplying of overhead charges, the decrease of purchasing power for the masses, and then the shut down of plant. But when these economic virtues are called out to build a social plant, commonly owned, they take on a different character and move in another direction.

Industriousness becomes a mutual obligation and not a debt owed for wages and therefore not only the management but all the active workers, and beyond them the active youth in the community, are united against idleness and absenteeism. Thrift becomes social, not personal. The Savings Banks, with a poster drive to increase savings, are maintained only partly to enable the workers to buy things like pianos but also to provide the government with more funds to build more plants. The response of the population is evident in the fact that personal accounts amounted to one hundred and twenty-one million rubles in the first six months of 1931 against one hundred and thirty million for the previous year. But thrift becomes chiefly the avoidance of waste in the factories. To this end in 1931, the workers in one of the textile mills addressed an open letter to all textile workers, appealing to them, and also to railroad workers and all who handle textile products, to make effective the slogan, "Not one kilogram of cotton must be wasted." Similar drives proceed in the metal industry to lower the proportion of scrap.

Honesty becomes not the best policy but a social necessity—the keeping of faith in the common toil, and a conscientious attitude to work. The Soviet system has its own need for contract morality, as it always puts the obligations between organisations and also the pledges of individuals for shock work into detailed contract form. The General Secretary of the Komsomol in his pamphlet, "The Komsomol-One Shock Brigade," goes out of his way to say, *The worst thing about the Shock Brigade movement is that there are those who parade the thing, who make solemn assemblies and mutual greetings, assurances and vows before one another and nothing more.* So the determination to see that contracts are carried out means that the workers are to be subjected to the same discipline of keeping one's word that capitalism in its best days instilled in the traders and bankers. Also when the kulak becomes transformed he finds a new meaning for some of the habits which before made him a social enemy. In their changed form they make him a valuable asset to the socialist cause.

Truth-telling also becomes obligatory in a planned system in order that the planners may not be deceived and misled. So contrary to the belief that one can see only the best, there is now a manifest desire to show the visitor the worst as well. "We want only to tell the truth," said one Russian American worker. "Not to tell it would not be nice." At a labor meeting to discuss plans for improving the food supply of the workers, there were complaints of dirty dishes in the factory dining room and the interpreter added, "They are dirty. Why should we say they are clean if they are not?"

Lenin knew how badly the land of *nitchevo* (it doesn't matter) and *zaftra* (tomorrow) would need both economic virtues and an efficiency movement. The

a more careful application of business method in all enterprises . . . labor power must be so distributed that every group of workers will be responsible for its work, its machinery, its lathes, and the quality of its work. And again: *Some comrades seem to think that depersonalisation can be abolished by incantation, by widely broadcast speeches. It appears to me that it would be far better if our business leaders, instead of incantations and speeches, spent a month or two at some mine or factory, studying every trifle and detail of labor organization, put an end to depersonalisation on the spot, and then went about spreading the experience thus gained to other enterprises.*

One of the Communist leaders tried to develop a socialist rationalisation of labor by putting the principles and methods of Taylor and Ford with those of Marx and Lenin. This has been strongly opposed by many labor leaders. The General Secretary of the Komsomol says:

The Komsomol has fought and will fight the founder of Russian Taylorism and his movement because of its emphasis upon mechanisation. We stand for emphasis upon the creative impulse in industry.

A planned economy develops of necessity its own type of efficiency movement and its own brand of rationalisation. It requires cost accounting and better management and the greatest possible co-ordination of processes to produce the greatest productivity at the lowest cost. The purpose of the Gosplan is to *combine the maximum of production with the minimum of expenditure in the shortest possible time.* The first Five Year Plan was characterised by speed and quantity, the second will be marked by quality. As Kuibeshev, head of Gosplan, announces, *Foremost in our task is improve-*

ment of quality in production. Quality must be placed before quantity. And Molotov repeats it before the Central Executive Committee of the Sixth Congress of Soviets, *The chief tasks before us are the reduction of production costs and the improvement of quality.*

Already results of the drive for efficiency and quality can be noted. One runs into them everywhere. The Russian office worker was notorious for wasting time but, "Since the plan came in we start work in our office on time and in the afternoon we pay no attention to the whistle if our work isn't done." The American foreman of the tool-making department in a watch factory showing me his udarnik book added that he got it not for speed but for conscientiousness. Taking a die out of the hands of a youth he pointed out its delicacy and accuracy. "I call myself a good mechanic," he said, "but I can't beat that, and he is only three years from the village." At Selmashstroi I heard the candidates for admission to the union examined on their records for lateness, absence, and thrift in use of materials, all of which are posted on blackboards in every department. Also at the union election, the visiting labor leader from Moscow set forth the responsibility of the "actives" in the membership for getting every one to work and to fulfil the plan in time, quantity, and quality. "Our trade mark must mean the best work." In conversation a worker from the United States annotated the point: "Under capitalism you think always whether you have a job, how to pay rent and taxes. Now you think only how to produce better." Thus does the leaven slowly work to change the whole inert lump.

When it comes to the wider aspects of efficiency, to securing a rationalisation of industry, agriculture, transportation, and distribution in the interests of the widest social well-being, the socialist economy has certain natural advantages. It is not limited by the demands of profit nor hampered by private property rights. It has not to support any idle class, neither at the bottom nor at the top. It suffers now but little from sabotage and has no bill of costs for long strikes. Against this must be set the waste from inefficiency and bureaucratism. But this will have to be enormous to offset the other savings. In addition, a planned economy can secure the most productive distribution of credit. It can build the biggest and best equipped enterprises. It can use its machinery up to the operating point of the law of diminishing returns. Allowing for that, the Soviet Union can use its agricultural machinery one hundred per cent, the United States only forty per cent. Also a planned economy permits for the first time a scientific development of natural resources. In the oil fields for example the spacing of the wells at proper intervals, according to the stratum being followed, is in striking contrast to that of the older wells which are sometimes close together on either side of a boundary line in order to tap a competitor's flow. Similarly a national plan for agriculture enables distribution of crops on a scientific basis according to soil and climate. Underneath all this, as the enabling fact and therefore a steady stimulus toward the greatest economic efficiency, is the new form of property.

SOCIAL OWNERSHIP

When capital plant is built up under the stimulus of personal profit and private property the result is a vast burden of debt upon the shoulders of the great majority of the people. They inherit a debt to the few owners of the capital plant just as peasants used to inherit a debt to landlords and contract tenant farmers still do. Finally they have to earn dividends on fictitious capital.

When the Russian Revolution brought in a thoroughgoing system of social ownership it put into operation a form of property stimulus which had never been tried on a large scale. Instead of the overhead drive of capitalism, from its managers, foremen, efficiency engineers, and personnel workers, there is substituted the pull of socialised self-interest. All capital plant is amortised and when paid for is owned free and clear by the government, which is the workers, according to the formula. To put it exactly from the standpoint of the intellectual, "The worker feels he is working for the state of which he is an important part." Therefore Soviet economists consider that the first stimulus to production, and the most important, is the consciousness of ownership. But just what is the consciousness of social ownership and how is it to be developed in workers fresh from the villages, where the love of private property is the strongest factor in keeping forty per cent of them out of the collective farms. "If I have only one hen," they tell you, "I want to know it is mine."

The teaching of social ownership begins in the schools. Says Krupskaya, the widow of Lenin and a leader in making educational policy, *The first aim of polytechnical schools (now universal) is to educate children to become at the same time workers and owners of industry.* The director of one of the big educational combines that are organised in the new industrial plants states its aims to be: (1) *To make the worker class conscious.* (2) *To make an effective worker for social production; to teach him that production belongs to him.* The new party member is taught: *A conscious attitude to industry is the first distinguishing feature of the party member. He regards the enterprise with the eye of its owner, having a lively interest in all details of industry and not only in his own shop. When the peasants come to work in the sovhoz,* an interpreter who lived at several told me, *at first they say, "See how these Communists live." Then after about two months they begin to say, "We have been wrong, this belongs to us." Then they go back to the villages to tell about it.*

It is also the business of the labor unions to develop this sense of ownership. In its resolutions, the Sixteenth Party Congress declared:

. . . The most important task of the labor unions is to inoculate the conscience of the broad working masses with the idea that the workers work not for the capitalists but for their own commonwealth, for their own class; the realisation of this fact is a mighty motive power in the development and improvement of industry.

In and through the union, the older workers carry out this task for those newly arrived from the villages, in the state farms as well as in the factories. At first they work only for wages and are slow to realise that the machines, the new cow barn and chicken houses "are truly theirs." At first, and it is the same with new students in the technical schools, they talk about what "they" do, meaning the management. Then the older ones will say, *Where do you think you are, you talk like a stranger; this is ours.*

I will see our director and arrange it for you, was the answer of a fellow guest at the sanitarium. At Kuznestroi when Glenn, the American engineer, could not get the practice of putting ice and frozen snow in the concrete stopped by appeals to the foremen he finally accomplished it by going to the workers directly and telling them it was their plant, and their interest demanded quality. *In my brigade*, said a foreman, *when the men are spoiling a blue print with their dirty fingers, I say to them: "This costs money. Soon it will be no good if you handle it that way. It's ours. Take care of it."*

There is no doubt about the growth of the consciousness of ownership among Soviet workers and about its power as an incentive. The captain of the Soviet ship in which we went to Leningrad told me the sailors were working better than before the revolution. *Why? Because now they work for themselves.* The day after an American journalist had told me this phrase was more rhetoric than fact I was going through a factory with an American foreman. As we came to one department he said, *We had a row here last week. The director changed the machines around without consulting the workers. You should have seen what they did to him. They called a meeting and put him on the carpet. They said "Who do you think you are, changing these machines around without consulting us? This is our factory, not yours."* An interpreter remarked that she was tired because the night before forty per cent of the "Intourist" staff had been sorting potatoes from eight until twelve in a dirty, wet basement, as their free work. I asked why. *They belonged to everybody and should not be wasted.* In his sketch "Building the Stalingrad Tractor Works," Peter Vorobyev, one of the shock brigade workers who has begun to write, says:

A peasant from the village of Lebedyan, in the province of Tambov, came along with me to work. Ivan Tulupov, as he was called, frowned at the first sight of the giant building. He couldn't understand just yet the proletarian pride of ownership. But soon the greatness of the construction gets hold of him too. "That's fine now. A big works. Never saw such a one in my time. It must be about five kilometres around, and more." And his rugged, furrowed face melts into a smile.

A journalist watching some Bashkirs digging the ditches for the new plant at Kuznetstroi wondered if these backward tribesmen knew what it was all about and asked one of them. He answered, speaking Russian with difficulty: *I work in Kuzstroi. It is my plant. The plant will make iron, machines, and everything we need in our kolhozes.* When I enquired of an executive worker responsible for preparing party propaganda why the Soviet workers, as I had observed, read posters and charts more than is commonly done elsewhere, even at exhibits, she answered, *Because it's their industry. If some one wrote of your home, wouldn't you want to see if it was right?*

"But the other industries where they don't work?"

They understand how they all belong together. No transport! No coal, no bread.

There is spreading through the population a sense of working for themselves that is quite different from that of working for the state as an employer. The two are being unified. Phrases to express it are becoming common usage: *Eto gosudarstovennoye. Eto nashe.* (This is the state's. This is ours). This attitude was emphatically expressed by a former worker in the United States:

This is a workers' government for the worker. You can see it in me. I am forty-four years old and my hair is turning gray. I was kicked out of the United States where I had worked four years. They found me at a workers' meeting and the policeman took me from Indiana Harbor to East Chicago and put me in jail. I have worked here seven years. Then they said, "We will send you to school and make you a manager." I said, "I am too old, what can I learn?" But they said, "You can learn so they won't put anything over on you." So now I am at school. The government gives me full pay, two hundred and fifty rubles a month for my family and one hundred and ninety for myself. I think only how I can study so as to pay back to the workers what they have given me. Here your family is taken care of. You never think of losing your job or of money. You think only of how to make the work better or better to explain something.

This growing sense of social ownership is different from the consciousness of public ownership in capitalist countries, where such enterprises are managed by politicians who are quite often beyond the reach of the workers. *But when you worked in New York you owned Central Park and the Public Library,* I said to one of them. *Did I?* was the answer, *I didn't know it.* Another in a different part of the country said:

I feel the same about the library. I could use the books there as I can here. But at the factory it's different. You cannot have a comprehension of how we feel if you think according to the capitalist system. "It's mine" does not mean that you can come and take the coal in the mine as you could if you said that in the United States. If I don't get enough coal I go to the union and they attend to it. If I see a fellow getting too much coal and trading in it I report him to the union. They call him to the meeting and make him ashamed and bashful. You can burn up things that belong to you in a capitalist country. Here we cannot destroy. It is mine means it is ours. There are laws of the organisation. We have discipline, that decides what to do. The man from the village is used to putting things this way or that way as he likes. So he leaves his tools about. Here we have a place for them. So he learns. What is mine is ours in production but not in distribution.

The essential thing in ownership is that a thing does not belong to somebody else. So over and over again Soviet workers will tell you, *What we are building does not belong to the capitalists, and never will. We may not be getting much out of it just now but at least we are not working for anybody else.* The further reality of social ownership is expressed in the fact of joint control of the process of production and of the ends for which it is used. Thus the head of an important trust, technically trained in the United States, writes me out of his experience: *All of industry is under constant control of the working class, the directors of the enterprises, the administrators as well as the technical leadership, are regularly accounting for its work before the workers.* More than once workers and directors have told me that the workers had power to get the directors discharged if there was just cause. Social management is the essence of social ownership.

The Plenum of the Central Committee of the Central Council of Labor Unions in Moscow December, 1931, ascribes the huge advance in Soviet industry largely to the close co-operation between labor unions, industrial trusts, and the government: *It is due to the fact that Soviet workers are the masters of industry. Any increase in industrial efficiency means better conditions for the workers.* One American engineer says the endless workers meetings used up lots of time but they spurred inventive efforts and encouraged co-operation. *After all it's their factory.*

Lenin foresaw this development and its meaning when he wrote in 1918 in his "How to Organise Competition":

Only now has the possibility for wide and really mass display of enterprise, competition and bold initiative been created. Every factory from which the capitalist has been ejected, or at least put under restraint by real workers' control, every village from which the landowner exploiter has been smoked out, and in which his land is confiscated, is now, and only now, a field in which the working man can reveal himself, straighten his back and feel that he is a man. Now, for the first time, after centuries of working for others, of subjection to exploiters, it has become possible to work for oneself, and moreover to do work with all the conquests of modern technique and culture. . . . Certainly this greatest change in the history of mankind—from involuntary labor to working for oneself— . . .

Krivitsky in his "Capitalist and Socialist Co-operation of Labor," puts the power of the latter form squarely upon the fact that:

. . . the means of production are in the hands of the collective of direct producers. . . . The collective does not represent individuals who are tied to one another by exterior ties particularly in relation to capital as is the case in capitalist society. Their inner solidarity consists in the fact that the means of production are not an alien force to them but are their own property, the property of the ever growing collective, and hence their toil is not a forced labor for others but work for themselves.

The claim that workers do more and better work when conscious of working for themselves is exactly the argument that was made in defense of the capitalist system in its early days. But in the building of socialism it acquires a wider sweep. Under universal ownership it operates without limitations because the essence of ownership expands throughout the population instead of contracting. Also it is reinforced by another principle which in emergencies has always proved more powerful—the principle that people will do for others what they will not do for themselves. This is the law of sacrifice upon which in the last analysis the future of humanity depends. True to its basic philosophy of the unity of opposites, Communism seeks for the most effective coordination of the egoistic and altruistic tendencies in human nature by developing a system of ownership which makes it true that when a man works for others he is also working for himself. Thus it has a chance to avoid the futility of capitalism, which tried in vain to unite the same tendencies in the reverse order by saying that when a man worked for himself he also worked for others.

That way of doing only enlarged the possessive appetites whereas when the order is changed they tend to disappear. Thus when I asked in an agricultural commune, whose founders had brought their capital with them from other countries, if there was not a tendency to regard themselves as owners of a separate community, they told me at first a number of them said and felt, "This is ours," but that attitude gradually disappeared as they were tied more and more into the larger national plan for socialising the countryside. A young agricultural engineer, graduate of one of our colleges, remarked that he was beginning to be afraid even of co-operative ownership of an apartment because it might interfere with his willingness to go where he might be needed. "We regard ourselves as mobilised," he said.

The necessity of this spirit was set down by Lenin in "The Great Initiative":

Communism begins where the unselfish and difficult work of the people is devoted to increasing the output of wealth, to preserving every bushel of corn, every hundredweight of coal and other necessities, destined not for the producers themselves and their "nearest" but for those who are "distant," for society as a whole, for the millions of human beings at first living in separate socialist countries and later united in a League of Soviet Republics.

When the legal essence of private property—exclusive control—is abolished, when it is impossible for people to keep things away from others, there is nothing left for the possessive appetite to feed on. Even social ownership becomes a misleading term; it is not ownership at all in the old sense. It simmers down in fact to joint use and management and perhaps had better be called what it really is—social control.

SOCIAL APPROVAL AND DISAPPROVAL

Far more, however, than by personal or material rewards the Communists achieve their ends by using the stimulus of social approval and disapproval. This is the most important shift in incentives—the transfer of the tremendous power of common judgment and public opinion from money making to socially useful labor. The resultant change in the psychological atmosphere is one of the things that causes the visitor to realise that he is in a new world. In the capitalist world, of course, practically all the agencies of public opinion are engaged in strengthening and sanctifying the spirit of money making, but much more indirectly than the Communists picture the process. In the Soviet Union naturally all the controls are thrown the other way—to get exploitation shunned as dishonorable, to get productive labor accepted and glorified. This is done directly, and according to plan, by the use of all possible forces of education and all available means of publicity, exactly as all the agencies of public opinion were mobilised to get the people of the United States to support the War.

A great campaign is now in progress to glorify labor. Its key-note is a much quoted phrase coined by Stalin in his report to the Sixteenth Party Congress when he was dealing with socialist competition. He said that its most remarkable feature *consists in the radical revolution it has wrought in man's views of labor, because it transforms labor from a disgraceful and painful burden, as it was reckoned before, into a matter of honor, a matter of glory, a matter of valor and heroism.* He then stressed the fact that in capitalist countries social approval is given to income, to property, and freedom from toil and in contrast declared: *Here in USSR on the contrary the most desirable course which earns social approval is the possibility of becoming a hero of labor, a hero of the shock movement, surrounded with the glamor of the respect of millions of toilers.*

All the means which have heretofore been used to romanticise the heroism of war are now being employed to glorify the activities of economic toil. At the exit from one department at Selmashtroi I was halted by a huge banner which read: "Today the 30th at 7 A.M. the axle brigade of Grishinev overfulfilled its monthly task and gave 936 ends over the quota." The shock workers have their badges which the stricter sort of young Communists refuse to wear, saying, "We do not work for praise." Their achievements and pictures are posted at the entrances to the factories and on special bulletin boards on the walls of the clubs. They are even sold in albums. They appear, of course, in the factory papers and the great dailies also carry portraits of the best of them. This is an exception to their general rule of printing no personal items. Then for good measure the exploits of the shock workers are broadcast over the air.

The deeds and spirit of the shock workers have also become the subjects of the new proletarian literature and the theme of the new proletarian music. Where aristocratic literature went to manor and castle for its characters the socialist writers go to the factories, the mines, and the collective farms. The magazine of the Russian Association of Proletarian Writers (No. 2, 1931) announced in an editorial: *Among our proximate tasks is to reveal to the masses the heroes of the constructive period in shock work and social emulation.* The Secretariat of the Russian Association of Proletarian Musicians passed a resolution in 1931 "To Create a Song about the Heroes of the Five Year Plan" which mobilised all its composer members for that task, sent some of them in brigades to the factories, asked the poets to join in a conference, and started "a mass creative competition" among the members of musical circles in factories for the best song about the shock workers.

The Komsomol and Young Pioneer organisations print the exploits of shock workers in articles and booklets and the youngsters reading them are moved with the spirit of emulation just like those who read of deeds of valor in defense of fatherland or the stories of poor boys who became millionaires. One Komsomol booklet tells the story of a young hero of labor, the youngest driver of the Possosharsky Machine Tractor Station, who in an emergency worked from sunrise to sunset overcoming great difficulties and once went ninety-six hours without sleep. He received the Order of Lenin, which is the highest public decoration. A decoration of the second rank is the order of the "Red Banner of Toil." Last year at the season when presentations at court were being made in Great Britain, and honorary degrees awarded in the United States, a number of these decorations for the people who toil were announced at Moscow. They went to a British engineer and an American agricultural worker; to workers in factories who had outstripped the Five Year Plan; to four women—a tractor driver who had nearly cut in half her allotted time for sowing the crop, a worker with cows who had greatly increased the production of milk, two swineherds who had worked day and night to save their pigs from an epidemic. Thus is history being rewritten.

It is also the custom to give victory banners to the best department in factories and to the best class in an educational institution. In one oil field in the Baku region the workers proudly told of three flags which they had received for fulfilling their year's plan in eight months. One from the Kharkov Soviet, away in the Ukraine, was won in socialist competition. Another was given by the Central Committee of the Party in their own Azerbaidjan Republic. The third came from Germany, from the paper "Rote Fahne," but this they had passed on to another oil field for bringing up production from a very low point.

The stimulus of these flags is dramatically shown in

one of the recently successful plays which uses strongly the effect upon the workers in a constructive enterprise of hauling down the red flag which signifies keeping abreast of the plan and putting up the burlap flag which advertises failure. It is shown again in a little book by Mikhailov, worker in the Serp Molot Works, entitled "The Fight for Steel." The author says he is not writing about heroism but "simply the conscious Communist attitude toward labor." He tells the story of the three hundred and seventy-two men working in the sheet-rolling shop who became ashamed because it had the worst record in the plant. So they drew up a plan and started socialist competition under the slogan of an English foreman "Our shop has got to be the best in the whole works." The first month, helping and watching each other, they succeeded in fulfilling the plan one hundred and five per cent. This shop, that some months before had been jeered at, now declared itself a shock brigade and was awarded the red flag of labor. To keep that flag the men of the shock brigade had to exceed in skill, courage, initiative, and helpfulness.

This policy of dramatically throwing public approval upon those who do the best work in socialist construction comes to a national climax in the park of Culture and Rest at Moscow. One of its walks has recently been lined with great busts of the "Heroes of Labor" who have helped to win the Five Year Plan. One is included for helping to liquidate illiteracy and there are several engineers. Despite some romanticising of the features, their proletarian lines stand out in strong contrast to the usual figures of generals and statesmen in public places in other lands.

The importance attached to this dramatisation of labor is shown by a Decree of the People's Commissars of the USSR, issued October 19, 1931, which "Izvestia" promptly put on the front page:

The working class must not only know but preserve for the future the names of those leaders and best workers . . . who by their sacrificial labors . . . vouchsafe the victorious advance of the cause of the building of socialism. . . .

In the chief constructions and new enterprises there shall be placed in a prominent place tablets of honor upon which are to be marked the names of those who designed the construction, its chief builders and consultants, and particularly the prominent shock workers. . . .

This campaign to throw the glamor of heroism around common toil is carried on under the slogans: "A land should know its heroes." "A land is known by the heroes it honors." "The country must know the heroes of Pyatiletka." Now over their gallery of shock workers the factories are putting these slogans with their own name in place of "the country." Thus even the love of the limelight is socialised.

All this can of course be compared in its social results with the use of agencies of public opinion to glorify war. Also it furnishes a counterpoise to the pressure of the mass upon the individual, which is inevitably inherent not only in the socialist scheme but in the very nature of the machine age. Radek was quick to use this point in his reply to the critics who sneered at this "mass production" of standardised heroes: *Neither Marx nor Lenin regarded the mass as the sum total of individuals. And for them history was not the struggle of a disintegrated, anonymous mass.*

Furthermore this tribute to labor is saved from the unreality of similar glorification by preachers and poets by having more substantial awards attached to it. The

"Red Banner of Toil" entitles the owner to a free pass on Moscow trams, a pass to travel twice a year to any point in the USSR, and a pension of thirty rubles a month. Also it brings the regular pension nearer by adding so many years to the service record. "Heroes of Labor" also receive an additional pension. Persons can be raised to this rank by special decision of the Central Executive Committee of the All Union Council of Soviets or of a federated republic, at the request of the labor organisation, for outstanding service in the field of production, scientific work, or service to state or community. As a rule persons are rewarded with this rank if they have thirty-five years of service but in exceptional cases this condition may be waived.

In like manner all the forces of social disapproval are thrown against those who are not doing their share in socialist construction—the shirkers, the absentees, the lazy, the drifters (from one department to another or from factory to factory), the snatchers (of pay), the wasters (of material). They are caricatured in the wall newspaper and in the factory paper, which in the larger plants does for all what the wall paper does for a department. Along with pictures of the shock workers it carries caricatures of the slackers and delinquents. Here are the inscriptions under some of them taken from a number of issues of the paper of the Ball Bearing factory, Moscow:

Concrete mixer. Bezruchkin, F. D. Frequently appears for work drunk.

Savin from the brigade of Begunov disorganises the discipline of the brigade by his "belly rubbing" self glorification.

Here is the fellow who breaks the tempos of the blacksmith shop. The earth digger Pentulin by his loaf-

ing makes impossible the accomplishment of the production task of the brigade.

The earth digger Misytov likes most of all to sit near the barrel (to smoke) instead of working. In this manner with crossed arms almost the whole day.

Factory Rabbit Lukashevich "23d group" is a vicious loafer and slacker.

Such caricatures will be found on special signs throughout the factories. At Selmash I was stopped one day by a sign over the washroom: "This is where the lazy fellows smoke the machines away." Another day on a blackboard in the plow shop were three columns headed "Drunkards," "Absentees," "Lazy Fellows," Underneath were the names of the delinquents. They were caricatured—the drunkard with a big bottle, the absentee sleeping in bed, the lazy man with his head tied up, pretending a toothache. The big score-board in the harvesting machinery department contained each man's name and his record for fulfilling his quota in the plan, for scrap, idleness, and absences, his classification as udarnik and his premiums. In front of the plant a giant worker was pictured with an enormous hammer under the slogan, "Smash the drifting and careless, the false udarnik."

The drunkards and slackers have to get their pay at a special "Black Window" where they are jeered at by onlookers. Sometimes the place for receipt of wages is a hole cut in the middle of an enormous black bottle. At Selmash it was the mouth of an enormous red-nosed drinker with a sign, "At the Black Pay Window all the lazy, absentees, drunkards, and snatchers will get their pay on—(date)." To get it they had to mount steps and pass along a raised platform in full view. The children added to this publicity by coming into the factory and drawing caricatures of drunkards for the notice boards. They even wrote biting phrases on the box of cigarettes to be sold to the delinquent and then the other workers would say "Aren't you ashamed? Look what the children write about you." Such procedure is a part of the Pioneer training. One of their picture story books for children is entitled "The Pioneers and The Loafers." In the illustrations the children come to the factory and see the machines idle. They are told the workers are drinking. They make a red board and a black board. They paste on house doors "Here Lives a Loafer." They parade through town holding up a vodka bottle inscribed, "Here is your Enemy." Their banners read: "Shame to the Loafers. You break down the Plan." The parade, with pictures of the guilty, goes to the drinking place. Ashamed, the loafers return to work. No more idle machines. Finally the factory goes on the red board for fulfilling its quota in the Plan.

With simple people such methods are very effective. Says one observer, "I saw an old woman who actually wept when a wooden elephant, the symbol of shameful sluggishness, was hung in her department." Practically the only fear operating among the workers in the Soviet Union, insofar as production is concerned, is the fear of public censure and the reprimand of the organisation to which they belong.

This fear of censure is used in more sophisticated ways. In the metal industry there will usually be found at the main entrance to the factory, also in each department, boards with pieces of scrap—parts ruined by poor work—together with the name of the brigade, foreman, or worker responsible. Similar exhibits of spoiled consumers' goods in Moscow stores are called "windows of disgrace." In one factory the agitation and propaganda brigade carried on its fight against shirkers by providing them with a special pay window with a picturesquely ornamented screen with inscriptions and figures showing how their deficiency in production had deprived all of the right to a rise in wages. The payment of wages was accompanied by the acting of three marionettes which developed in conversation, limerick, and song, the consequences of shirking. The names of single shirkers were loudly announced through a speaking trumpet.

Similarly photo brigades distribute pamphlets with photographs they have taken of shirkers, drunkards, waste goods and their producers. At one railway base an engineer who had broken a locomotive when drunk came to the brigade and promised to get drunk no more if they would not reprint his picture. Some of the Moscow tramway workers at one terminus would come to dinner ten minutes early. Photographs of these "embezzlers of working-time," eating while the clock showed only 11.50, brought forth such jeers and jokes that the practice soon stopped.

It is doubtful if there has ever in history been such an organised conscious attempt as this to change the customs and habits of a people, certainly not since the great days of the Roman Church. Now the authority that has been taken away from church and state is given to the crowd made conscious of its needs. All the mass force of social approval, the force that few even of the bravest dare defy, mobilised by all the arts known to modern publicity and propaganda, is being thrown upon socialist production, and the results are far-reaching. As one watches the tides of humanity flowing back and forth along the streets of Soviet cities, so like and yet so unlike the millions in other lands who go their way practically oblivious of the powers that mold their destinies, he cannot but wonder if these masses also are inert and indifferent to the changes being projected around them. Is it after all the inertia of the human mass that gives to a few bold spirits, the power and the right to manipulate destiny? The answer lies in this unparalleled mobilisation of the forces of social approval and disapproval to make the masses conscious participants in the program that is changing their lives. The *mores* are being altered in accordance with a definite plan.

CHAPTER III

THE COMING OF THE NEW

In what new direction are the folkways turning? What new forces are now shaping their course?

A NEW ATTITUDE TOWARD WORK

It was my custom everywhere to ask children and young people what "Building Socialism" meant to them. One of the best answers was given by a sixteen-year-old boy in the factory school of the Ball Bearing Plant in Moscow. "It means national ownership, national planning, and a new attitude toward labor." This is more than a different estimate of the place of work in life which makes it an honored service and therefore willingly accepted instead of an imposed, unavoidable task to be escaped from as soon as possible. These attitudes belong respectively to new communities opening up fresh fields of production and to old societies living on limited resources by long-established methods. Work had a different value in the early days in America, Canada, Australia, and New Zealand than in the older lands with their ascent from manual workers to white-collared workers, professional and leisure classes, each of which represents a rung in the social ladder. This is the difference between a society controlled by the producers and one in which the exploiters have come to power, with their scribes to write for them legends about work being a punishment and a curse. Therefore in order to make forever impossible the rise of a leisure class the Communists put beneath their first Soviet Republic a revolutionary foundation. In the "Declaration of the Rights of the Toilers" adopted by the All Russian Congress of Soviets on July 10, 1918, it is written:

The Russian Socialist Federated Soviet Republic recognizes labor to be the duty of all citizens of the Republic and it proclaims the principle "He who does not labor neither shall he eat." Article Four of the Constitution entitled "The Right to Vote" begins: "*The right to vote and to be elected to the Soviets is enjoyed by the following citizens, irrespective of religion, nationality, domicile, etc., of the Russian Federated Socialist Soviet Republic, of both sexes, who shall have completed their eighteenth year by the day of election:*

a. All who have acquired the means of living through labor that is productive and useful to society, and also persons engaged in housekeeping which enables the former to do productive work, i.e. . . .

b. Soldiers of the army and navy of the Soviets.

c. Citizens of the two preceding categories who have to any degree lost their capacity to work.

This difference in the place of work in life, so that it becomes something to be embraced and honored instead of contemned and avoided, is one of the two big differences between the psychological atmosphere of the Soviet Union and that of other lands which at once impresses the observer. This change of valuation leads to far-reaching alterations in the structure of society. It is for instance playing the decisive part in determining the place of woman in society and the nature of family life. The new attitude toward work is not developed easily. Thus Yakoklev reports on the situation in the collective farms to the Sixteenth Party Congress:

There will still be thousands of instances of a grafting attitude toward work and toward the distribution of the income in socialised farming. There will be thousands of cases where the kolhoznik will look on the common work as work which is not his own, as work to be got rid of, where he should shirk as much as possible or get out of it completely. . . . In 1919 when the bourgeoisie was completely expropriated, Lenin put, as the main problem, the struggle against the old habit of looking on work as something one does only under duress . . . the struggle against the idea that one must always try to avoid work as much as possible; that work is only a means of getting something out of the bourgeoisie, failing to understand that the character of work is entirely changed by the passing over from the capitalist to the socialist system of economy.

The process of education which is changing the old habits and saving this new valuation of work from being another abstract ideal begins in the school, where work is an inseparable part of education. The child is educated to become a worker in a workers' society and taught from infancy that it is an obligation which he owes to society. This process of education is carried on in a thousand ways by the factory and the kolhoz. From the beginning of the Industrial Revolution the factory has been an instrument for remaking people from the country; sociologists have charted the changes after they have occurred without being planned or desired. In the Soviet Union the factory is consciously used to change the standards of life of the people from the villages. The regular workers speak of those who regard it only as a place to make extra earnings in the winter time, as not having yet "been through the factory melting-pot"; they have not yet been freed from the "egoistic instincts of petty ownership and a slavish attitude toward work." Now the kolhoz is used in the same manner. In a pamphlet on the Red Army, in the section on the relation of the soldiers to collectivisation, occurs this phrase: *Collective labor not only convinces the peasant that kolhoz economy is more advantageous than individual economy, it also teaches him to submerge his own private interests in those of the proletarian state.* It is required of the labor union that it should educate the workers in the new attitude toward work and this it does in various ways later to be described. The party instructs its new members at the outset that, *The foundation of the new life is the new attitude of the worker to his labor, to industry, to the socialist structure.*

This new attitude toward work has two characteristics which are constantly reiterated. It is both "conscious" and "conscientious." The former is psychological, the latter is ethical and includes the former. The Soviet worker is being educated and trained to be conscious of his work in relation to the task of the factory as a whole, to be conscious of the relation of his factory to the entire national economy, and then to be aware of the inter-relation between this and a world ecenomy, both now and in the hoped-for future of a socialist world. He, beyond all the workers of the world, knows what he is doing and why. He has a purpose and his work has a meaning. It is the depth and breadth of this consciousness that distinguishes it from the results secured by welfare and personnel workers, and industrial psychologists, who try, under a capitalist régime, to create an interest on the part of the worker more vital than that contained in the pay envelope.

The "conscientious" attitude of the Soviet worker toward work involves his acceptance of obligations which are stronger and more far-reaching than the obligation to give "a good day's work for a good day's pay." They arise out of his comradeship with fellow workers, they emerge from those bonds in the recesses of his nature that tie him to future generations. Several times Russian-American workers have told me, "Life is harder here but more interesting. Here we have less interest in our pay and more in our job and improving our qualifications. And there is more to do after work." Here are two of "The Experiences of a Soviet Efficiency Expert":

"I quit. Don't want to work. Pay me for the lot according to the fifth rate. I won't do it according to the third." This is the sort of thing Ivanov used to say only two months ago. But this is what I overheard him say recently to an apprentice in his department: "Say, you ought to go back to the village and play marbles. Here we have no time for fooling. What do you think of yourself? Aren't you ashamed to fall down on the job? You so young and strong." He used himself to be a slacker. Now he never stays out and never refuses to work when necessary. He pledged himself to stay on the job until the end of the Five Year Plan.

The plant finished the program of the first two years ahead of time. Now a new brigade is formed to go ahead of the collective agreement. Shop meetings are held and a special committee is appointed to go over the details. The day comes for report. . . . I begin to criticise myself and the weak spots in my department. This roused the meeting. The workers pointed out their own mistakes. The resolutions declared we will reduce absences to zero, etc., etc. One spoke against the high norms and low prices: "I am not going to kill myself working. I get my minimum and I am satis-

because have a standard to meet (american)

fied. At least I won't get tired." . . . *"What, you will fool around and get paid for it. How will you face your comrades?* . . . *And what will you tell your folks at home? That you were playing? And will they praise you for it? While your comrades are building you are stealing the bricks. No, we don't need such workers. Go ahead and look for a job where you can have lots of rest. And we'll work. We'll build. We have no time to sit around and wait." The effect was profound. He felt ashamed. He sat with bowed head and rubbed his nose.*

In the Soviet system, work is a gospel as well as the law, it becomes both the "means of grace and the hope of glory." Ask young Communists how they expect to avoid the heretofore irresistible tendency of all human organisations to create a separate office-holding class and they will tell you, "When we see any signs of that attitude developing in our organisation we send the person back to the factory. It will cure him in two years." A young engineer who had been selected with the picked group to go abroad for training was not sent because it was discovered during the last period in the language school that he had not outlived some bourgeois tendencies. He was sent back to the factory. If he made good in two years he might go on with his specialist training. Those whose stay abroad is noticed to have affected their personal habits are sent to difficult tasks to get cured, usually in a remote district. A grafting contractor, whom I met in a prison in 1924, was in 1931 in an important executive post. He had been sent to Central Asia to take part in a big development of flax cultivation and had made good. The famous engineer-professor Ramzin, sentenced in the famous Prom Party trial, was not kept in jail but sent back to his lecture room every day, at first under guard and then unattended. He lost his house, his automobile, and his prestige, but not his job. If he continues to do that well his prestige will return.

The OGPU not only eliminates the incurables, it also assists in transforming those capable of reformation. Among its many activities it conducts a reform colony for thieves and prostitutes, teaching them real trades. Many delinquents are now in "working and living communities in isolated places" in the Soviet Union. On their own initiative and volition they have taken as their motto the words of Lenin, "To be a member of a commune means to behave so as to give your strength and your work for a common cause." Down at Tiflis, in the Factory of the Ten Commissars, the young Komsomols who were showing us their department where every worker was both Komsomol and udarnik told us with pride that ten of them had formerly been hooligans. At Selmash I saw two former *beshprezorny*—homeless boys—admitted by the shift meeting to the classification of udarnik. The chairman made a special point of describing their former condition and their changed habits, telling them that their comrades expected them to continue worthy of the privilege being awarded them. One of the most powerful propaganda films in the Union is directed against syphilis. In the end the young man who has lost his wife and his reason by producing an idiot child is restored by the discipline of work in the factory. One of the best of the recent short stories by proletarian writers portrays the transformation of a horse thief who accidentally got charge of a kolhoz stable.

The far-reaching significance of this new use of work and this new attitude toward it, is that the ethical sanctions which have moved the few to become sacrificing servants of the common weal are now moving the many in their every-day work. When the control of the economic means of life is democratised it involves also the democratisation of its highest ethical values.

THE CREATIVE PURPOSE

One of the most obvious expressions of this change is the fact that the workers have at last acquired what the machine age under capitalist administration has given only to a few—a creative purpose. Of all the general forces at work moving the people of the Soviet Union this is easily the first. They do what they do, and as they do, because for them the world is young; the former things are passing away, all things are becoming new. In the early dawn of this new day Lenin told them that, *The organising talents of the peasantry and the working class are very great and these talents are just beginning to reveal themselves, to wake up, to draw close to the living, creative great work, to undertake the construction of socialist society.*

The sense and feeling of a new life are everywhere evident. Stalin told the Industrial Managers, *It would be silly to think that the production plan led merely to an enumeration of figures and tasks. In reality our production plan is millions of workers, creating a new life.* An American miner in Siberia was not an exception when he declared, *I came here not to get rich but to build up this country and through it the workers' world.* An interpreter, of the former intelligentsia, when asked what were the most significant changes between the old and the new Russia put first: *The greatest change is that the people now know what they want.*

The masses formerly were not persons, now they are self-conscious. A young Armenian engineer, trained in one of our state colleges, in talking over his work in the tractor stations said, *I feel part of a great social welfare enterprise. I feel that I am also myself, creating. That is what gives me satisfaction.*

When it sets out to accomplish a classless society, the Second Five Year Plan not only gives the people a stirring goal but it also plans to extend the sense of a creative purpose in life and work. The Seventeenth Party Conference (January, 1932) declared:

The Conference holds that the chief political task of the Second Five Year Plan is to do away completely with the capitalist elements and with classes in general. . . . Both the industrial workers and the collective farmers in this country are already overwhelmingly in the ranks of the active builders of socialism. The task of the full liquidation of the capitalist elements and of the classes generally is at the same time the task of the transformation of the whole toiling population of the country into conscious and active builders of a classless socialist society. . . .

It is of course the Five Year Plan that has brought the building of socialism down out of the air and made it a concrete reality, in which the workers can feel that they are participating every day. Now it means heavy industries and mechanised agriculture; next, light industries and better living conditions and all the time more cultural gains. Here are definite objectives set down in figures, not vague hopes and promises. These things can be measured, also they necessarily expand and call for further activity. This is the first time in history that the masses can consciously create by scientific standards; heretofore they have been used by the great builders, not knowing what they were doing. Now they build themselves, for themselves. What else should science mean but this, and how else shall it be justified?

It is in the nature of social-economic planning that it both requires and gives a purpose. Those who first conceive it must possess the purpose, then as the plan is worked out it develops purpose in the masses. *Inasmuch,* says the State Planning Commission, *as we are realizing a purposive economy . . . the whole, working collectively participates consciously in the aggregate social production . . .* This is spoken theoretically, actually it takes a terrific campaign by party, labor union, kolhoz, and Komsomol to bring about this consciousness. In a myriad of ways the worker is told: *Every works, every mine, factory, workshop, is a part of our socialist structure, a cog in the Soviet machine. If a single cog is spoilt the whole suffers.*

These ideas have gripped the masses, the head of one of the trusts told me. *Now the party is welcomed at the factories. Formerly "Building Socialism" and "The World Revolution" were words; we got only a pound and a half of bread where we should have had two.*

How they permeate the countryside is shown by the way the chairman of a village Soviet, aged twenty-eight and formerly a farm laborer, writes about their collective farm:

Our kolhoz is only a small link in the general system and the object of that system is to build a socialist society. Our collective farm is a good one but, taken by itself, it is only a farm after all and that is not enough for socialism. The members of every collective farm must be aware of the place it occupies in national economy and of the obligations which each worker must ful-

fil in connection with the whole Union and the political problems of the Soviet government, both at home and abroad.

Among the material which the Soviet delegation took to the World Social Economic Congress at Amsterdam, August, 1931, was a statement about the futility of proposals to introduce the principle of planning into capitalist economics. The chief argument was that the competitive and class nature of capitalist organisation made it impossible to extend planning beyond a very limited area. But in the Soviet Union, in contrast to the sense of frustration that afflicts so many people elsewhere, those who come within the orbit of the plan and participate consciously in socialist building move on a big stage and are aware of great destiny. They feel they are actually taking part in the world revolution. They expect now to bring it about by such improvement of their own conditions that the workers of the rest of the world will demand the same. Stalin tells them:

Our progress must be such that the working class may exclaim looking at us, "There it is—my vanguard; there it is—my shock brigade; there it is—my workers' power; there it is—my fatherland. They are carrying out their cause—our cause. We must support them against the capitalists and help on the cause of world revolution."

In the same key a Komsomol leader told me: *By active participation in socialist construction in the USSR we get the perspective of the international socialist revolution. Our success consolidates the international revolution.*

Thus the significance of the Plan is that it gives the masses that which our liberals are so afraid of, that which life has not had since the break up of the Middle

Ages—a central purpose. In so doing, it puts the balance of power into the hands of the constructive energies of mankind. And if in the long run man the builder is not greater than man the destroyer, if his periods of building are not longer and more effective than his mad moments of destruction, if the constructive motives are not more powerful than the disintegrating, then there is no meaning to life and no future for society. Heretofore the social organisation has always betrayed the creative capacities of the workers, turned them toward greed and war and death. Even science has driven up the same fatal road. Now a form of society appears which calls man to the greatest creative task of history, the remaking of his institutions and his nature. This is the continuing social revolution—a vast constructive possibility.

NEW ANTAGONISMS

To realise this possibility the Communists call upon the fighting spirit. The whole constructive task of building socialism is dramatised as a great war. The party member is told that *he must fulfil in the factory the duties of a rank-and-file soldier. Just as in the civil war the workers fought (with arms in their hands) against the Czarists and bourgeoisie, the proletariat of the Soviet Union is now carrying on at the bench the new fight for socialism against the capitalist world.* So he is enlisted in shock and storm brigades, in the light cavalry for industrial or agricultural emergencies, or in the cultural army. When the program is not fulfilled in a department, a staff of action is formed and the battle-cry is, "To the attack of the crisis."

An example of such methods occurs in a report by

Professor I. Borozdin on "Ten Years of Construction in the Crimean Republic and the Kalmuck Autonomous Region":

In connection with the tenth anniversary of the Kalmuck Autonomous Region there was organised a "cultural attack" which was carried out with great success. Not only liquidation of illiteracy and introduction of general education were the subjects of the attack, but also other elements of cultural work. Five thousand soldiers of the cultural army, armed with textbooks, economic, cultural, and political books, now fight for liquidation of illiteracy, general education, pre-school education, hygiene, agro-minimum, zoo-minimum, etc.

Another instance occurs in the story of the "Pervaya Pyatiletka Kolhoz." Evlampy Fedorovich Solkov, former Red Partisan, writes:

In 1930 I was mobilised in accordance with a resolution of the village Soviet and the board of the collective farm to start an economic and political campaign. A general staff was formed at once, since neither the board nor the Soviet could do anything without the workers' assistance. . . . A shock-group of thirty men, formed around the general staff, were called "the whole-hearted" because every one of them was wholeheartedly devoted to collectivisation and ready to struggle for it . . . we decided to form our most active public-spirited workers into a storm regiment . . . two hundred and eighty men . . . divided into companies. There was a company to each collective farm brigade and each company had a political instructor and cultural instructors. . . . We issued military orders and the whole work was done with great speed. And thanks to the work our regiment did, we were the first in the region to complete our spring sowing, delivering one hundred thousand poods of grain exactly as the plan provided.

The Communist is called to fight against a number of foes. In the field of international socialism he wages constant warfare against the Social Democrats whom he calls "Social Fascists" because *when the World War broke out, this section of the labor parties went over to the side of the bourgeoisie and openly betrayed the cause of the working class;* because they are opportunists working *for reconciliation with the bourgeoisie and endeavoring to hinder the proletarian revolution;* because they *are now the most rabid foes of communism, the revolution, and the dictatorship of the proletariat.* The new member is also exhorted *to struggle actively against deviations within the party. He who does not struggle against right, left, and opportunist deviations is no true member of the party.* Against the *lefts,* of whom Trotzky was the chief, he must struggle because they *wanted to rush ahead on seven-league boots and also in fact rushed into the arms of the bourgeoisie;* against the opportunists and rights because they would slow down the tempo of socialist construction and make concessions to the kulaks, thus bringing back capitalism.

Against capitalism of course the Communists wage unending battle. This is regarded now as a war of defense. In poster and in print the capitalist world is portrayed as preparing its armaments and its intervention plans against the Soviet Union. There is nothing the young Communists believe more powerfully than this. Logically they know it must be so. Their papers tell them continually that it is so. Then the Russian worker hears constantly that all over the world the class struggle of the proletariat against the capitalist system is increasing. *The proletariat is preparing for its last de-*

cisive fight. The success of the industrial-financial plan is the success of the proletarian victory over capitalism. Thus, as in the fight against bad habits, antagonism is enlisted for productive purposes.

The portrait of capitalists that is held up before Soviet citizens is the counterpart of the picture of Bolsheviks drawn by the reactionary press of other countries. New party members are taught that:

The worker in bourgeois countries is a veritable slave, dragging out a wretched existence, doomed to undernourishment and to life in miserable hovels without any chance of enjoying the benefits of culture in his spare time.

Sufficient facts can of course be selected from the news of the world to make this picture concrete. So the use of hate as a motivating force is regarded as a justifiable attack upon evil. Also Communist hate is supposed to be impersonal, like the attitude of scientists to noxious insects; but popular propagandists are neither saints nor scientists, especially when the war against capitalism becomes concrete in the fight against the *kulaks*—the elementary capitalists of the Russian villages. Then, when even the children are drafted in the class war to report the enemy and especially when the kulaks start actual attacks on Communists, there emerge all the human passions—spite, envy, malice, fear for self-preservation.

This warfare against capitalists and capitalism is the class struggle, which for Communists is the determining historic fact. The first chapter of the "Handbook for New Members of the Party" is devoted to it. Lenin long ago warned the party that:

The dictatorship of the proletariat is not the end of the class struggle; it is the continuation of that strug-

gle under new forms. He told them that after the power of the bourgeoisie had been broken the class struggle in the transition epoch would *consist in protecting the interests of the working class from those handfuls, groups, and sections of the workers clinging obstinately to the traditions of capitalism and continuing to regard the Soviet State from the old point of view of "giving too little and asking too much." Are there not plenty of such rascals?* He added: *To destroy the classes means also to make an end of the petty-goods producers, and they cannot be driven out or suppressed. We have got to live with them; they can, and must, be re-educated; and this can only be done by prolonged, slow, cautious organising work.*

It is precisely these aspects that the class struggle is now taking in the Soviet Union. Since the socialist sector assumed the dominant position in trade and in agriculture, the capitalist remnants have no economic strength with which to fight. Nevertheless in asking the Seventeenth Party Conference to approve the slogan of a classless society by the end of the Second Five Year Plan, Molotov anticipated that this would lead to an intensifying of the class struggle, *especially in some districts and points of socialist construction.* Every one to whom I talked about it agreed with him. This is first of all because the decision means the liquidation of the remainder of the kulaks and speculators. These people will not accept economic extermination without a struggle, and the kulaks especially will renew their war in the villages. Already there are reports of the killing of Communist organisers. But beyond this Molotov specified *the inevitability of the preservation, and in some instances even intensification, of bourgeois influences and of their still permeating for some time to come some of the workers and even some sections of the party*. He also expected that the necessary enlargement of the administrative machinery would lead *to a certain fresh influx of bourgeois elements*, although *the chief nests of the "wreckers" have been destroyed.*

Thus the class war, by a strange turn of the wheel, is carried into the ranks of the labor unions and the party. In the former it becomes a struggle against anti-social attitudes and habits on the part of the workers and technicians, who are constantly warned against becoming class enemies. Many of the American engineers are focal points for the Russian capitalist remnants in the factories and their attitude of working only to earn their pay—by good service—with no interest in the social meaning of their job is a symbol of the old order. In the party the class struggle becomes merged into that bitterest of all fights—a heresy battle. To be unorthodox is to be "petty bourgeois," or "a tool of the kulaks." There is however reality to the class war in the realm of ideas which goes far beyond the question of method in getting rid of capitalists or kulaks. A teacher in a language school technicum tells me that the faculty divides regularly along class lines on the question of teaching technic. Those who come from the former bourgeoisie, with a background of classical university education, insist that language must not be profaned by teaching the newer idioms; and in teaching methods, they do not want conversational discussion but the formal procedure, by way of grammatical drill.

A new turn was given to class relations within the Soviet Union by Stalin's speech in the summer of 1931 to the managers of industry. Speaking of the necessity of recruiting the industrial and technical intelligentsia not only from the higher schools but also from the leaders of socialist competition and shock brigades in the factories, he said:

We must not ignore and overlook these workers with initiative but advance them boldly to commanding positions, give them opportunity to display their capacity of organisation and extend their knowledge, and create suitable conditions for them to work in, and not spare any expense for this purpose.

Many of these comrades are not members of the party. But that should not prevent us from advancing them boldly to leading positions. On the contrary, it is particularly these comrades who are not party members who must have our especial solicitude and must be advanced to commanding positions so that they may be able to convince themselves that the party knows how to appreciate ability and talent in the workers. Certain comrades think that only party members may hold leading positions in the mills and factories and for that reason ignore and hold back non-party members who possess ability and initiative and advance party members instead, although they are less capable and possess less initiative. Needless to say there is nothing more stupid and reactionary than such a policy. . . . It is our policy to achieve between workers who are members of the party and members who are not an atmosphere of "mutual confidence," of "mutual control" (Lenin). Our party is strong among the working class it should be stated, just because it pursues such a policy.

The new state of affairs (ending of interventionist hopes by Prom-party trial) was found to bring about and actually has brought about a new mental attitude on the part of the old bourgeois intelligentsia. . . . But from this it follows that we must change our policy toward the old technical intelligentsia. If during the height of the wrecking movement we adopted smashing tactics toward the old technical intelligentsia, now when these intellectuals are turning toward the Soviet power, our policy toward them must be one of conciliation and solicitude. It would be wrong and dialectically incorrect to continue our former policy when conditions have changed. . . . And so our task is to change our attitude toward the engineers and technicians of the old school, to show them greater attention and solicitude, to display more boldness in inviting their co-operation. . . . We must alter our policy and display the maximum care and solicitude for those specialists, engineers, and technicians who have definitely come over to the side of the working class.

The meaning of this declaration is that all engineering and technical personnel working directly in production have the special privilege of being classed with industrial workers in the matter of receiving supplies, that is they are in Category 1. The results were soon manifested in a changed temper. Shortly thereafter I heard the chairman of the Workers' Committee in the Hammer and Sickle factory in Moscow exhort the workers to show more consideration to the engineers. All my American acquaintances confirmed my feeling of a different atmosphere. One told me of a Russian engineer friend who remarked to him, *Now we can work. At last they treat us like human beings. I can now get my child into the school I want for him.* At Selmash one of the workers said that the engineers had started out to work honestly and the workers helped them by giving better conditions. To understand this change, one must take into account the remark of an American engineer of Swedish extraction that neither in the United States nor in Sweden had he seen such a class difference between engineers and workers as between those in Russian factories and the old-time engineers. *If there is a piece of scrap to be carried to the office for testing they will not touch it but must call a man away from his work to carry it.*

Now that the class struggle is being modified, the fighting spirit of communism is being concentrated against anti-social factors. They are personified in posters exactly as the older religions personified evil in their devils, they are listed like the deadly sins in slogans—bureaucratism, illiteracy, inefficiency, religion, alcohol, nationalism. Young Communists are told that "the struggle with bureaucratism is one of the most important forms of the class struggle." Seeing the inevitable bureaucratic tendency in the socialist form of administration, Lenin early called on the proletariat to abolish bureaucracy. In 1930, Yakoklev reported its growth in the kolhoz movement:

When the members leave the collective farm because they see in the farmyard more stablemen than horses; and there are foremen, sub-foremen on duty, and assistants, and persons in charge of removing manure, and managers over them, and fodder-getters and purchasers, and men in charge of orders, and with all this the horses are standing knee deep in manure, then there is only one means against resignations: to free the collective farm from the excess apparatus and really help the collective farmers organise their farming.

Stalin also brings this evil home to the party in his report to the Sixteenth Congress:

The problem of fighting bureaucracy—it tries to counteract the creative initiative of the masses, binding them hand and foot with red-tape. . . . The danger is represented not only and not so much by the old bu-

reaucrats, derelict in our institutions, as particularly by the new bureaucrats, the Soviet bureaucrats, among whom Communist bureaucrats play a far from insignificant rôle. I have in mind those Communists who by office instructions and decrees, whose virtue they worship as a fetish, try to replace the creative initiative and independent activity of the millions of the working class and peasantry. The problem is to smash bureaucracy . . . and clear the road for the utilisation of the reserves of our social order, for the development of the creative initiative and independent activity of the masses. In this struggle against bureaucracy the party works in four directions: development of self-criticism; checking carrying out of decisions; cleansing apparatus; promoting into state apparatus from below loyal members of the working class.

Against religion the Communist is called to fight because it is held to be the instrument of the exploiting class, turning the attention of the workers to another world when they ought to be changing their conditions here. Hence, *the Communist cannot be a believer and must not take part in any church ceremonies whatsoever, he is bound to struggle for the complete emancipation of the workers from religious confusion.* The fight against religion is tied in with the fight against alcohol in a joint campaign because in the Russian orthodox religion the family ceremonies and feast days were not properly celebrated if people did not get drunk, and the priest was often the first, because as he visited each house in the village to chant a prayer he was given a drink. The Communist Party on the other hand *struggles resolutely against alcoholism in the interests of the health and cultural development of the working class.* It expels members for heavy drinking.

The Communists are calling their people to fight against nationalism in two forms—a revival of "great-power chauvinism" and a tendency in the constituent republics toward local nationalism. The brunt of this struggle falls upon the proletarian associations of writers and musicians who continually call upon their members to fight on the "ideological front" against these nationalistic tendencies. The present race equality of the USSR, and its democratic internationalism between its one hundred and fifty odd races and nationalities, is in striking contrast to the attitudes and policies of Czarist Russia. Its slogan was coined by Lenin, "A culture, national in form and socialist in content." This means in practice the subordination of the national movement to the class struggle and the development of national languages, literature, and art.

Thus, in some ways the Communists are doing what the idealists have long desired, they are turning the battle spirit of man into constructive channels. It is upon the development of this aspect of the proletarian revolution that the future hangs. Eastward as well as Westward it is opening up the last great reservoirs of undeveloped human energy at the bottom of society. From these depths successive waves of human endeavor have arisen as the peoples have moved to new continents. Now begins the last and the greatest migration. The toilers, who have always been builders—terrible in destruction when they have been led or outraged by those in power—are on the march in search of a new home for the spirit of man. They are following the vision rejected by the mighty, they are trying the methods refused by the wise.

PART TWO

THE INITIATIVE OF THE MASSES

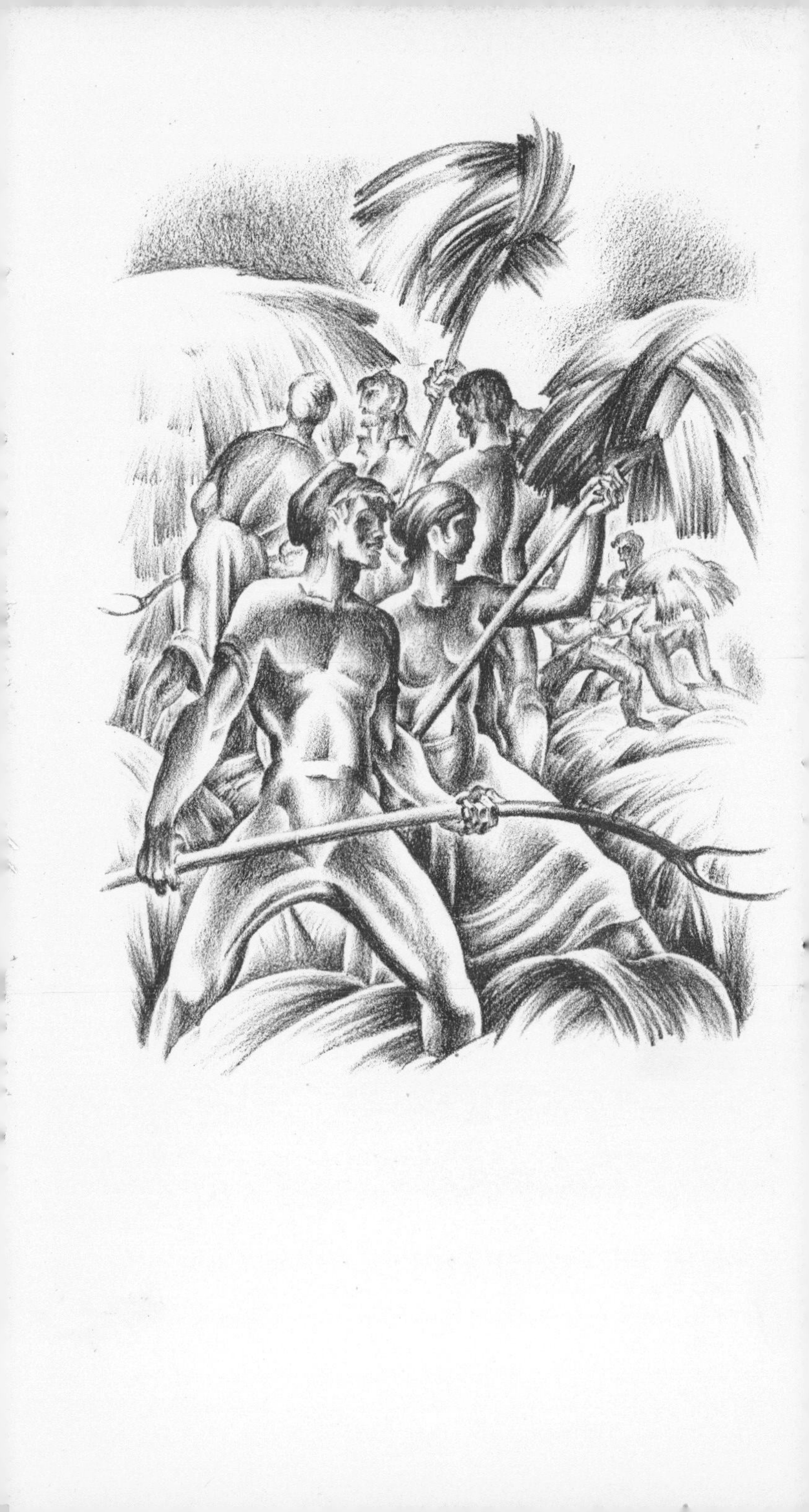

CHAPTER IV

NEW FORMS OF SOCIALIST LABOR

Instead of the private initiative upon which capitalist society has relied for its development, Communism puts its faith in the initiative of the masses. In his "How to Organise Competition," written in March, 1918, Lenin enlarged upon the possibilities that socialism had *of really drawing the vast majority of the toilers into work in which they can develop their abilities, display their talents, which are still an untapped source and which capitalism has trampled on, crushed, and strangled.* That faith is one of the intangible forces that are making it possible to carry through the Five Year Plan. In the Library of the "Komsomol Propagandist," one of the issues of 1930 was entitled "Overtake and Surpass —The Five Year Plan of Development of the National Economy," by A. Loginov. Its purpose is to show the youngsters that the policy of the Party expressed in the Plan is scientifically correct, historically corroborated, and despite mountains of difficulties can be accomplished if only they will have faith. The ground of belief in the great work of socialist construction offered to those of little faith, and to unbelievers in the great work of socialist construction, is that, *The enthusiasm of the socialist construction has gripped the widest circles of the working class. The proletariat finds again and again new sources and means for the industrialisation of the country.*

It is to the same forces that the Communist leaders constantly attribute the results that have been achieved under the Five Year Plan. Thus Stalin to the Sixteenth Party Congress:

The success of the Party in building socialism in industry and agriculture is possible only by the vast activity of the working class and the toiling masses . . . socialist competition and shock brigades. . . .

Again to the directors of industries:

No other government in the world enjoys such support among the workers and peasants as does the Soviet government. This is shown by socialist competition, shock brigades and strechny (workers') plan.

Molotov repeated this in his report on "Results of the First Five Year Plan" to the Seventeenth Party Conference and the resolutions therefore reiterate it:

These achievements are all the outcome of the colossal growth of the revolutionary activity of the broad masses of the working class and the toiling peasantry, a result of extensive socialist competition and organisation of shock brigades.

Consequently the leaders rely upon the same spirit to meet any attack from the outside.

SHOCK WORK AND SOCIALIST COMPETITION

These two forms of voluntary labor grew up together and are intertwined. Their forerunner, still surviving and vigorous, was the practice of *subbotniki* or Saturdaying which grew up during the crucial days of civil war and intervention when groups of workers would give their Saturdays to work in an emergency. The workers of the Kazan railway were the first to do this, and Lenin hailed their act as "the great start." It is now a regular practice and is often called "free work."

Every fall in Moscow a large part of the population turns out to help unload potatoes and vegetables, and again in the winter to dig the city out of a snowstorm which has stopped traffic. In one issue "Moscow News" reports a group of villages organising subbotnoki to make school furniture for illiterates and an American lumber specialist writes that in an emergency in the woods one hundred and twenty men turned out and by free work did in four and a half hours what would ordinarily have taken those responsible for it eighty working days. American engineers report that the new tractor works at Kharkhov could not have been finished on time if the citizens of all sorts had not come on their free days to do such unskilled work as clearing away rubbish. One says that on some afternoons it looked like an excursion getting off the cars and he estimates that thirty thousand in all participated.

A shock worker, or udarnik, is one who rushes into the breach in an emergency to do extra work or to lead and organise others; or to enable the fulfilling of the plan, takes upon himself special obligations in speed, faithfulness, and quality. Without formal organisation, the udarniks have become a company of real Knights of Labor, admission to which is determined by vote of their fellow workers. What is expected of them can be seen from objections made to candidates for admission to the order and its privileges in a meeting of one shift in the welding department of Selmashstroi. The first thing examined is, of course, the worker's record on filling the quota. Then:

How much scrap you got?
Why were you absent the other day?
Why do the sledge hammer men run away and don't want to work with you?

How much did you sign up for on the loan?

The whole brigade complained, "he gives quantity and not quality."

He didn't attend political circles.

In some places there are two and even three degrees of udarniks—ordinary, better, best. In a brigade meeting of a shift in another department at Selmash, to revise the list of udarniks and make promotions, my notes show among others the following questions and comments:

Why were you late the other day?

Does he know his equipment?

Is he active?

Is he making economy?

She keeps her belt in order and if she has any spare time she picks up parts.

It took two before on that job, now only one.

She keeps valuable equipment clean.

His production is good but he is not a good group organiser.

He gave suggestions for rationalisation.

Have you liquidated your illiteracy?

He has dirt under the rattler; he takes care of his own hide and doesn't help others.

Then they come to the brigade leader, and the chairman exhorts:

Don't hide the criticism. Show his mistakes.

So they begin:

I worked with him—he is always good.

He goes round with the workers and helps them.

He works like the devil and shows others what to do.

Even if he can't get help, he always does it.

But discipline isn't as good.

It is—he never fools with us.

The brigadier says he will pull up the discipline and they vote to make him a "better udarnik."

Naturally some quarrels develop over these elections. Also, as udarniks multiply in some plants where they are most numerous, to be one is to be regular, not to be one is to be odd. With this standardisation there appears the "false udarnik" who wants the honor and the privileges without the obligations. He is made the object of constant censure and caricature on blackboards, in wall and factory newspapers. In very grave cases he is given a "social model trial," partly as a warning to others. The final penalty is expulsion from the labor union, one of the heaviest forms of ostracism.

From shock workers this expression of mass initiative grew to shock brigades, then to shock departments, and finally shock factories or farms. A brigade is composed of all the persons engaged in one operation. It is the equivalent of the "gang" in unskilled work in the English-speaking world. It may run from a dozen workers in a factory department to several hundred on a big farm. Describing his work, the brigade leader on a collective farm, a former poor peasant, writes:

There are three hundred and four people in my brigade and I must know every one of them personally, to judge what sort of work he is able to do. There are fifty shock-brigaders in my brigade and they can always be depended on. Most of them are quite young but some are thirty and over. They are ready for work at any time, whenever needed.

A shock brigade is one whose every member is a udarnik—the goal of the Komsomol in brigades made up entirely of youthful workers—or, like the shock department of factory or farm, it is one that so declares itself, in meeting assembled, for the purpose of repairing a breach in production or over fulfilling the plan.

How the shock brigades work is shown by some extracts from an account of the work of the Komsomol nucleus in a kolhoz, written by two of its members:

We formed shock brigades for making preparations for the spring planting, repairing harness, collecting fodder, treating seed, and organising public feeling. We had "light cavalry" detachments for checking the work of shock brigades and stable tending. We took on the care of the stables, selected fifty of the weakest horses, which were unfit for work, and by dint of proper feeding and care had them in good condition in three weeks' time.

For industry the procedure is illustrated by a section in the report of Kosarev, General Secretary of the Komsomol, published under the title "The All-Union Komsomol—One Shock Brigade."

Comrades, a peculiar self-sacrificial movement is developing out of these shock brigades. There lies before me the rules of the shock brigade of the Komsomols of the weaving mill of the great Dresden factory. It is very characteristic and I will read it. These rules have been devised by the boys themselves without the knowledge of the management or the central organisation of the Komsomol, and without any suggestion to them. They write: "The shock brigader must know that the work of the shock brigade is a concrete affair of carrying out the problems laid before them, to which they are called by the party and the Lenin Komsomol. The shock brigade is the advancing line of socialist work. The shock brigader facing the working class gives his vow to the Party and the Komsomol that in his work he will do the following things: Never miss a day or be late. Accomplish the norm of output of goods by all means, not less than the norm which has been fixed by the administration, also increase it to an nth amount of per cent. Reduce scrap to a minimum. Reduce the leisure of the machine to a minimum (idle time). Participating consciously in the building of socialism, the shock brigaders must be among the first to do what they vow to do. . . . Every shock brigader who has signed these rules is bound by the class discipline of the building of socialism, and he will brand any one in his group who will transgress these rules, and he promises to turn over such comrades to the social court of the organisation as a deserter on the socialist front."

It was the All-Union Congress of Shock Brigaders that sent out the slogan which the whole country took up, "The Five Year Plan in Four." The newspapers are constantly reporting records broken by shock brigades. Here are two: the first from "Izvestia" in 1931 under the head, "American Engineer Made a Mistake."

"Izvestia" of October 11 reported the arrival from America to Leningrad of a shipment of powerful railway engines. These engines were turned over for assembly to the Proletarian Plant. On October 14 the shock brigade from the Proletarians commenced the assembly of the first American railway engine. Comrades Lasberg, Semenov, Dulin, Binder, Nefrazov, Volin, Egorov, Petushinkov, and Shatalov commenced the work from the outset by a fighting tempo. According to the calculations of the American firm which filled the order for these engines, the assembly of them was to take forty-eight hours.

The representative of the firm, an American engineer, Draper, said at the shop meeting before the beginning of the assembly: "Perhaps before we begin we at once shall add to the forty-eight hours indicated by the firm another twenty-three hours, then the affair will be surer." "No, we propose not to increase the forty-eight-hour term but on the contrary to cut it down by several hours," replied the Chairman of the Factory Committee, Comrade Serov.

The shock workers on the first engine beat the American time in spite of a number of difficulties and the assembly of the first engine was completed in thirty-one hours. On the second engine the norm of the Americans was left far behind. Its assembly was brilliantly completed in eighteen hours.

A few days after, the paper reported the completion of the job in less time than the workers had estimated. Tests showed only one engine defective, and that not seriously.

The second instance is from an account of the great steel plant at Kuznetskstroi in "Pravda," November 11, 1931. A group of Bashkir tribesmen, who had never seen a factory chimney nor an auto truck before, were working on excavation. Finally one brigade beat the world's record. Every man in it dug 33.5 cubic metres of earth instead of the six required by the norm. The old leader was given the honor of turning on the switch that lighted the huge red star with which the entrance of the plant was decorated for the celebration of the October Revolution.

From agriculture I take several instances from a number collected by the Proletarian Writers and published in their magazine. Bashta, a former farm hand, made a world record by sowing eighty-one hectares in one shift. Soboleva, who at twelve had been an underfed worker, at fifteen one of the unemployed, then a Soviet cook and now a tractor driver, drove her machine with a string of seeders for fifty hours without stopping except for supplies. This she did because, first, the administration forgot to send the relief shift, and next because an incompetent driver came and she was bound to keep her section in first place in the sowing campaign. Datukeshvilli, Georgian farm laborer, whose slogan is "keep up with the best," when Alazan Sovhoz had seven thousand five hundred hectares of cotton to be sown and a shortage of drivers said, "Give me the men. I'll teach them." So by night he repaired tractors and by day taught peasant lads to drive them. At sowing time, with forty-three new drivers, the seven thousand five hundred hectares were plowed and sown in the allotted time.

The strain of these emergency activities, a draft upon the sub-conscious reserves of vitality, is in large measure compensated for by the satisfaction of taking part in a great and high purpose. This, and the extent of it, is what distinguishes the high speed of Soviet labor from similar examples in capitalistic industry. It is part of the general tempo—one of the most used words—for whose necessity all citizens and children are taught the reasons. The two best known are first, among six, given to the Komsomol:

1. The capitalist surroundings compel us to be ready to defend the country from imperialist invasion. 2. Our technical and economic backwardness compels us to overtake and surpass the foremost capitalist countries, without which it will be impossible to construct a socialist society.

It is among the executives and educators that one finds the pace that kills, or sends them to the sanitariums. From the beginning, the Soviet leaders have proclaimed that they would build socialism by substituting the most scientific and intensive exploitation of natural resources for the capitalist exploitation of the physical and spiritual energy of the workers. American workers say that the udarnik pace is just about ordinary American speed, that it goes beyond it only in crises. Said one foreman, "If I worked here all the time as I had to at home I would get two udarnik books instead of one."

Speed is the characteristic of the days of construction of plants; when production begins, the need for quality comes to the front. In building, as in our wartime construction, quality has too often been sacrificed to speed. Yakoklev reports the same thing in the first days of the kolhoz:

You may find as many such examples as you wish. The plowing is done quickly but there are so many unplowed strips left between the furrows that the machines will be broken to pieces on them. What good does that speed do? You may sow rapidly and get through at the proper time, but you use up six poods of seed instead of five. You put up as many shocks of hay as required, but leave a tenth of it scattered on the field. You thresh all that you are expected to do and get through with it on time, but a lot of grain is lost in the straw.

In some of the industries the amount of production below standard was shown by reports of the Workers' and Peasants' Inspection to be serious. My morning paper uses quotations from such reports, sent out by a university research bureau, to show that the Five Year Plan is failing. These extracts really show that the same spirit which built plants in record time is now expressing itself in a far-flung drive for quality. Again the initiative of the masses came into play. In the very beginning of the third and decisive year of the Five Year

Plan the workers of the "Electroapparat" in Leningrad sent a letter to "Pravda" (January 20, 1931) appealing to strategic groups of workers and to *all the working class of the USSR,* to organize an all-Union campaign for *the improvement of the quality of all our work, to decrease the cost of production, to raise the efficiency of labor. . . .*

Then under five heads in detail they give the measures they have deemed it necessary to put in practice in their factory.

Later in the year, following Stalin's appeal for the mastery of technical knowledge, special Stalin-brigades were created in the factories to increase the technical knowledge of the workers and to improve the quality of their work. Everywhere the unions began to call special meetings for this purpose. Such a gathering, in a shop that made patterns or models for the clothing workers of Baku, began with a brief statement of its purpose by the organiser from Labor Headquarters—a woman. It appeared that workers of other trades had written a letter to the paper complaining of the quality of the clothes they bought. First, there were a few speeches from workers named by the chair. Then came volunteers, one after another, declaring themselves udarniks on quality, and some offering to go to the clothing shops and instruct the workers. Finally a resolution declared the whole shop udarnik, ordered brigades organised to go out and instruct the clothing workers, a delegation sent to Tiflis to study methods there, and invited the shoe workers to enter into socialist competition in a campaign for quality. The quiet woman organiser then secured the appointment of a control commission to draw up the agreement in contract form and supervise and report on its execution.

This activity of the more energetic, whose eagerness and enthusiasm have to be seen to be appreciated, does not separate them from the others as does private initiative. On the contrary, it ties them to the slower and weaker in various forms of co-operative endeavor. There are planning brigades to assist in working out and carrying out the Plan for the factory by bringing it down to each machine and organising six production conferences per year in each department, and chain brigades, uniting various shops, and even plants dealing with the same process of production, to see that all parts come through on time. Then there are towing brigades to pull along the weaker by assistance and instruction and finally the community tow in which a forward factory brings its experience to the assistance of a backward one. For instance, the Taganrog works in Leningrad undertook to tow the Parostroy works in Moscow and gave it sixty-three workable rationalisation suggestions, with necessary drawings, which accomplished a saving roughly of 100,000 rubles. During a recent harvest a Kolhoz Centre executive reported, *Collective farms in those districts which have already taken their quotas of grain to the gathering points and elevators are giving a hand to more backward districts.* The Forest Commune Equality reported such a world-beating record for felling timber without mechanical contrivances that the Professors of the Leningrad Forest Academy refused to believe it and the newspapers were afraid to report it without investigation. It was finally found to be correct, and to be accomplished within the eight-hour day and without strain, through a new system of division of labor and conscientious work. Sixteen forest papers then reported it and immediately the workers and managers of the other communes began to ask why their record was low. The Red Partisan Commune sent a squad of experienced fellers to work side by side with one of Equality in competition under identical conditions. They were beaten but learned the new methods. Then the brigade organised by the Northern White Sea Railway Forest Department for the study of brigade methods of labor was sent to investigate and thus the new methods spread throughout the district.

Besides exchanging their knowledge and skill, the shock workers sometimes use the whip of censure on the laggards. On April 23, 1931, "Pravda" published an open letter from the workers of Krasny Putilovetz Plant in Leningrad addressed to the Stalingrad workers: . . . *The tempo of your work does not keep pace with the development of socialist construction, the growth of industry and agriculture. You are not fulfilling your program. We fail to understand why an up-to-date plant like yours, equipped with the best of machinery, should fall back in its production.* On October 22, 1931, "Pravda" announced that Stalingrad had made a record by turning out a hundred tractors a day for the past few weeks. The next day it printed a six-column reply to the letter of April 23 from Stalingrad workers, headed "We Have Kept Our Word." It began, *It was painful to read your letter in "Pravda." We realised that your criticism was justified. It was futile to reply with promises. We decided to reply with tractors and we have kept our word.* Then, characteristically enough, the letter closes with an appeal to other workers, first indirect and then direct: *We have also learned that tractors are not produced within the boundaries of the plant. The fate of the tractors is decided in the workers' stolovayas (dining rooms), in the workers' city, in the co-operative stores, and in the homes of the workers. Poor living conditions hampered efficient production at the plant. . . . We now appeal to kolhoz workers to increase the quality of their work, to strengthen organisation, and fulfil the plan of grain collection.*

Socialist competition grows naturally out of the example of shock workers, which inspires emulation. In one village meeting at plowing time, Ivanov, an individual peasant, who is not yet in the kolhoz, rises to say, "The kolhoz ploughed all the ends of their strips. We should propose to the whole village to plough the upper ends of our strips; we could get there five hectares." And Yudin Iven, also "individual," adds, "I cleaned a place of bushes without waiting till they proposed it. We must urge the rest to do the same." At the Electro-Apparatus works in Moscow the German workers were sufficiently moved by a campaign for the improvement of quality to organise two shock brigades and twenty out of seventy-six agreed to remain in the industry until the end of the Five Year Plan.

Emulation develops into organised competition. One brigade challenges another, then departments and factories. Individuals challenge individuals through the plant newspapers or announce their own purpose to beat the norms of the plan. Such an agreement between two foreign workers at Selmash contained nine points: *To systematically overfulfil norm. To reduce the cost of operations ten per cent. Not to be absent without sufficient cause. Not to come late, etc.*

Competitive agreements are also entered into between farms and between factories and farms. When the Turk-Sib railway connecting Siberia and Turkestan was being built, the workers entered into socialist competition with adjacent villages. The villages increased their tax payments, eliminated illiteracy, completely returned the seed grain loans and increased their contribution to government loans. The workers raised the level of productivity by eleven per cent and decreased costs three per cent.

At the Seventeenth Party Conference, Comrade Vareikis in an amendment to the theses of Molotov and Kuibeshev on the Second Five Year Plan promised to double the harvest of the Central Black Earth region in the course of three years. He also challenged the delegates from the Ukraine to organise a competition in the matter. Molotov replied, "The initiative of the comrades from the Black Earth region should be supported in every way."

Curiously enough one result of the "forced labor" outcry and campaign against the Soviet Union was to stimulate socialist competition in the lumber industry, against which particular charges had been made. In direct answer, the workers in the Karelia district proclaimed March, 1931, a storm month for executing the program of output, increasing socialist competition and shock work, and raising the productivity of labor. The daily output rose immediately. By the end of the month two other districts had beaten their record. When they read the tales of forced labor, the lumber-workers of Teretulmsky forestry in the Leningrad region laughed and said, "We are shock workers not slaves." The same day they organised a socialist competition with the workers of other forestries. Down at the other end of the country the lumbermen of the Tartar Republic did the same thing; in two weeks they almost doubled the number of shock brigades and increased by half the number of workers in individual competition. In Vologda a "red caravan" a kilometer long, flying red flags, came bringing two hundred twenty loads of wood as a present from the lumberworkers to their patron, the power station, to demonstrate their protest against the "forced-labor slander."

"Socialist competition," said the vice-president of the big Oil Trust at Baku, an old oil worker, "is now the backbone of all our work," and the saying can be extended to cover the whole work of the country. In agriculture it appears in competition between kolhozes, between them and factories as also between factories and sovhozes, on the fulfilling of their respective plans. Also in the North Caucasus the labor unions of three rayons signed an agreement in 1931 for competition in helping farms to put through the best crop in the Third Decisive Year of the Five Year Plan. It covered such things as hoeing a certain number of hectares, aiding in organising piecework and cost accounting, supplying a specified number of men for specified tasks in harvesting and storing grain.

Here, in condensed form, is a sample agreement between district organisations of kolhozes printed in "Izvestia," August 14, 1931. It was signed at the Selmash Harvester Factory.

Agreement of Socialist Emulation of the Collective Farms of the Central Volga Region (*Around Samara*).

Under the leadership of the Party of Lenin, the working class and the kolhoz peasantry of the Soviet Union successfully construct socialism. The Soviet Union completes the construction of the foundation of socialist economy. 518 large new factories and plants and 1040 machine tractor stations are beginning operations.

On the basis of the success achieved in industry the collective movement in the village is aggressively developing. . . .

We consider it to be a matter of honor, a cause of glory and of heroism to complete as soon as possible the plan of grain delivery, the plan of fall ploughing, the plan of fall sowing, and the programs of developing socialised cattle breeding. Following the socialist emulation among ourselves and with the collective farms of the Northern Caucasus, the Ukraine, the Central Black Soil region and the lower Volga we take upon ourselves the following practical responsibilities:

THRASHING *to be finished not later than August 20. The kolhozes from left bank of river take upon themselves to transfer the surplus machinery to those on right bank. (There grain ripens earlier.) Economise every gram of grain; for which purpose they will go over the fields with horse-drawn and then hand rakes. Each kolhoz to organise brigades for the gleaning of the grain, using Pioneers, women, and school children; also to do the utmost in preserving the grain from loss during thrashing. A norm of daily output for each machine to be completed.*

GRAIN DELIVERY *to be not later than September 5. Not one single bushel to be sold to the private market, exclusively to State elevators. Exceptions can be made only in cases of collective farms which are over sixty kilometers from railway. Grain to be delivered according to the method of the socialist conveyor, directly from under the thrashing machine, for which purpose special transport brigades are to be organised with fixed norms of work for each day. Each farm takes responsibility for helping individual farmers in their delivery of grain (that is outsiders).*

Fall Ploughing *to be done with every effort to double plan given by Commissar of Agriculture,* i.e., *nine million hectares instead of four and a half. Norm per plow, quality-depth, to be done. Tractors and horses will be passed on from left to right bank.*

Fall Sowing *in time and of quality.*

Cattle Breeding (*New here*). *To be popularised as in decree of government by educational campaign. To create capital fund by January 1. Ask for voluntary contribution of two cows with calves from each three households. Two sheep, one sow for each ten households. Excursions to be made to other collectives where this has been done. Special brigades for care of cattle. Building weatherproof cattle sheds. Silos. Ten-day campaign to popularise these decisions. Union of kolhozes to be judge. No formal document but campaign plan. To ask "Izvestia" to control by brigades of correspondents and publicity.*

From the collective farms, from which many of the workers come, as well as from the factories, the methods of shock work and socialist competition have spread throughout the lumber camps of the Soviet Union. Numerous examples are reported in "VOKS" 1931. At the local Party Conference at Sukum a Negro delegate from a group of Negro lumberworkers up in the mountains of Abkhasia who had emigrated there for "freedom's sake" reported, "Now the workers of the sawmill are fighting like leopards for the industrial and financial program and they have fulfilled it with excess like *simba* (the lion)."

In the storm month for lumber, March, 1931, the

chairmen of the kolhozes of the Olonetz district in the Karelian Autonomous Socialist Soviet Republic sent out an appeal to all their members in Karelia calling their attention to a deficit in their felling program and to the appeal of the Party and the Government for the "Decisive liquidation of the break in our felling program."

In response to this appeal we undertake the following obligations:

1. We give to our forest work one out of every five able-bodied kolhoz members (the official excluded). From those districts where constructions are going on, we give one in every ten able-bodied kolhoz members.

2. We take in tow individual peasants for forming them into brigades and join the competition in forest work, organised by the newspaper "Red Karelia."

3. We sign a contract for floating with the district forest industrial economy. Taking into consideration the importance of the arrival of rafts to the main waterways on time, we propose to the sub-district forest economies to make piecework contracts for the floating of timber on the tributaries with individual kolhozes.

4. We give for secondary work . . . kolhoz members who are not able-bodied and boys.

On behalf of the membership of all kolhozes in the Olonetsk district we appeal to them all to send without delay these additional forces to the forests. Kolhoz members must be propagandists of an all-round application of the brigade method to forest work. In these decisive days of the felling season, kolhoz members must simultaneously make preparations for the floating campaign.

By energetic work let us give a rebuff to the kulaks

and their supporters attempting to hinder us from fulfilling our felling program.

(*Attached to this were forty signatures of Olonetz kolhoz chairmen.*)

The drama of the lumberjacks under new socialist forms of labor can be seen in this condensed extract from "Shock Workers of the Forest," by F. Konichev:

In the forests between Vologda and Archangel is the village Gora, numbering about forty households. It is now passing through the period of cleaving in two: one part of the village is in the kolhoz "Red Gora," the others—individual peasants—are "simply Gora." So they divide themselves everywhere—in the cooperative store, in the district, in the village Soviet.

In the winter they work in the forest. In the season of 1930–31 an instructor came to organise them in the new method of brigade work for the first time. The meeting took place in the house of Shamovkin, an active kolhoz member and a progressive lumberman. Last year he not only fulfilled but exceeded the program of felling, finished it before the date fixed and returned home from the forests with a red banner.

To a running accompaniment of questions, mostly from the individualists of "simply Gora," the instructor explained how the forest brigades must be organised, how they must work, how they help to augment the output, to raise the wages, to improve food and goods supply to the lumbermen. He told the men that prizes would be awarded to the best shock workers.

On the motion of Shamovkin the "Red Goras" put all their names down on the brigades' lists, including women and boys. The "simply Goras" decided to wait and "see first what they'll do."

Not an hour had gone by after the meeting had dis-

solved when a fir stake, breaking the window pane, flew thundering to the far end of Shamovkin's room. "That," thought Shamovkin, as he blew out the lamp, "is because my name is at the head of the brigades' list."

In the morning's light he discovered a second warning; a slip of paper was pasted with dough to his wicket door; on the slip some one had written in print: "This hand will not tremble even to shove you under the ice."

In the autumn the "Red Gora" kolhoz people moved into new, clean barracks in the forest. Shamovkin had taken upon himself to organise three brigades. Their organisation was extremely simple. The men were distributed between different specialties according to their strength and skill. Every brigade included one marker-brigadier, 2 fellers, 2 men for the hewing off of boughs, 2 for hewing the trees into logs, 2 for marking the logs, and 4 for heaping them. The stamping down of the snow and the hewing under of trees was given to women and youngsters. Shamovkin's brigade was proclaimed a special shock one and the others had to dress according to its work.

The first day one of the men said, "It is less convenient to work this way, the 'individuals' will outstrip us."

"Next time," said Shamovkin, "we'll arrange with the fellers to fell the trees before the others come to work. There will be no crowding and the whole business will go with a swing."

After supper the younger generation began learning by heart "The Lumberman's Song" from a crumpled copy of the Archangel "Northern Commune":

"The early dawns come
To wake the barracks up,

They call upon the men
To enter competition.
We'll go out
Into the forests.
Thud on and glisten
My well-sharpened axe!"

Shamovkin was late. He had been measuring the logs. When he came in the lumbermen surrounded him.

"How much have we cut?"

"My brigade produced 3 cubic metres per worker, Lobanov's brigade two and seven-tenths, Plothikov's only two and a half."

"No-ot mu-uch," drawled the men.

"Yes, but the 'individual's' average is less than two cubic metres. We've outstripped them the very first day and later on, when we adjust ourselves, it will be still better."

Next day the brigades did 4 cubic metres per worker.

"The devils, how much they cut!" the "simply Gora" were saying with amazement.

By the end of December the "Red Gora" had raised their daily output to six cubic metres per worker and were saying, "Even six cubic metres becomes too low a rate for us."

On Christmas Eve an antireligious propagandist came from the district town. "What have you come for?" said the "Red Gora." "You may keep your throat in order for others. We have already decided unanimously here not to leave the forest on Christmas. We'll produce seven cubic metres a day, and the money we'll give to the fund for the airplane against General Miller, we remember him well, the bitch. We have in our brigade some men who were Partisans in the time of the Whites, who beat Miller and drove him into the White Sea."

The propagandist began to praise them. "As to praising us, wait some time. Wait to the end of the felling season to see the results. We don't work for praises' sake. You'd better print in the paper how to work with the American spring-saw, 'compis' or what is its name; they write about it, but too little and not clear enough."

The example of the "Red Gora" made the "simply Gora" men pull themselves together. They also abstained from celebrating Christmas and resolved to form a brigade, regretting that they had not done so before as they had lost much money by that way.

The new socialist forms of work have permeated the educational world as thoroughly as they have the spheres of industry and agriculture. Students and faculty, separately and jointly, make agreements in socialist competition to finish their work in shorter time and to improve its quality. In Baku I found an agreement between a master craftsman and a student, the former to get the plan fulfilled in his department one hundred per cent without break, the latter to be one hundred per cent lesson perfect. The soldiers in the cultural army, which is recruited among workmen, kolhoz members, and young people to do volunteer work in extending popular education, enter into cultural relay races. The companies are given tasks called itineraries, which include visiting schools, homes of illiterates, and organising centres of universal education; also attaching schools to industrial and agricultural enterprises for mutual aid, in accordance with the plan for polytechnic education. As each task is started it is passed on to another company to continue. The race finishes on a certain date and the results are publicly announced.

In the arts also the methods of socialist competition are used. The art students of Moscow held a conference in 1931 on making the city beautiful for the celebration of the October Revolution and promptly challenged the artists of Leningrad to compete. Substantial prizes were offered for the best plans. The theatres too use similar methods for improving both the artistic form and the intellectual content of their work. The Little Theatre in Moscow has been given the shock workers' banner for its exceptionally active social and professional work.

The spirit of emulation touches the widest aspects of national life where it is expressed in the slogan, "To overtake and surpass the most advanced capitalistic countries" in technical equipment and knowledge, and to do it in a definite time—the Sixth Congress of Soviets said "within the coming decade," that is by 1940. The same spirit is imparted to the youngest children. District organisations of the Young Pioneers enter into agreements to draw the parents of their members into socialist competition. The children themselves sign competitive agreements with their fathers and mothers. Their fulfilment is checked in the Pioneer circle. A group of ten youngsters visit the home for this purpose. They know what goes on in the factory from frequent visits there in connection with their school work and their social work. The record shows an average of ninety per cent fulfilment on both sides. While I was asking the secretary at Selmash for a sample agreement, a boy brought in the following to be filed:

AGREEMENT ON SOCIAL COMPETITION OF PIONEER LEVA GOVAROVA WITH HIS FATHER IVAN, A BENCH WORKER IN TOOLROOM.

I, Leva Govarova, Pioneer of Third Division (ten

years) call out my father to social competition on the following points:

1. Not to be absent or late without reasons.

2. Take care of factory equipment and tools.

3. Not to make scrap from fault of yours.

4. Be active in all department campaigns.

5. Keep always a udarnik book so that you will have the honor of being called udarnik.

6. Have competition with comrades for better work.

7. Do active work against "snatching."

8. Not to have any break in machinery by your fault.

For my part I take upon myself:

1. Not to be late to school.

2. To learn well.

3. Not to have one absence.

4. To keep discipline, to be one of the best Pioneers, to be an example to unorganised kids.

This agreement to run from November 7, 1931, to January 1, 1932.

Signed LEVA GOVAROVA, *Pioneer.*
IVAN GOVAROVA, *Father.*

Efforts are made to teach even the kindergarten children the new forms of work. The Leningrad pre-school pedagogical station has put out through its pedo-methodological sector, a brochure dealing with socialist competition as a pedagogical method. One of the reasons given for the claim that it has great possibilities among children of pre-school age is that it enables the unfolding of individual abilities upon a collectivist background of work. A questionnaire was put out to discover what were the problems of socialist competition and how far the children were acquainted with them. The brochure concludes with suggestions as to kinds of competition most suitable for children of six to seven years and the best methods for organising it, along with shock brigade work. It must be voluntary, with leaders chosen by the children themselves. The program must be for a specific time, with definite obligations. Responsibility must be both collective and individual. There must be monthly check-ups.

New forms of socialist competition are appearing faster than they can be recorded. In one engineering institute the students this year started a "technical study loan." The competitors subscribed to a premium fund and assumed obligations to attend a certain number of lecture hours and acquire a certain degree of technical knowledge. All those who fulfilled their obligations drew for premiums, which enabled the winners to take further study or a vacation spent in travel. On December 23, 1931, "Moscow News" printed an announcement from sixteen collective farms of Dergachev village:

We have successfully fulfilled our economic plan. Our sixteen kolhozes and our individual peasants have turned over to the government 126 per cent of the grain expected. We fulfilled our vegetable campaign 100 per cent, our autumn sowing and winter fallow, and the mobilisation of savings. Now together with the preparations for spring sowing we also give our aid to socialist transport. Our village is on a main line uniting the Ukraine with the Red Capital—Moscow. On this important line with 200 trains daily, we shall not permit any holdup from snowdrifts. . . . We have divided our members into brigades, each one attached to a particular point of the road and responsible for that part. . . .

Comrades! The accurate working of the railways is the guarantee of fulfilling the mighty plan of socialist construction. . . . We call on all village Soviets located near railroads to join an All-Union competition in the war on snowdrifts.

These new forms of work are changing life in the remote parts of the Soviet Union. One frequently reads incidents like the following, which is condensed from an account in "Literature of the World Revolution" (No. 3, 1931):

Away down in Turkestan there suddenly appeared last May, for the first time in eleven years, a barefooted courier and herald—the jarchi. After sounding a trumpet longer than himself he announced greetings, hearty and glowing, to Kolhoz Yash-Dekkan from Kolhozes Kzyl-Bairsk and Illifak, also "this precious and dear gift and they beg you to love and favor, cherish and guard it. . . . They inform you that in seven days and six nights they have plowed three times over with European plough 231 hectares of land, have sowed it with first-class seed, and within the week are going out to cultivate the cotton for the first time. Having learned that you have fulfilled your plan of 130 hectares by 67 per cent, and that in untiring labor and ardor, squatting over the teacups in the teashop, are plowing 2¼ hectares a day, the men of the Kolhozes Kyzl-Bairsk and Illifak, as a sign of sympathy, have requested me to hand you this relative of yours. She was captured yesterday by children near the kolhoz. Probably she lost her way because of fatigue and accidentally strayed over our way." Then out of his red saddle bag he pulled a tortoise and flung it into the arms of the President of the kolhoz.

In other days that would have meant fight. But now

there followed an extraordinary assembly at Kolhoz Yash-Dekkan for better mobilisation of their work. Three days later everybody, including women and children, turned out to field work. They worked nights by the light of bonfires. In three days they finished the plowing, and exceeded the sowing plan.

Both the spirit and methods of socialist competition are spread by appeals in the papers from groups of workers to others. One of historic significance, both because of the crucial time of its issue and also because of the way in which it reveals in definite forms the initiative of the masses, is the following appeal from a factory in Tula, a city where in Czarist days there was a high tradition of skilled craftsmanship in metal working:

THE APPEAL OF THE TULA PLANT NO. 1 TO ALL THE WORKERS OF THE USSR, TO ALL THE KOLHOZES.

Comrades: The second year of emulation comes to an end in the USSR (April, 1931). Leninist competition and shock work proved in the hands of the working class to be a mighty lever by which they pushed forward the matter of reconstruction of the country, making it from a backward country of small producers and individual peasant farmers into a country of advanced technique and most progressive agriculture in the world. In the process of competition was born the slogan "The Five Year Plan in Four," advanced by the workers themselves. This slogan was accepted by the workers as obligatory not only before our country but also before the international proletariat. The accomplishment of this slogan became for us a matter of honor, of glory, of sacrifice, and heroism.

Have you heard that this year we must put into operation 518 new factories and plants? Have you heard that we must organise this year 1040 new machine tractor stations? Think over these figures of our greatest victory. . .

(They then describe the situation in their own plant.) In 1931 we shall double the program of 1930, increase the productivity of labor by 35 per cent and lower the cost of production by 18.5 per cent. We shall give the country 3.2 times as many tools as in 1930 from the tool-making plant. This will save the country 14 million rubles in gold (Former imports).

But now comrades how about you? Have you completed your program for the first quarter? How many workers have been absorbed by social emulation and shock work? How many shock brigades do you have? Do you use the method of the social tow? Do you have any through shock brigades? How do you struggle for the quality of production? Have you taken any measures to abolish scrap? How have you accomplished the instructions to cut down cost of production? And to what extent have you developed inventiveness and the work of production meetings? What have you done to carry out the slogan of Comrade Stalin to master technique? How many workers have been absorbed into technical study and how is the study being carried on? What use do you make of your imported equipment and how do you master the advanced foreign technique?

We propose at the end of the first quarter of the third year of the Five Year Plan to organise through "Pravda" an All-Union reporting plan of factories, plants, new constructions, soviet farms, and collective farms along these lines:

1. We propose to make known to each worker and collective farmer the figures of the greatest achievements of our country in order that everybody shall know that so much strength and energy has not been expended in vain. Our savings of blood and sweat have not been wasted but have been invested in the construction of new powerful giants of socialist industry and socialist agriculture. Let there be exhibited upon the city squares, placards, diagrams, and expositions, on theatres, cinemas, clubs, and workers' dwellings, and red corners these pictures of our victory. These figures 518 and 1040 must be known by the wives and children of the workers, by the collective farm workers, by the middle and poor peasants who tomorrow shall be collective farmers. These figures must inflame with new enthusiasm our hearts, pour new force and energy into each toiler for new victories.

2. We request the newspapers of the fraternal Communist parties abroad—the "Rote Fahne," "Humanité," "The Daily Worker"—to tell in detail the workers of capitalist countries of these, our victories and achievements as was done by "Pravda." Let the workers of the West know that we with Bolshevik firmness and decisiveness build victoriously socialism in one-sixth part of the world's surface.

3. We propose in honor of the new enterprises and the new machine-tractor stations to declare a recruiting of shock workers in honor of the 518 and 1040. Let a new thousand shock workers enter into emulation in honor of each new enterprise at this first of May of the second year of socialist competition. This would give us over half a million new shock workers. Let there appear in honor of each new machine-tractor station a new thousand of shock collective farm workers. This would give a new shock army of workers of socialist agriculture of 1,200,000 men.

4. We propose to develop a mass fighting campaign for re-examining the norms of output during the second quarter of the current year. The existing norms of the present time are in most cases out of date. These norms were gauged by the output of the average worker during the old technique but we must fight for norms proposed by the workers themselves, for the norms which have been set up by the best shock workers, brigades, and shops. We must gauge ourselves by the norms of output of the shock worker. We must take into consideration all the enormous technical improvements and social rationalisation which we have carried through. Only under these conditions will we be able to carry out the task of increasing productivity of labor by 28 per cent throughout the USSR. By this method we can accumulate surplus and strengthen our financial system.

WE SHALL PRESENT YOU MINERS OF THE DONBAS A SPECIAL BILL

Systematically from month to month you do not do your duty before the country. Last year you held back many millions of tons of coal. The Party and the Soviet Government has undertaken measures to give you better conditions of labor, improve the food supply of the Donbas and supply you with articles of first necessity. It has expanded the construction of dwellings, has raised your wages by 20 per cent, particularly for the workers underground.

All workers expected that this would mean a turn in the work of the Donbas but this is not the case. During the first quarter your debt to the country has again grown to two million tons and perhaps more. Particularly bad is the situation in the mechanisation of output. By the mechanised output you give but half of what you should. You also have slackened down on the hand output. How long will this shameful deficit in coal continue? It is a black spot upon our Donbas.

Is it possible that the heroic example of another army of miners, of the old men of Baku and Grozny, will not be a contagion for you?

Having completed their Five Year Plan in two and a half years, the oil men have advanced the USSR to second place in the world's output.

Have you heard, you miners of the Donbas, of Kuzbas, of the sub-Moscow and other coal regions, of the victory of the proletarians of Baku and Grozny? This victory fills our hearts with proletarian pride.

We see how practically is being realised the slogan "To overtake and surpass" the capitalist countries. In oil we have already overtaken all of Europe and are only behind America. In pig iron we still in 1928 were in the sixth place. In 1929 we overtook Belgium and got into her place, the fifth place in the world. According to the plan we must give this year 8 million tons of pig iron and overtake England which at present occupies the fourth place in the world in the production of pig iron. This year we must wrest from her this fourth place and press England back into fifth place and then we must overtake Germany.

But how are we going to accomplish this task if our All-Union coal centre is not doing its part? Coal as a fuel is the basis of our metallurgy, the basis of our heavy industry.

Comrade miners, you old honored proletarians, the

best specialists of the Donbas, you see what enormous responsibility rests upon you. We are convinced that with the aid of the proletarians of the USSR you shall find in yourself sufficient strength to purge the Donbas from opportunists, loafers, grabbers, labor tramps, and absentees, in order to establish in the Donbas an iron proletarian discipline and compel the brains, the machines, and the hands to work at full speed.

Comrades, in entering upon the second quarter of the current year, we appeal to all the workers of the factories and the plants of the USSR, to all agricultural workers, and to all the collective farmers:

We have all the possibilities to complete the program of the third, the decisive year, of the Five Year Plan. Let us show then that we are able to carry out these possibilities. Let us mobilise all our energies, all our will, let us concentrate all our reserves and press forward with the might of many millions. Thus under the leadership of the Bolshevik Communist Party and its Central Committee let us accomplish and surpass the national economic plan for 1931, and complete the laying of the foundation of a socialist economy in the USSR.

Signed at the request of the general meetings of the workers of all shops and departments of Plant No. 1.

(*47 signatures.*)

Results immediately followed this appeal. In reply to the challenge of the oil industry which had offered a banner of honor to any industry for going over the top as they did, and in reply to the Tula challenge, the coal miners of Shcheglovka Minelin, Donbas, appealed last May Day to all of the Donbas miners to devote May 2 (holiday) as free work. In one district even women came out to help husbands. Some even worked all May Day and paraded after returning from work. One mine reports it exceeded production on Easter Day and will do the same on May 1.

In reply also to the Tula challenge, a group of 7,000 students and scientific workers at Moscow Institute of Engineering Transport answered, *Call was heard and it raised enthusiasm in our ranks.* So they challenged proletarian students and professors to give technical aid to industry and agriculture in getting their program over. They themselves organised 729 shock brigades and 150 engineers who completed courses before time and 70 *groups of eighth-hour workers to which we give technical instruction. 44 Professors work to prepare programs for these circles. 372 students work with illiterates.*

Another response to Tula, from the Frolov Kolhoz, indicates how such methods are co-ordinating industry and agriculture:

We shall commence the sowing campaign on 100 per cent collectivised basis and we shall prove by facts that the collectivised peasant is a firm and dependable supporter of the Party and of the working class in the village. There are 4200 shock workers. All accepted the plan of piecework. (Then comes an appeal also to all other workers and collective farmers of the Soviet Union.)

A similar appeal from the workers and engineering technical personnel of the Moscow Stalin Auto Plant (Amo.), printed on the front page of "Pravda," April 6, 1932, shows how specific results are being achieved: *Comrades: . . .*

Exactly three years ago the workers of Red Vyborzhets and the Kamensk paper mills sent out their com-

radely appeal to all workers to combat slackers and disorganisers who were doing great harm to our economy. Their appeal found hearty response among the millions of workers, resulting in the spread of socialist competition.

(*They recount the growth of "Our Plant."*)

. . . *Mass socialist competition between the different departments, shifts, brigades, and individual shock workers was the method of our work. It brought us the victory. We shall turn out 25,000 heavy cars a year.*

We reduced the cost of the machine from 11,078 rubles in 1931 to 6775 rubles and we shall continue in this manner.

In mastering technique we have surpassed American standards in 659 operations.

Scrap is reduced from 15.5 per cent to 6.7 per cent.

(*Then follow accounts of accomplishments of other big plants.*)

Lenin's idea of competition is gripping the masses. It has become that gigantic force which is transforming the world and creating a mighty socialist order.

The history of socialist competition shows clearly the combination of forces that is behind the building of socialism in the USSR. There appear the pressure of immediate need, the initiative of the masses, the insight of Lenin, the guiding hand of the Party, the influence of the press, the executive capacity of labor unions and Komsomol. In 1920 the Ninth Party Congress passed a resolution which declared, *Competition must be a mighty power to raise the efficiency of labor . . . Competition between factories, regions, factory departments and workshops, and individual workers should be a matter of careful organisation and attentive study on the part of the labor unions and economic organs.* Lenin had early set down the organisation of competition as one of the tasks of the Soviet state. So it was practised somewhat during the period of NEP. With the coming in of the Five Year Plan it rapidly became popular, largely through the efforts of the Komsomol. Also it grew naturally out of production conferences. With it grew the shock brigade movement. The Komsomol declared that the member who does not participate in it is a backward element. The Central Labor Council organised a drive for shock brigades in connection with the anniversary of the death of Lenin. When production fell down in 1929, the Central Committee of the Party charged the Central Labor Council and also all Party members and Komsomols to promote socialist competition and shock brigades. These instructions were reiterated by the Sixteenth Party Congress in 1930. Meantime the Party had discovered and published Lenin's article, written in 1918, on "How to Organise Competition," whose keynote was:

Now that a socialist government is in power, we must organise competition. . . . Socialism does not do away with competition; on the contrary, it for the first time creates the possibility of applying it on a really wide scale. . . . The talents of the working class and peasantry are as yet untapped and they are enormous. . . . We must organise competition among the practical workers and peasant organisers. . . . Every commune, factory, village, consumers' organisation, supplies committee, must come forward and compete with the others as practical organisers of accounting and control of labor and the distribution of products. . . .

With the words of Lenin behind it and the practical necessities in front of it, socialist competition ran like a prairie fire from border to border of the vast Soviet territory. Everywhere is the struggle to meet norms and the fun of challenging others to do likewise. It is a huge game, with a high goal. It gives zest to work and spirit to life as the Plan had given them purpose. In spreading it, the Press played a leading part. It treats the news of the fulfilling of the Plan as papers in other countries treat sports, and the records have similar interest for their respective readers. The socialist competition agreements in agriculture are often signed in the office of the local paper; often it is made responsible for, and always given a leading part in, checking the results and deciding the winner. Hence the provincial and agricultural Press, just like "Toil"—the daily of the All-Union Central Labor Council, is filled with accounts of progress of socialist competition agreements. Here is a typically frequent headline: "The second check-up on the collective agreements of the enterprises of the Northern Caucasus is not satisfactory."

Krivitsky in his "Capitalist and Socialist Co-operation of Labor" summarises the function of the Press:

The common purpose which is outlined and focussed by the national organs "Pravda" and "Izvestia" then goes through the whole system down to the smallest shop, kolhoz, or pioneer paper. . . . Also the process runs in reverse direction as a counter response from mass initiative, and sometimes as original suggestions from the millions of correspondents who reflect the mind of their group and community and bring it to bear upon the formation of party purpose. In this manner most of the new forms of labor co-operation sprung from the masses and were recognised by the leaders.

Solotov points out in his pamphlet on socialist competition that the essence of it is publicity and good example. To this end all the power of artistic advertising, particularly through posters, is brought into play with the same result that follows in the case of the Press; its propaganda has a constructive purpose and therefore a social value.

Because of the difference, both in nature and consequences, between socialist competition and its capitalist forerunner, some Soviet writers are trying to change its name to socialist emulation. While this correctly represents the dominant element in it yet there is a residue of real competition. Sometimes its undesirable concomitants appear, though not as much in industry and agriculture as in trade, where the interweaving of the old forms with the new produce—fortunately at a declining rate—such abnormal phenomena as competition for market and supplies between various state enterprises, expenditure on advertising, middle men, commission agents. Instances of the temptation to cheat that lies in the competitive method appear in the account of "Building the Stalingrad Tractor Works" by shock worker Peter Vorobyev:

(*He tells how one brigade of rivetters sent a scout to see how another with whom they were competing was getting along. Their rivals deceived the scout into believing they had accomplished much less than the real record. As a result his brigade took a rest, got to talking, and let the forge go out. It was too near quitting time to get it going again.*) *As they got up to the control gate Mishka* (*the brigadier*) *noticed a crowd round the board where the results of the socialist competition were always announced. Somebody shouted at him and jeered as he came up: "Mishka, you've slid down from the first to the tenth place. First from the tail end. Ha! Ha! That's a lad, bravo!"*

The laugh cut Mishka to the quick. . . . Natolka's

brigade occupied first place on the board. It had made a record of six hundred and three rivets.

Mishka turned on Artyushka and cursed him angrily:

"What sort of a scout are you, anyway, damned fool! I told you to be careful how you asked. And you believed what they told you, like a fool. Ay, you'll stay a candidate for the Komsomol for ages yet."

Artyushka shrugged his shoulders. "Oh, all right, Mishka, you needn't be so mad! We'll outdo them tomorrow, by jiminy, we shall."

. . . .

The approaching winter threatened to stop the building of the tractor works. The workers said: "No. The frosts won't cool our enthusiasm." And they declared parts of the work a shock brigade front. The seasonal workers were drawn into the socialist system of competition. Whole families of them laid the brick walls.

The bearded old Ipat laid his bricks evenly, quietly. His wall grew ever so slowly. His son—Mishka—challenged him to competition through the newspaper "On with the Tractors!" "Ay, the blackguard," said his father.

Sweat, mixed with cement dust, rolled down his face. A dormant aptitude and swift-handedness awoke in the old man. Instead of the usual three hundred bricks a shift, Ipat lays six hundred. The wall rises quicker and quicker. Then, it seemed that the old man [illegible] frizzled out and Mishka challenges again: "Six [illegible]ed and fifty."

[illegible] strains every nerve and lays six hundred and [illegible] bricks. Mishka challenges again: "Seven hun-

dred!" Then Ipat spat and swore—"Go to the devil, you and your bricks!"

Mishka felt a bit sorry for the old man. He admitted quietly—"I cheated you twenty bricks, dad. I couldn't lay more than six hundred and fifty myself."

"Ugh, crook! An' I was thinking, and what if he really lays more'n me." Pleased with his superior efficiency, old Ipat goes on laying brick on brick with assurance.

It is in its extent that socialist competition between groups of Soviet workers differentiates itself from similar rivalry between gangs of capitalist wage earners trying to reach first the centre of a new bridge or the meeting place of a new railroad track. It is in its purpose also that it removes itself far from the salesmanship competitions of capitalist business organisations. But its chief distinguishing characteristic is the extent to which it unites the principle of mutual aid with that of emulation. Stalin popularises this as meaning that some work better, others not so well, and each must help the other. Examples appear everywhere. The agreements between sovhoz and kolhoz require mutual aid, the sovhoz sends tractors for plowing, seeding, and harvesting, the kolhoz sends workers. A kolhoz centre reports, "Already this year—1931—the older kolhozes have sent thousands of organisers to help the newly formed collectives." The Moscow Auto workers gave voluntary first aid to tractor stations. The foreign workers of Selmash drew up and published in the plant paper a resolution, with specifications, to help their Ru[illegible]sian brothers with their best work and knowledge[illegible] Mass Meeting of Workers at the Pervaya Py[illegible] Farm, Millerovo District, Northern Caucasus, [illegible]ised an appeal, "To all Individual Farmers, [illegible]

Women, To all Members of the New Collective Farms," as an introduction to the little book about their life the work written by a number of their shock brigaders. Among other things the appeal said:

We want to impart our experience to other collective farm workers and individual farmers by means of this book. We want to tell them about our mistakes, which is one way of learning, and we ask all individual farmers, farm-hands, poor and middle peasants to join collective farms.

We further appeal to the members of the collective farms which are not yet running properly to increase their strength by means of organised labor, piecework, and socialist competition.

We want everybody to know that we shall never abandon our work in the collective farm, and that we no longer have the slightest desire to live as individual farmers.

There are several interesting and important by-products of this extension of mutual aid in connection with socialist competition. One is that it is removing the former inferiority complex of the Russians as they acquire strength in and for the technique of socialist construction. Another is that it develops joy in work, it brings back into labor the song that the coming of industrialism drove away. One chilly November evening we asked a small company of kolhoz workers who were loading cabbages for market why the kolhoz was better than individual farming. One woman spoke up first: "It is merrier to work together." Often they go forth to the sowing or the harvest and to their free work in cities with banners flying and with songs. Also this joyous, competitive, mutual work promotes solidarity. It gradually ties the whole diverse multitude into a fellowship, including nationalities who were formerly at each others' throats in pogroms and race wars. The Pioneer educators claim to have found this concretely among the children. A paragraph in one of their publications is headed "Socialist Emulation as the basic method of Communist Education":

Both in city and village the Pioneer Organisation has been pushing Socialist Emulation, not attempting to transmit mechanically the methods of work among adult organisations, but trying to adapt it as a principle of education in collective habits. . . . Two surveys which have been made to check up this work have shown that socialist emulation strengthens the solidarity and comradeship among the children and draws them to the tasks of socialist construction.

The mutual-aid aspect of socialist competition comes to its fullest expression in the *sheftsvo*—or patronage—agreements, in which some institution or organisation becomes the patron of another. This is also spoken of as the process of adoption. In earlier days this meant merely doing social work. For instance, the little village reading room in which, in 1924, I answered the questions of the peasants about the United States, was provided by the Police Union of a neighboring town, which had taken shefstvo over that village. Today this means an agreement for competition and mutual aid in fulfilling the Plan. The most universal form of such agreements is between factories and nearby collective farms and communes. For instance the oil industry at Baku has sixty-six such agreements, the harvester plant at Selmash has thirty-three. In working out this patronage, the Party supplies political education, the labor union technical aid, the Komsomol youthful leaders. The kolhozes to be adopted are divided between the departments, even the gas station takes one. The work is done through a sheftsvo society organised in each department with a membership fee of ten kopecks a month.

Besides binding the factory workers to send skilled men to put in order the agricultural machinery before seedtime and harvest and to carry on specified cultural work in the villages—such as organising kindergartens, libraries, nurseries, and playgrounds—these agreements bind both sides in competition to fulfil and sometimes surpass the norms in their respective plans. For example, in the agreement between the drill department and the Pervaya Pyatiletka Kolhoz the latter agrees among other things:

To increase the area of spring sowing by adding 4015 hectares. To increase the crop over last year by 11 per cent. To lower production cost 15 per cent. To increase working oxen to 50, horses to 55, milk cows to 51, pigs to 31 and to get 2 full-blooded sows.

The drill department, for the factory, agrees among other things: *To lower production costs 15 per cent from the previous mean; to reduce absence without reason to .03 per cent and drifters to 3 per cent; to get 50 per cent of all workers on hozraschet by January 1 and 75 per cent by May 1.*

The kolhoz also agrees to increase its own cultured activities, such as putting on social competition to liquidate illiteracy and organising technical courses. They also agree to adopt, jointly with the workers, a jail for political prisoners in Poland.

Both factory and kolhoz papers print from time to time the joint accomplishments under the agreement, which specifies the time of calculation, with a representative from an agricultural paper as judge. At the end prizes are given, with a great celebration. In this case the factory did not reach the mark set, the kolhozes went past theirs and made a national record for seeding, for harvesting on time, for threshing in twenty-four hours, and for sending a great "Red Haul" of wheat from the thresher to the elevator. As a result their deeds were chronicled in a book entitled "Heroes of Millerovo."

Separate departments in Selmash also patronise, respectively, a company of sailors, an aviation corps, and a section of the OGPU. The factory workers helped the latter in cultural activities and the OGPU helped them to find out why production fell down. The factory had also—and it is becoming customary—taken patronage over a section of the Red Army and delegates were going back and forth to get acquainted with each others' work. At one factory celebration which we attended, the applause of the evening was given to the delegates from that corps of the Red Army over which the factory had taken sheftsvo. The Theatrical Workers' Union is the cultural patron of the Red Army, organising performances in barracks and camps, soldiers' excursions to theatres and amateur dramatic circles. Some factories also have taken patronage over theatres, taking an active part in their repertory plans and their artistic-political councils. The theatres in return help in the dramatic work of the factories. The "Krasny Bogatyr" factory is patron of the Moscow Art Theatre, the Electro Factory of the Meyerhold Theatre, etc.

Another form of patronage agreement is that which the textile factory Trehgorka, for example, signed with a kolhoz, promising to train effectively for trades the surplus workers whom the kolhoz promised to send to the factory. There was also the usual mutual agreement to increase production. In the lumber industry the sawmill workers constitute themselves patrons over neighboring villages, giving them aid in farming, repairing machinery, organisation of socialist forms of labor, and cultural activities. This method reaches down to the children. Sometimes a Young Pioneer takes patronage over a certain machine in a factory. He then has to see if the worker carries out his agreement not to drink, be late or absent, and to keep the machine clean and oiled. On the other hand the Pioneer assumes obligations in his school work. The furthest reach of patronage work is where it becomes a productive bond between the biggest factories and the agricultural district which supplies them with raw materials. For example, the textile workers have adopted the cotton district of Central Asia. Through such agreements the organisational experience of industry is transmitted to agriculture; it learns how to develop shock tactics, the new socialist forms of labor, and the methods of socialist competition; it becomes socialised as well as mechanised. Thus socialist competition, instead of dividing people into classes like its antecedent in the capitalist world, is one of the shuttles running back and forth between the various sections of the population, weaving them into a unity of knowledge, purpose, and accomplishment.

STRECHNY PLAN

The highest form of socialist competition, according to the Central Committee of the Party, is the strechny plan. There is no satisfactory English equivalent of this term. Literally it means "meeting plan" because [illegible] comes from the verb *vstrechat*—to meet, and is [illegible] plan of the workers themselves, with which they meet that made by the planning authorities. It is usually translated "counter plan" but that term has a suggestion of opposition, whereas in fact the workers' plan usually exceeds the one offered to them. Therefore it seems best to use the Russian term and to drop the *v* which is almost silent.

This form of mass initiative started in the Karl Marx metal factory in Leningrad. It followed from the instructions of the Party and the Government that the preliminary Plan should go to each department and be discussed by each worker in terms of his job. The First Plan sent out from Gosplan headquarters is only an outline, consisting of general estimates, called control figures. This is sent to local planning commissions and by them to the planning departments of factories and other institutions to be filled in on the basis of local knowledge and sent back to Moscow for revision and co-ordination. When the workers in the Karl Marx factory took part in this filling in, according to instructions, they began to say on the basis of their experience, that they could do more than the control figures suggested. So they drew up a plan of their own and submitted it to the management. As a result the program for the year was increased by 120 per cent. Then they began to pledge themselves to exceed this. Comrade Ojojin wrote to the Temporary Control Commission:

Three months ago I produced 50 cylinders a day, now I make about one hundred. The former cost of production was 13 kopecks a cylinder, and now it is 8 kopecks. In the industrial financial counterplan I pledge myself to increase production by an additional 40–50 cylinders, and to reduce the cost by 30 per cent. Take this into consideration when you draw up the new industrial plan.

Then the workers of the Karl Marx factory addressed a letter to the whole proletariat in the Soviet Union in which they said: "The strechny plan should be taken over by agriculture which is being reconstructed on a socialist basis." A group of the leading members of shock brigades in Moscow plants addressed a letter to "Pravda" suggesting that the industrial financial counterplan ("strechny") be introduced on the collective farms. The more progressive kolhozes soon answered the appeal of the workers. The Kolhoz Blucher wrote as follows:

The plan which is projected by the government should not merely be subdivided for each kolhoz, but in line with the example set by the leading workers of the industries, a strechny plan should be drawn up by the kolhozes, which should thus assure not only the fulfillment of the government quota but that it would be surpassed.

Thus the strechny plan spread rapidly throughout the country and is found working today in every institution. For instance the workers in a refinery at Batum read in the paper that a factory near Odessa had put in a strechny plan for each shift. At once they do the same and in eleven days over-fulfil their plan. They write labor headquarters at Baku and propose a Trans-Caucasus conference to make the method universal. The strechny spirit is evident in the fact that this region, formerly a colony exploited for oil and manganese, is now developing for itself and the Plan various minerals, water power, silk and cotton growing, canning factories, and chemical plants. It has finished most of its Five Year Plan in three years with thirty per cent surplus for the last year. Almost always the workers' proposals go beyond those of the official plan, but sometimes they reduce them. The Komsomols usually lead the advanced proposals but their executives say they are not so instructed, that their actions express the natural enthusiasm of youth. Sometimes they add wisdom to zeal. At one of the refineries in Baku, the workers proposed a strechny plan and the Komsomol brigade said, "on the basis of our rationalisation experience we know we can't make that." The others went ahead—and failed. But the Komsomols overfulfilled the original plan.

This method means not only that the workers are competing against standards which they have set for themselves but also that they make a substantial contribution to the planning process. As the plan comes down through the factory it gets broken up into smaller units and set for shorter times. The planning department will work it out for a three months' period, the planning brigade in a shop for one month, and the working brigade for ten or five days, and sometimes for each day. Also the figures that go back to headquarters become much more exact as the workers fill them in from their experience. For instance, a young engineer in an electric factory tells me the plan will call for ten million lamps at 42 kopecks, the workers plan may total up to nearly fifteen million at 30 kopecks. *Why? Because the drafter, not knowing the machine, puts down 1000 parts for it, the worker says, "We—the machine and I—can do 1223" because he knows just what he has been averaging.*

The director of one trust tells me that besides making the strechny plan, the workers pass on every aspect of the official plan. They take it first to small groups of activists, then to larger meetings and finally to a mass meeting. "They say 'yes' or 'no' or change it, even to the amount of costs and profits." The labor unions have the responsibility for getting the workers' plans included in the plans for sections of industry and in the general economic plan for the country; also of keeping the process free from undue standardisation and bureaucratic control. One of the national secretaries. Shvernik, reports:

Sometimes we have cases where they (managers and union officials) try to force this movement, which includes the most complex process of developing the creative initiative of the working class, into the framework of formal planning from above, and instead of help and guidance for the movement they display an unnecessary and troublesome guardianship over it.

The kind of interest that the making of the strechny plan develops is seen in the notes of a shift meeting in one of the departments at Selmash, to consider the plan for 1932. The chairman proposed a ten per cent increase and the men at once began to comment:

If we are to do that, the foreman must explain things better.

We must get parts on time and they must be better prepared; the holes must be accurate and without burrs, the nuts must fit.

The tools must be kept sharp.

The conveyor must be fixed. ("We'll get a new one," says the foreman.)

We must have three days' material ahead and an uninterrupted supply of tools.

The equipment for rivetting should be attached to the machine.

I asked for a drill and got one without a socket.

There is a break in transportation.

The office workers should go on hoz raschet (socialist cost accounting). The accountants too—so as to calculate quicker our socialist competition results.

There should be no rotation but keep each man to his machine.

They then voted the ten per cent addition and ordered it worked out in detail for each machine and compared and co-ordinated with the plans of all the shifts.

A further development of workers' planning occurred at the Djerzhinsky steel plant. When it was ordered to restore the blast furnace in fifty days, ten of them were lost in confusion in making plans. A group of Komsomols conceived the idea of a graphic strechny plan, based on such plans from each department and brigade; then they got them to check up the capacity of each machine and the productivity of each worker, and determine the period in which all materials and equipment for the furnace should be turned out. With the results they made a graphic plan that pictured to each brigade what it had to do and its relation to the whole job. The management of the foundry department refused to reduce the time for making knobs for pillar supports. The Komsomols talked with moulders and foremen and called a meeting of casters of knobs who drew up a strechny plan pledging themselves to produce the knobs in two days instead of four. In each department those who lagged behind were assisted by those who wanted the plan to succeed. Grandpa Morpan—a lathe hand for thirty-eight years—ate breakfast and dinner at his machine for five days. He ground the belt for the furnace in five days, whereas his own counterplan had reduced the time for the job from fourteen to eight days. In the end the graphic plan reduced the time of repairing the blast furnace by ten days. It was used again with similar results in laying gaspipes from the coke furnaces to the steel plants and soon found its way into all the construction plants of Kamensky region.

Examples of the increased enthusiasm and efficiency that strechny planning has developed in the workers are legion. I select only two, condensing them from accounts in "Pravda" and in "VOKS" respectively:

Kuznetskstroi, the largest steel plant yet built, was erected in a wilderness in 18 months. The Gary plant, the largest in the U. S., was finished in two years in a centre of industrial development with everything available. The French engineers at Kuznetskstroi estimated the time for laying 23,000 tons of brick for the coke batteries at 121 days—the shortest time in the experience of the West. They figured that at least 40 per cent of the workers would be of average skill, 40 per cent of high skill and 20 per cent exceptional. But it turned out that 60 per cent had to be common laborers, mostly young people, who were taught right on the spot. The workers studied the graphs and rejected them, saying that 121 days was too high, 80 days was enough. The French shrugged their shoulders and said: "Well you can write anything since paper is very patient." The first battery was finished in 76 days, the second—delayed by accident—in 87. The French engineers checked the work and accepted it as excellent.

The Electro Factory in Moscow carried out its Five Year Plan in 2½ years and the executives ascribe the result to the higher forms of socialist competition, leading to the mobilisation of all forces for carrying out in-

dividual tasks, for direct participation in planning, rationalisation, and for active endeavor to master technique. Planning brigades composed of engineers and workers elaborated the control figures in detail for each machine, then went over them in six production conferences in each department for each year. The women workers distinguished themselves. Their program from the Gosplan was 48 million lamps. The manager suggested 51, the women raised it to 60—without extra investment, on condition that supply of materials be improved and that workers' rationalisation proposals and inventions be adopted. The management said supply was difficult. The women sent brigades to the glass factory and stirred them up to needed improvements. Then they sent a delegation to the highest authorities and stirred up a row in "Izvestia." Supply was improved. If the control figures did not come through on time the workers made their own calculations. One group included one-day planning and if production lagged called a flying production meeting to find out which operation was responsible and if necessary regrouped the workers. (Since adopted elsewhere.) The cap section was put on the blackboard for disrupting the factory. It called a production conference, organised a storm brigade, rejected the administration program, proposed 35,000 more and actually turned out 40,000 more. To do this it had to send a brigade to the brass factory to get a proper supply of material, and "put sentinels in the narrow places" (every school child knows what this slogan of Stalin means) to see that extra orders came through on time.

With such evidence—and it can be multiplied—Krylenko the famous prosecutor was amply justified in saying in his pamphlet about the Industrial Party trial, that *the wreckers were beaten by the enthusiasm and creative power of the proletarian masses. They had forgotten that the plans were checked from below. So testing from below is the best method of counteracting the wreckers.* Also of course this method develops the economic possibilities of the planning system as the technicians alone could not possibly do. Thus Kuibeshev, head of Gosplan, recognised this in opening the meeting of its Plenum in 1931 by saying, *The first step toward improving the plan is to attract the masses of the workers. This has already been accomplished in strechny plans.* Their influence on the whole planning program is seen in the fact that at the Seventeenth Party Conference, where the preliminary Second Five Year Plan was discussed, Mirzoyan moved as an amendment the strechny plan of the Ural Workers on pig iron. And Molotov in accepting amendments that "appear to be indisputable" included a suggestion to the presidium from a group of non-ferrous metal workers for redrafting more accurately and minutely the section on non-ferrous metallurgy.

The social economic plan of the Soviets was not thought out and superimposed by a few people at the top. It grew up gradually in the course of years—after the first electrification plan so strongly advocated by Lenin—as the natural result of the union of two forces, the inherent nature of the socialist economy and the practical necessities of the situation. The first draft plan is *merely tentative and provisional* say the Gosplan authorities. It is *subject to thorough discussion, critical examination, revision and amendment in accordance with the proposals made by the central and local bodies, public and business organisations and the millions of workers in each respective district and factory.* They report that the importance of this local planning work and the number of people participating in it increases yearly. *The plan of national economy in the USSR is a plan of the millions. The millions draw it up, carry it out, and closely watch the course of its fulfilment. This is the basis of success of planned economy, this is the fundamental advantage of the Soviet system of economy.* Thus the Plan provides the masses with more than a concrete aim and a unifying slogan. It gives them opportunity for developing their initiative.

HOZRASCHET

The next step in the development of socialist forms of labor was *hozraschet.* Again the term has no English equivalent. It is sometimes translated "socialist business basis" and sometimes "self-paying basis" or "administrative self-cost." The planning authorities explain it as the socialist form of the principle of rationalisation, that is, securing the greatest possible economic results for the least expenditure, and for social ends. For this purpose, naturally, the technique of cost accounting is employed, and this is implied in the phrase. But the important thing is that this technique is used by the workers as well as by the management and for ends which they have chosen. In the factories they say that hozraschet means that every operation of each machine, department, factory, and trust must pay for itself, and provide its quota of socialist accumulation.

Lenin knew how necessary this would be: In his "How to Organise Competition," he said:

. . . *accounting and control, carried on everywhere,*

only twelve cutters in his lathe instead of fifteen. On the other hand, the agreements specify that in no way is the responsibility for losses to be placed on the workers, outside of the terms of their union agreements. This refers mostly to the making of scrap; the union reasoning is that it is the responsibility of the technician to prevent that. On the other hand, the premiums for savings and increased production are fully applied to the hozraschet brigades. Thus it appears that the stimulus is completely positive. The agreements do not hold the workers to their responsibility with the threat of loss. They stimulate initiative on both sides, again with a combination of mutual aid and competition in reducing costs. But the worker's interest in that process runs far beyond the pay envelope, he is using it to accomplish bigger ends.

The pamphlet above referred to makes it clear that the rationalisation movement, which in other lands was developed by financiers and technicians, appeared in the Soviet Union on the initiative of the workers themselves:

One of the leaders of a brigade of shock workers, Kapkov, by name, working in the Lenin plant in Leningrad, and independently of him a certain Nikoliav of the Baltic plant and a certain Davaines of the Sevkabl plant, all in Leningrad, observed in their work that much of their enthusiastic efforts in maintaining tempos in production and quality were frustrated by inefficiency. Quite independently of one another, they came to the conclusion that to maintain the tempos and the enthusiasm, it was necessary to have a scientific analysis of the process of their own work, dividing it into definite operations with definite equipment, material, and auxiliary help.

They learned from analyzing their work that there was much waste in the use of material and irrational application of effort, and that very often failures were even not due at all to the workers but to the shop administration, which failed to supply the workers on time with the necessary parts, material, auxiliary help, proper working conditions, and the like.

These men, therefore, in discussing the situation in their own brigades, decided to make a proposal to the administration to sign special agreements with shock brigades, in which, in simple but exceedingly definite terms, the mutual obligations and responsibilities of the parties concerned were to be laid down. In this manner it was possible to make a check on the process of the work and fix responsibility for failures and also for improvements.

The experience of these brigades . . . passes through three definite stages:

First: The shop administration works out, on the basis of its plans and calculations, the quantitative and qualitative norms for the brigades, with an itemizing of the overheads, auxiliary materials, and the like.

Second: The brigade finds out the productive capacity of its equipment, calculates what amount of material is necessary for the production of each detail, what kind of overhead is needed, etc., and on the basis of these estimates, it presents a strechny plan . . . particularly in respect to the norms of output, of scrap, of expenditure of material per unit of production, of losses, etc.

Third: The brigade and the administration jointly meet and discuss both the plan of the administration and the strechny plan of the brigade, and formulate an agreement and a preliminary estimate of costs . . . later expanded into a similar agreement for the whole shop. All these plans for determining norms and lowering costs must be accompanied by a more detailed plan of rationalization within the brigade work.

The results achieved by these hozraschet brigades are set down first in lowered costs and increased output. The initial brigade in Leningrad accomplished 100 per cent of the Plan whereas the whole foundry achieved only 67 per cent. Over against the savings must be set statements by American engineers of increased overhead for accounting that in some cases more than eats up the savings made by the workers. But this will be counteracted by the fact that the workers now have in these agreements a detailed check on the administration and can hold it responsible for results. In the other direction it leads them to support administration plans when they see in detail what they mean. The workers in a kolhoz near Saratov supported the movement to build a central stable and grain warehouse when cost accounting analysis showed them the problem and the results of their labor: Said one of them: *Now we see our situation as in a mirror. And we are especially surprised at the proportion between labor in the fields and behind the lines in the care of property.*

Also the training that the workers thus get in scientific analysis of their problems conserves the advance first made by emotional initiative through the shock brigades and enables it to go further by putting it on a sound business basis. A director of a factory in Tiflis was reporting to the workers' meeting: "There are no figures on the results of hozraschet," he said.

A worker raised his hand to wave some papers, saying: "We have them. You didn't take them."

"Last month I took them and found them wrong,"

was the answer. "When you work with figures you must be more serious."

Obviously an attempt to reduce production costs that starts from the workers will go in the long run much further than one which is originated by management for its own ends. In the former case it becomes a strechny plan in savings. For example, the administration at Selmash proposed for 1931 a savings' plan in the toolroom of one and one-half million rubles. The workers analysed it and proposed two millions because each one said, "My machine can save so much." Thus the initiative which started strechny plans and hozraschet works up to larger measures of rationalisation.

WORKERS' RATIONALISATION

Socialist rationalisation has several advantages to begin with. No property rights stand in the way of the most efficient co-ordination of the various parts of the national economy. There is power to restrict or to prohibit the production and sale of commodities for which there may be a considerable demand but which public opinion regards as harmful or unnecessary. But most of all it is able to draw to the fullest upon the initiative and co-operation of labor in other matters than the reduction of labor costs in particular operations. For instance during the campaign against "drifters" from plant to plant whose restrictive regulations occasioned the "forced-labor" outcry in other countries, the "Red Triangle" factory of Leningrad issued a statement in the press, and at the All-Union Labor Conference, proposing "a fortnight of labor reserves" during which a resolute campaign was to be waged against irrational use of labor in industry. The editor of "Pravda" took

the first place in Europe regarding the volume of industrial production and consumption of textiles, the level of the electrification of industry, the provision of mechanical power for labor and the efficiency of labor in industry. . . . The last circumstance is of decisive importance.

This increased efficiency has had to be gained against the handicap of a load of inherited inefficiency among the white-collar workers and not a little sabotage. When the assistant director in the Production-Planning Department at Selmash—a worker elected by the workers—was asked why production fell down the year before he replied: *Lack of machines; supplies of steel and lumber did not come through on time; the plan was not perfected.* A group of Leningrad engine fitters mobilised to stop the slump in coal production down in the Donetz basin found about fifty per cent production in certain pits and discovered that boring-machine workers were occupied only four hours daily for lack of tools to make repairs. They requested three simple lathes, some tools, and a few litres of chloric acid: *If we receive the same, we Communists take upon ourselves first to put all this equipment in order, of course making no charge for this work to the mine management; second, we positively agree to stop the slump.*

It was for mismanagement such as these workers corrected that a Labor Court in Moscow, March, 1931, found several factory managers, engineers, and other officials guilty of being "grave diggers of workers' initiative." In his "How to Organise Competition," Lenin, who knew his Russians, had warned the workers what to expect. *Intellectuals give the best advice and guidance but are laughably, ridiculously, disgracefully incapable of carrying out the advice and directions, of exercising practical control, and seeing to it that the word is transferred into action.* Hence as the technical staff for the building of socialism gets manned with the younger men and women, trained in different methods and imbued with a different spirit and purpose, it may be anticipated that the efficiency and productivity of the Soviet workers will increase even more rapidly.

The transformation of the habits and attitudes of the workers is counted by Soviet leaders the most significant result of the new forms of socialist labor. They *strengthen the first elements of Communist consciousness in the working class,* says Molotov. In his "Socialist Competition" Solotov concretes this:

. . . the worker becomes conscious of his worth as a member of the collective in which each works as links in a chain. Some of the backward workers reason as follows: "Well, what do I, a single locksmith, mean? I do little work and if I do not do it the USSR will not suffer." When we bring the agreement about competition to the workbench it becomes clear to every one that the Five Year Plan is the result of our common work and of our individual exertions.

Professor Krivitsky also emphasises the consciousness that grows in the worker as he realises that he is a member of *an ever-growing collective which is building the socialist economy.* Thus the bond of solidarity in socialist co-operation of labor is not external but ties deep into the centre of the worker's being.

CHAPTER V

OTHER EXPRESSIONS OF WORKERS' INITIATIVE

In the framework of Soviet institutions there are other opportunities for the expression of initiative from the masses besides the new forms of labor which the workers have themselves devised.

PARTICIPATION IN GOVERNMENT

Justice in the USSR is less formal than in other lands. It is not yet encrusted with precedent but is guided by the desire to achieve social ends. In the People's Court there is a bench of three judges. One is legally trained, the other two—often one man and one woman—are workers, released for a month for this purpose from factory, farm, or office, with pay. Naturally these courts increasingly deal with economic matters. In Baku in the Auditorium of the Factory House of Culture we saw one trying seventeen managers and workers in a co-operative on the charge of a grafting scheme. Through the improper distribution of purchasing books, goods had been secured and sold on the speculators' market. In Abkhasia, an engineer acquaintance had to go to court to answer for exceeding the amount appropriated for a new building. At Selmash the administration was about to be tried for not repairing the machinery during the October Revolution holiday, according to its hozraschet agreement with the workers.

Then there is the Comrades' Court, less formal still, dealing with matters less serious than those which go to the People's Court. For these, for example, violation of discipline, abusive language, assault without wound, spreading lies, stealing up to the value of fifty rubles—the worker is tried at the place where he works, by his comrades. The judges are selected from those who, nominated by their department committee, have been elected by the works conference to help the one chosen in the same way to administer this procedure. He has an office where he hears complaints after hours. Also, since his orders from the higher legal authorities are to concentrate on putting through the Promfinplan, he may start proceedings on his own initiative if, for instance, as one of them said, he sees a bunch of scrap (imperfect parts) that the foreman has let go through to be assembled. He had on trial that day the manager of equipment in a dining room who had been rebuked for unsanitary conditions, and threatened with a fine, by one of the doctors—a woman. He was tried for using abusive language to her. Then in the larger centres there is the Labor Court which hears complaints, usually from the workers, for infraction of the labor code. The cases are less since private employers have decreased. There are no costs and each case must be considered within five days. The bench consists of a judge, an economist, and a representative from the labor union.

Also there is the "House" or "Tenants' Court" elected by and from the tenants of an apartment house to handle disputes or quarrels arising within it. It can impose limited fines and public reprimands, and its decisions are final. These courts are very popular. They handle thousands of cases formerly brought before the "People's Courts." They teach the masses self-control and social mindedness. They are a more powerful corrective than forms of professional justice because the culprits feel so keenly the social reprimand or isolation from their own circle of daily associates.

The workers have a still wider expression for their initiative in the Workers' and Peasants' Control Commission. This was an invention of Lenin's to enable the masses to check the government. It was formerly a commissariat or cabinet department. Just before his death he secured its reorganisation, uniting it with the Central Control Commission of the Party, which has charge of Party discipline and ethics. His idea was to unite all controls in a very small organisation with large numbers of voluntary workers. The union between the two commissions is personal, rather than official, and informal, the same man being head of both. It is expressed by a hyphen between the initials of the two titles: CCC–RKI, but it is in the latter that the workers function and by which it is known to them. Its functions are investigation and report. When these are concentrated on a particular institution they are known as a "cleaning" because the disloyal and inefficient are cleaned out. In 1929 following the split in the Party and the discovery of sabotage among engineers and administrators, a general "cleaning" was ordered, first of the Party and then of all government offices and institutions. There is no department of the government too high to be cleaned. One member of the bureau has the OGPU for his work.

When an institution is being cleaned, meetings of

open for evidence of bad management and they also help to "liquidate misunderstandings." Complaints go to the bureau for investigation. Decisions are made by the department group on cases for which a rebuke is sufficient. If discharge is involved it must be affirmed by the regional bureau. An investigating or cleaning commission may order a job to be found for a man elsewhere or he may be forbidden to take any job in government employ, or be turned over to the procureur of OGPU, according to the seriousness of the offense. In one factory for instance RKI volunteers found a department selling for firewood lumber that could be used by a furniture factory. Others noticed metal in the sand being dumped from the forge shop and eventually over two hundred tons were recovered at a time when the supply was short. The general office is under the eye of the RKI organisation of the trust that operates the plant but in each office and department within the factory itself there is one man under the workers' control, especially prepared and appointed in the production conference, to give them a check on its efficiency. The RKI can and does order cuts in office staffs.

The work of the RKI, joined with the persistent efforts of the Party to mobilize the masses in the fight against bureaucracy in the state machinery and in the Party organisations themselves, has led to a more extensive expression of the initiative of the workers in government. It has become an established practice everywhere for the labor unions to take sheftsvo over some piece of state machinery. The most celebrated instance is that of the Electric works in Moscow in 1929 adopting Narcomfin—the Commissariat of Finance. About 3000 workers participated with RKI in the cleaning of the nations' financial centre. As a result three hundred officials were removed as aliens to the workers' state and three bureaus were eliminated as unnecessary, saving several million rubles. The staff was cut twenty-eight per cent and the "chair warmers" were sent off to jobs in the provinces and collectives where they were badly needed. Special brigades—three hundred of them—checked the tax lists and finally collected over four millions given up as hopeless. This practice spread to other cities until the workers had collected over twenty-five millions of back taxes. In 1930, the Moscow electrical workers also took part in investigating the finances of several organisations collecting funds from workers, such as co-operative banks and housing co-operatives. For good measure they collected over one hundred millions in back rent due to the municipality. Each shop in the electric plant has now adopted some section of Narcomfin. All this took long, hard courses in economics and public finance for many of the workers; as a result ninety-four have been moved up to important posts in the finance department, some of them being assistant chiefs of bureaus, while others stay as unpaid workers in their free time.

Another factory in Moscow has taken sheftsvo over Narcompross—the Commissariat of Education. In its offices, as one expression of the policy which unites productive labor and education, the workers are welcomed as inspectors and advisers. Their particular purpose is to see if the decisions of the Commissariat are always carried through. Indeed always the sheftsvo is a cooperative relationship, entered into willingly by both sides. In this form of it the workers are getting education in administration. In 1930, Moscow unions reported sheftsvo over thirty-five different government offices, and Leningrad recorded twenty, including the Gosplan. By the end of 1931, the practice had become so general that it was regularised in a decree of the Commissars—a striking example of how the masses are actually making the government. For the first half of 1931, the RKI had listed over 4000 workers executing administrative jobs in their free hours which were formerly held by paid officers. In every city we visited this practice was in vogue. In Tiflis, the railroad workers have sheftsvo over the railroad administration, with eleven hundred workers taking part. As one result, all directors and managers appointed in the last two years have been former workers. In 1930–1931, the unions of the Soviet Republic of Georgia recommended to responsible positions in State, economic, and co-operative organisations, 2545 men. Selmash adopts the regional office in charge of stock raising and pasture work. It sends nine men to work there—one for each division—on their free day. One is assistant manager in the finance department and one has full power to give orders and sign papers in the absence of the manager. These workers report back to the Party and to the general factory meeting. Some will be promoted to permanent jobs.

Labor headquarters at Moscow reports that over five million workers have taken part in meetings for cleaning government machinery, that the unions have already nominated twenty-five thousand workers for government posts and are preparing many others by volunteer work. It also mentions the part that workers have taken in studying and criticising plans for public buildings and in supervising their erection, as an especially valuable form of "proletarian self-criticism." The commission on the building of the Moscow Palace of the Soviets, before making its award in the international competition, held an exhibition of the plans in several factories, in order that the workers might participate in the decision through their criticism and suggestions.

This increasing participation of the people through these sheftsvo workers in the operations of the government—the growing detailed knowledge of its affairs which they bring back into the union meetings and present to the kolhozes, the constant infusion of new workers into administration staffs—is the main reliance of the Communist leaders in their fight against the besetting sin of bureaucracy. As Molotov told the executives of the Third International in February, 1930, *The motive force in the reconstruction of the state machinery is the participation of the mass of the workers in the administration of the state.* Lenin set forth this aim in "The State and Revolution": . . . *we must attract all the members of the Soviets into actual participation in government. . . . Our aim is the free execution of government obligations by every worker after the eight hour lesson.*

On the legislative side of government, the Soviets are organs devised to express the workers' will. They were initiated by the masses themselves at the time of the first revolution, when the Czarist power fell, and the Bolsheviks at once used them for the seizure of power in the name of the proletariat. Their outstanding characteristics, which strike every observer, are first the youthfulness of their members and then the fact that most of them are direct from the factory and the farm. Recently one of the younger generation of Russian novelists, who has been disowned by the Proletarian Writers on account of his bourgeois tendencies, became quite rhapsodic in print over the fact that his cook had just been elected to the local Soviet, a realisation of Lenin's famous saying, *Every cook, every common laborer should be drawn into the conduct of the government.* Lenin claimed for this form of organization the widest possible democratic base:

This is a power open to all, working openly, available to the masses, derived straight from the masses. . . .

Secondly this apparatus is a bond with the masses, with the majority of the people, so close, so indissoluble, so easily checked up and renewed that it has no match in the former government apparatus or in history.

Stalin, with a longer experience of the working of the Soviets behind his words, characterises them in more detail:

Soviets are the most comprehensive mass organisations of the proletariat, being the only organisations to which all the workers, without exception, belong.

Soviets are the direct organisations of the masses, consequently the most democratic, and therefore the most influential mass organisations; thus they are able to have a maximal effect in the way of inducing the masses to participate in the upbuilding of the new State, facilitating its administration, and to the greatest possible extent, developing the revolutionary energy, the initiative, and the creative faculty of the masses in the struggle for the destruction of the old order and the upbuilding of the new proletarian order.

The Soviet power, uniting legislative and executive authority into a single organ, and replacing territorial electoral areas by electoral units based on production (factories and workshops), establishes direct ties between the workers and the laboring masses, on the one hand, and the administrative apparatus on the other, and teaches the former how to use the latter.

The local Soviet has executive as well as legislative functions; it is in fact a local Council of Commissars. At certain times, the Moscow Soviet may be more powerful in determining national policy than even the central government itself. Since the Soviets have become concerned with the carrying out of the Plan they have secured increased interest and participation from the workers and peasants. In the last general election, 1931, 61 million voters participated as against 47 millions in 1929. This represented 72 per cent of the voting population and 48.1 per cent of them were rural. These elections were conducted under the slogan of bringing all administrative machinery closer to the masses. In his report to the Sixth Congress of Soviets, Molotov claimed that they had brought into the Soviets fresh groups of *advanced people from the masses of workers, primarily from among the best shock workers of town and village.* A practical step toward more expression of local initiative was the disbanding of the county Soviets—one link in the chain—thus allocating more power to the urban and rural units. That it was needed is shown by the fact that the appropriations for road building in 1931 were not all used for lack of initiative and participation, so only 55 per cent of the plan was completed. In the discussion Molotov said that he regarded the strengthening of the smaller units as *positively essential in order to vitalise and utilise local resources and natural wealth and in order to really rely upon the activity of the whole mass of Soviet workers.* This move is part of a general policy of decentralisation which is breaking up the large trusts—industrial and agricultural—and the giant farms into smaller units. It follows upon a growing realisation, sometimes through costly experience, that the success of a planned economy depends absolutely upon the initiative and intelligent participation of the bulk of the population.

THE LABOR UNIONS

The labor unions in the Soviet Union—they should not be called trade unions because they are organised by industries, not by trades—give their members more things to do than ordinary trade unions, and their membership includes practically all the workers. The new tasks set for them by the building of socialism provide continually more room for the expression of initiative. They have complete control of the direction and administration of the social insurance system, which in 1931 covered 15,315,000 workers and spent 2,172,000,000 rubles. They also administer a large educational work, including full-time, part-time, day, and night courses. They train leaders for cultural activities in the workers' clubs. For this they expended in 1931 for 42,485 workers, 24,500,000 rubles. They have also taken responsibility, by resolution of the Presidium of their Central Council, March 21, 1931, for organising and heading *the movement of the millions of toilers for mastering technique, and to equip each shock brigade with technical knowledge, and to stimulate socialist emulation between the brigades . . . for the best possible assimilation of Soviet and foreign technique.*

These and various other forms of work have to be worked out in the factory by the continuous efforts of the active portion of the membership, which is by these very activities constantly enlarged. In one large plant the union was found to be organised in ten sectors: Organisation of Workers; Production and Planning; Salaries and Calculating; Housing, Living, and Working conditions; Cadres (a baffling word, meaning sometimes small picked groups of technically qualified persons and more generally the whole technically trained personnel); Co-operatives' and Workers' Supply and Nourishment; Work in Villages; Cultural Organisations; Agit Mass Work. These sectors all have representatives promoting their interests in each division of the factory, from the department to the brigade. Also emergency duties are assigned, as for instance when a "safety first" campaign is on.

A still larger field for the energy and initiative of the workers, however, is opened up by the coming of a definite plan for the building of socialism. This pushes further that change which took place in the nature and responsibilities of the unions when the Revolution released them from the war against capitalists and made them responsible for the administration and organisation of production. Their main task now is to increase the productivity of labor. The failure to recognise this on the part of the former union leaders was the basic cause for their removal in 1930. They were drawing collective agreements as though the main function of the union was still to protect the rights of the worker. But the new leaders at once changed the character of the collective agreement and made, as the first sectional heading of the model agreement for 1932 says, "Mutual Obligations in Fulfilling the Industrial-Financial Plan" its main purpose.

This process has been accelerated by the spread of the new socialist forms of labor and workers' rationalisation. This is made clear by the official union pamphlet on "The Collective Agreement in the Fourth, Final Year of the Five-Year Plan," by L. Kaufmann. The workers agree, as in their socialist competition agreements between themselves, to increase productivity and efficiency, reduce waste and absenteeism, etc., in definite specifications. In like manner the management agrees to provide the proper *engineering and technical management of production, to supply in good time raw material, fuel, instruments, machinery, spare parts, to make the program known to every individual worker, to prevent stoppages, etc.* Besides the former definite specifications for the supply of housing and clubs, the administration also contracts now to provide certain kinds of technical instruction for a specified number of workers.

To increase the responsibility and participation of workers, the making of agreements between the trusts and central labor bodies was discontinued in 1931 and they are now made between the local factory and the works committee. So the model agreement is not a standardised form; . . . *every enterprise may and should draw up its own collective agreement, adapted to the conditions of the respective industry.* Also there are to be supplemental agreements between departmental managers and labor-union committees. All these are discussed finally in mass meetings. So the area of participation and interest is still further extended. Also it is specified in the agreement that there is to be arranged a mass check up of its fulfillment every three months and, before the agreement for the next year is made, a committee checks the record of fulfillment for the year that is closing. Furthermore the time of renewing collective agreements is made the occasion of an educational campaign for extending the new forms of labor. In 1931 this campaign brought *hundreds of thousands of rationalising recommendations from the workers, which saved millions of rubles for the state. Hundreds of thousands of workers entered the ranks of the shock-brigaders.* The resolution of the Sixth Plenum of the All-Union Central Council of Labor Unions on this matter declares that the collective agreement campaign for 1932 must, among other things, *result in the organisation of thousands of new business accounting brigades.*

The defensive function of the union is now transferred almost entirely from the field of wages and hours to that of living conditions and cultural interests. In these areas there is no need to defend the workers' rights against any desire to encroach upon them, because there is no diversity of interest and purpose between management and workers, nor any difference of class psychology. As the workers say over and over again, "we are also the management." Here again are two opposites woven into a unity. It is then merely a question of seeing that the pressure of the present production program does not lead to an undue sacrifice of the workers' other interests. At certain points some aspects of the old defensive function of the unions remain—against managers engrossed in immediate results or in making a record. It was found, for example, that in times of stress some managers were getting workers who could be lured by the bait of extra pay to come to the factory on their free day. For this day the worker then got double pay. So the unions had to prohibit the practice on grounds of health. The educational union last year had to send a special commission to the Central Black-Soil Belt to look into infringements of the educational law, both in regard to buildings and salaries, and secured the dismissal of several officials. The stress of socialist building sometimes leads workers to disregard safety devices, as does the need to make more money by piecework elsewhere. From one of the new giant enterprises under construction come reports of disregard of health and life by both workers and management similar to that which obtained in the American Steel industry before its "safety-first" campaign. Also there may be found occasionally in official quarters an attitude like that of certain staff officers in a great war, which says that in the interest of future generations a certain proportion of this one must be sacrificed. But the attitude which is bound to prevail is that expressed by Stalin's emphasis on improving the living and cultural conditions of the workers.

The slogan under which the unions are now working—"Eyes Toward Production"—is made vital in the constant production conferences which are a regular part of the program of all enterprises. They will be found constantly in theatres and educational institutions as well as in factories and kolhozes. It is in these meetings that the general production consciousness noticed by foreign observers and broadly stimulated by posters and printed matter, films, and radio, is intensified and made concrete. These gatherings are stimulated by the government because, as the economists say—a trifle rhetorically—"the Soviet government is production." From general factory conferences, they have gone down through departments and shops to shifts and brigades. In emergencies especially, such as sowing and harvest season on the farms, they are held daily, taking from twenty to thirty minutes after work. In some places, the chairman of the general-production conference, elected in the works committee meeting, automatically becomes assistant to the director; in other places he is assistant to the manager of the planning and production department, with the special responsibility of seeing that workers' proposals for increasing and improving production are carried out. In some departments in Selmash, one worker in each department, shop, shift, brigade, is elected organiser of production; he gets and gives to his brigade reports on its progress, usually every five days. The brigade must call a production meeting every ten days, the department every thirty days. In other plants less frequent conferences are obligatory. *In them,* wrote the director of an important trust, in response to my question about workers' participation on the business side, *the workers discuss in detail not only the accomplishments of the plan in respect to the output of production and the productivity of labor, but they also discuss the plans of the commercial functions of the enterprise, its financial situation, etc. In this manner they take active part in the financial and commercial life of the given enterprise.* Says a rate-fixer, *A technically correct standard can be worked out only with the aid of the workers, so we explained the whole situation and the reasons for it to department meetings.* He adds that standards were set according to the shock brigaders because they understood that by working correctly they are useful to the state.

The union leaders everywhere say that this growing participation of the workers in all the business of management has not been checked by the recent policy of one-man responsibility. This innovation was necessary to counteract a general Russian tendency toward the evasion of responsibility which had been increased by the suspicions and penalties following upon failure under the Soviet régime, and also to overcome the bad habits and consequences engendered by committee control. Stalin told the managers:

The position at present is, that in the collegiums of a combine there are ten or fifteen men, all writing papers, all carrying on discussions. To continue to manage in this way, comrades, will not do. We must put a stop to paper leadership and adopt genuine, business-like Bolshevik methods of work.

It is further the contention of the union leaders that one-man management enables the workers to locate responsibility and so gives them more power to hold managers and engineers to the execution of their tasks. The workers also say that it cannot result in autocracy because there are so many checks through works committees and production conferences which the executives must attend, also through the union and the Party of which they are members. The director of one trust tells me, *If the workers are not with you, you had better quit. There will come criticism in the wall papers and plant newspapers. Then an article in "Pravda" and out you go.* Another writes, *In other words, while there is personal responsibility of the administrators, the collective thought is not eliminated. On the contrary it helps (through the production conferences) in the administration of the enterprise, both in the various plants and in the enterprise as a whole.*

Several times workers who had been years in the United States commented on the difference this collective responsibility made to them. Said one after his first two days' work: *It is so much more interesting here to have a meeting after work to talk over the results and our conduct. At home we were out of the plant as quick as the whistle blew and did not want to go back. Now I shall like to go back evenings to study. There I had no rights and no responsibility. All I knew was that the plant made twenty-six millions last year out of the workers. We wanted only our wages and they wanted only our work.*

Any one who sits in at production meetings or talks with groups of technical students will be struck by the intense interest of the listeners in everything that is being said. Nowhere have I seen such light in the eyes, such tense lines in the faces, outside of religious revivals or strike meetings.

THE CO-OPERATIVES

Before the Soviet Government came to power there was in Russia an extensive co-operative movement which gave the workers and peasants opportunity to express economic initiative in ways denied them by capitalist organisation. At first the tendency of the Bolsheviks was to view these organisations as mere "collective capitalism" because of their payment of interest to shareholders and similar features. But Lenin soon saw their possibilities and proclaimed them socialist enterprises when "built up on the land and with the means of production belonging to the State, that is, the working class." Particularly for the villages he threw out the slogan, "Through Co-operation to Communism." There followed an attempt to dragoon the whole population into co-operatives, which had to give way to more voluntary methods. In the days of NEP and still more with the coming of the Plan, the co-operative stores became a powerful weapon for the conquest of trade for socialism. By 1930 the co-operatives had 68 per cent of the retail turnover of commodities in the USSR which, joined together with the State trading, put 95 per cent into the socialist sector. So they now constitute the main machinery for the distribution of supplies. By 1931, 63,000,000 people, over 67 per cent of the adult population, were reported to be members of co-operatives. In July of that year the entire adult membership in the towns was claimed for membership. Nearly all factory workers belong to the local co-operative but membership is not obligatory. Most factories have stores where workers can buy without joining but membership permits additional purchases above the quota. As in other lands, the membership fee, which is proportioned to wages, draws interest but instead of being taken out by the members this is devoted to a Cultural Fund—for playgrounds, clubs, schools, etc. If a member leaves he can withdraw it. Profits do not go back to the members; they are divided between the capital fund and the State.

Recently there has been a wide campaign to improve the co-operatives and to draw the whole working population into their administration, particularly for the improvement of food supplies. Before the Sixteenth Party Congress Stalin indicted the co-operatives on several counts. He held the machinery of supply responsible, and the consumers' co-operatives in particular, for the inability to raise real wages higher than the record showed. He charged them with stocking goods—like haberdashery, in preference to the necessities, because they were profitable, with the result that the workers were forced to satisfy about 25 per cent of their need for agricultural products in the private market:

Apart from this, the co-operatives are concerned most of all with their balance sheets as a result of which they are difficult to move in the direction of the reduction of retail prices in spite of categorical instructions of the leading bodies. The result is that the co-operatives act in this case not as a socialist sector—they are infected with a certain Nepman spirit. The question arises who needs this kind of co-operative and what is the value to the workers of its monopoly if it does not carry out the task of seriously improving the workers' real wages.

Since then the growth in the purchasing power of the population—the wage fund for 1930 was 10.5 billion rubles against 3.4 billion for 1929—has outdistanced the growth in turnover of the co-operatives, part of which is due to a deficit of certain agricultural products and an inadequate collection system. In 1931, the co-operatives were again scolded, both by Stalin and the Joint Plenum of the Central Committee; also the Central Control Commission of the Party told them *to act as the socialist sector of trade and not as a commercial contagion.* The latter phrase had reference to the results of an RKI investigation summarised in Molotov's report to the Sixth Congress of Soviets. He spoke of *facts showing an impossible attitude to the consumer, and an utterly unjustifiable surcharge on various commodities. Some stores made a profit of 1000 per cent on confectionery. Others sold sandwiches at 10 kopecks that cost only 2 or 3 to make. . . . Co-operative stores have not yet been put upon the system of cost accounting and this constitutes a tremendous defect which ought to be promptly eliminated.* An economist comments that the *co-operatives may have sought undue profits to cover up individual speculation or mismanagement. They more probably followed the line of least resistance.* As a consequence they were ordered to enliven their turnover, reduce the rationing system to a minimum and create a base for socialised catering. A general exhortation was sounded: *The whole of the working people of our country must assist in the work of the co-operatives. Only through the wide activity of all the working people shall we manage to bring the consumers co-operatives into line with the general tasks of our socialist construction.*

This means an attempt to develop in the field of distribution the same forms of socialist work, the same initiative and enthusiasm, which has been recorded in the field of production. In this way, by making the local groups of workers and peasants responsible as far as possible for the efficiency of the machinery for supplying them with goods, it is hoped again to avoid the bureaucracy of a state system of distribution. If this can be done the co-operatives, like the unions, will enlarge their functions and become another creative expression of the initiative and will of the masses in the building of a socialist society. Already the Moscow Regional Union of Co-operative Societies reports a considerable move in this direction. They claim among their characteristics:

A wide participation of the mass membership in the organs of management and control and a close connection with the labor-union and Party organisations; also active support of other economic organisations included in the economic plan; a turning toward the socialist reconstruction of the material and technical base of the co-operative movement. "We are done with shopkeepers' traditions." (*They report their dairy farms, vegetable gardens, industries, and restaurants.*) *These have a social importance in helping the Moscow region toward a food balance, in accomplishing its socialist transformation from a consuming into a milk and vegetable producing region. Also they stimulate the movement of the peasants toward co-operation and collectivisation by the example of their higher productivity. (They also stress the influence of their communal feeding arrangements in factories, apartment houses, schools and technical institutes in emancipating women from kitchen drudgery and "introducing collective forms into everyday life." They also report devoting profits to children's institutions, maintaining in 1930, 11 creches, 25 kindergartens, 65 playgrounds, 1000 children in summer homes and forest schools, and providing textbooks and breakfasts for the poorer children in the regular schools.)*

THE KOLHOZ

The co-operative movement in the villages is the base from which collectivisation developed. The Soviet economists put it alongside mechanisation as an essential condition of big-scale collective farming. Consequently the Sixteenth Party Congress, in directing the attention of all Party organisations *to the necessity of undertaking widespread preparations for a mass collective farm movement in the Eastern republics and territories of the Union,* listed first in the preparatory work *the development of the co-operative organisation of the poor and middle peasants, beginning with the village co-operatives and special combinations for production and supply.* The kolhoz, or collective farm, is a socialist form of co-operation, and is sometimes called a co-operative farming association or an agricultural artel. It was preceded, not only by the village consumers' co-operatives which gave the peasants training in mutual purchasing, but also by a simpler form of co-operative farming—"The Association for Joint Tillage." In this organisation there was no joint ownership but only joint use of land, horses, and implements during the season of making the crop. In the kolhoz there is joint ownership as well as use of land, horses, and implements, seed supplies, herds of cattle, swine, sheep, and flocks of poultry. Cows, chickens, pigs, and other small stock may be kept also in individual ownership for domestic use, unless the kolhoz pursues dairying, sheep, or poultry raising as its chief end. In socialist language "only the basic means of production are socialised."

In the agricultural commune, which also preceded the kolhoz, there is "complete socialisation of the means of production," nobody has any private property except his personal possessions. Also there is a common dining room, and communal apartment buildings in place of the individual cottages of the kolhoz. The sense of ownership in relation to land and buildings is quite different. Being merged in a common owning group, the communar more easily merges into that universal ownership behind his group, which is now the State but will some day be something different. At first the kolhoz member felt himself the owner of the land which he had temporarily or experimentally pooled, and he was allowed to take it out if he left. But some began to use collective labor for individual enrichment by getting land that had been sown or improved by joint labor. So now a settlement with those leaving takes place only after the harvest and the land is indivisible. The statutes therefore declare, *The combined area of land belonging to the artel must not in any circumstances be reduced. . . . Members leaving the artel can receive land only from the free land reserves in possession of the state.* On this point Yakoklev reports, *I have talked with dozens of collectivised farmers on this question, asking whether this does not contradict the principle of voluntary joining the collective farm. They answered me with one voice: "The other way, you can't build a collective farm; free choice doesn't mean turning the collective farm into a gate of passage." And this we say openly not only to members of the collective, but to individual peasants wishing to enter.*

The kolhoz movement as an expression of peasant initiative has gone through three stages: first, a largely spontaneous growth of widely scattered local organisations; next, in 1929–30, a widespread campaign from the top, using all the arts of salesmanship and in some sections coercion, both economic and physical, which has since been officially disowned; and now, a steady increase based on spontaneity and economic advantages. The slogan is that individual peasants are to be regarded as potential members and are to be helped and educated into joining. The kolhoz is frankly a class organisation and a class weapon. It is designed for the poor and middle peasant, to emancipate both of them from economic bondage to the kulak. When the leaders of the movement are asked whether the country is not a loser from driving out the initiative of the kulak they answer first, that his initiative was too often in the form of land grabbing, exorbitant money lending, high charges for supplies and low wages; next, that the middle peasant lacked sufficient land to develop his abilities, while the poor peasant and hired men were still more repressed. They quote the successes of collective farms whose boards are wholly former poor farmers and hired men. They say that scores of their best organisers were formerly poor peasants. One official spoke of having come from a convention of farm brigadiers who had been transformed from former small farm individualists and said, *Collectivisation, like the revo-*

figuring out the day's work for a brigade, getting up working plans and making them known to the brigade concerned, and how to arrange conferences and questions on grain growing. About forty of our active workers took these courses, and afterwards the various groups let everybody have the benefits of this knowledge.

Thus the kolhoz becomes a training school in labor discipline and in the socialised economic virtues, both kinds of instruction being badly needed by peasants suffering from the heritage of feudal serfdom. As Yakoklev points out:

One must not idealise the members of the artel. An artel member was yesterday a small owner, a propertied man on a small scale. Consider his psychology. It is understandable that at first his design will be to escape from the lacerating labor of the small farm, to get more of the various goods of life, which he did not see on the small farm, but which the artel can give. He will often try to snatch at leisure, to be lazy, to shove work off on others, etc. These phenomena will, doubtless, have a serious character and a wide distribution for a long time. It is understandable that a certain time is needed for this type of collectivised farmer not only to see, but actually to feel, that by grabbing at leisure, by snatching and seizing, things simply cannot be done, that it leads to the ruin of the artel.

This necessary education is furthered by the contract system, through which the government advances credit and other helps to the kolhoz, while the kolhoz contracts to supply the government with a definite part of its crop at a fixed price. Under this general head some of the trusts contract with the collective farms for a supply of raw materials and undertake to pay part in advance—often in the form of selected seeds, fertilisers, or technical aid. Likewise the machine and tractor stations make contracts with the collective farms in their territory for working their fields. The Sixth Congress of Soviets stressed the importance of these contractual agreements as "an indissoluble part of the kolhoz plan of production" and instructed all kolhozniks and kolhozes to see that they "are promptly and conscientiously carried out."

In harmony with the general move for decentralisation the Kolhoz Centre administrators insist that everything is done to encourage local initiative and control. The booklet explaining the principle and rulings regarding distribution of income adds:

The mass meeting of the kolhoz is the real master of its income, and only this meeting can decide how to divide it. . . . The Kolhoz Centre is merely offering the general suggestion that the income be divided in accord with the quality and amount of the work of its members. . . . It is necessary to reach a condition in which every member knows all details about the spending and income of each family and their general financial condition, etc.

There are two local controls over the administrator of a big collective farm. Above is the Township Staff concerned with the total area and its crop; below are the constituent villages, each one of which must approve the plans before they are considered settled. The experts in the central office are continually asking and getting the advice of the peasants. The local organisations have representatives on the price fixing boards and can get prices changed if they are below the cost of production. The grain quota to be delivered by each kolhoz is determined by the district commission, which *mouths and send them up to the Murmansk coast to catch fish with their trousers.*

So the new forms of socialist labor and management become what the Communist writers call "a mass phenomenon." In and through them the masses have new opportunities to express initiative and, as controllers of the machinery and processes by which they live, to become the makers of their destiny.

HOW IT GROWS

This process is manifest in several of the foregoing examples of socialist competition, for instance the rise and spread of hozraschet brigades. It can be seen in any kind of gathering that has to do with some situation in which action is needed. Here and there the natural leaders will express themselves, a little group of the like-minded forms, then the whole company crystallises in sudden decision. This is the usual democratic procedure, but the Soviet system is peculiarly designed to extend its area and increase its effectiveness. It both provides for and encourages the expression of initiative from the masses. When it appears in socially useful form, at once all the powerful educational machinery and pressure of a centralised authority is put behind the natural forces of social imitation, in the endeavor to make it universal. The resultant expansion of the undeveloped fund of human energy is therefore much wider than that which occurred when the appearance of capitalistic industrialism and colonialism together loosed the bands that the mediæval system had put around the people at the bottom. That liberation soon reached its limits in the reappearance in a new form of the inherited class system.

A wider reach for the newer expression of initiative from the bottom of society is guaranteed by the nature of socialist society and the requirements of the machine age. Both of them require the fullest and widest possible co-operation of people who are all as intelligent as it is possible for them to become. Everybody's business must become everybody's, not nobody's—if a socialist society is to be successfully built. And this is exactly what is happening in the Soviet Union. As an American engineer said concerning the forms of activity which the youthful workers invented, when difficulties and delays threatened the construction on time of one of the great new plants, on which other industries depended: "No organiser could possibly have thought of the things they did." In the whole field of social organisation, the old proverb still holds true: "Necessity is the mother of invention."

The necessity that is behind the social inventiveness of present years in the Soviet Union must also be regarded as an expression of a wider compulsion—the need to discover modes of living that will realise the possibilities of the machine and of the whole range of scientific technique. Only a co-operative system of organisation can secure, by its harmonious co-ordination of human activities, the utmost results from the rhythm of the machine. Only a system that constantly evokes the widest expression and secures the fullest use of initiative is able to avoid the standardising effects of the machine and of machine-like human organisation.

An example of the grouping of the various forces that take part in drawing out initiative from the Soviet masses is the collectivisation movement. In the background is the pressure of the new industrial development; tractors are economically unprofitable on small holdings. There was also the need to feed the growing industrial cities, which made vivid in 1928 the urgency of agricultural reconstruction. In 1929 came a mass movement of small farmers in the south toward collectivisation with existing materials. Then came Party and government pressure. Then a reaction to a more spontaneous growth. But before any of these there was the example of the communes, organised in revolutionary days, and of the co-operatives which existed before the revolution.

WILL IT LAST?

The inevitable question concerning the initiative from below with its accompanying enthusiasm is, "Can it continue?" Is it an emotional upheaval following the revolution which, like the great historic religious revivals, will subside and be followed by reaction? Is it like the feverish energy of wartime, too intense to last, an overdraft on human energies and emotions which must entail a time of depletion? When one asks the young people of the Soviet Union whether they do not get tired or bored with the constant campaigns and drives, their first reply is that there is always something new. That seems to be the answer to whether the poster appeal is being overdone. Just as you get used to one series another appears on a new subject, with sufficient vitality of treatment to arrest your attention. It is the same with the plans, local or national. In the Baku oil field, where they fulfilled the Five Year Plan in two and a half years, the next year they went thirty per cent past the mark. The need still called.

The history of the religious communes in various lands is that they failed to hold their youth in later generations because they crystallised their movement into rule and rote and because the set of the world was away from them, its appeal and pressure too strong. The communist movement aims at the continuous expansion of all the possibilities of life; hence new tasks await new generations and offer fresh objectives to the inexhaustible fund of youthful energy. Also they have not withdrawn from a hostile world but more and more are shaping it to their plan, so that the forces of social approval and disapproval, expressed in more normal manner, are taking the place of mobilisation. If one is not to doubt the possibilities of life itself continually to draw out and make room for all the capacities of human beings, the only question is whether the Communists are providing sufficient room for their development.

PART THREE

NEW FORMS OF CONTROL

CHAPTER VII

THE SOCIALIST STATE

The greater part of the machinery of control which directs and limits the initiative of the masses in the Soviet Union is, as elsewhere, the State. But this is the first great socialist power in history and its essential, distinctive characteristic is that it is a proletarian State. It is in fact government of the workers, by the workers, and for the workers.

IS IT REPRESSIVE?

At its beginning this new power was, and now is, boldly proclaimed as the "dictatorship of the proletariat." Lenin declared it to be *in a new sense democratic (for the proletariat and the poor) and in a new sense dictatorial (against the bourgeoisie).* The new members of the Party are instructed that the proletariat *can only conquer capitalism, abolish exploitation, put an end to the division of society into classes and attain socialism, by means of an iron dictatorship.* The state is the instrument of this dictatorship, which is directed against all enemies of the proletariat, within and without. Molotov recently reminded the Seventeenth Party Conference that *the fundamental difference between the proletarian state and the bourgeois state is that the law, under the conditions of the proletarian dictatorship, protects the interests of the toiling majority and tends to suppress the class elements that are hostile to the proletariat.*

In Marxian thinking the state is the instrument for the oppression of one class by another. Lenin's version of Engels—the philosophic collaborator of Marx—says, *Its aim is the creation of order which legalises and perpetuates this oppression by moderating the collisions between the classes.* So the Soviet state is the capitalist state in reverse gear. As the latter uses all the forces of law and order to repress the rebellious workers, so the former uses them to suppress the plotting and revolting bourgeoisie and all their allies, conscious and unconscious. So poor peasants are occasionally prosecuted for being used by the kulak against the government. They are called "pot kulaks"—serving the interests of the richer peasants for the leavings in the pots, just as the "lumpen proletariat" of Marx are an auxiliary force for the capitalists even while they stand in the bread line.

Those in the capitalist world who talk of copying national economic planning from the Soviet example are apt to overlook the essential fact that there all power is given, not to a partially democratised capitalist state run by liberals, not to a socialist government which dare not come to grips with the money power, but to the workers' state, which has dispossessed the landlords and industrialists and is now dispossessing their progenitors—the kulaks and the petty bourgeoisie. Because there is now a great state corporation with which to do profitable business, hoping that it may slip back into capitalist ways, it is so easy to forget that all Soviet socialist construction rests upon the fact of confiscation and continues, by virtue of an iron will, to make that fact irrevocable by relentless suppression of all who seek to change it. This is what makes this socialist state more absolute than its capitalist contemporaries who are limited somewhat by democratic principles and practices. As long as the proletariat can suppress its class enemies it is, as its youth are taught, "Limited by no one and nothing." The only exception is the divisions that may arise in its own ranks.

But the repressive aspect of the dictatorship is only instrumental, its main objective is constructive. As Lenin said, *The purpose of the dictatorship is to establish socialism.* This is an evolutionary process. So Molotov recently defined the proletarian state as *the organisation of the rule of the working class and of the development of proletarian democracy, that is of the ever-growing active participation of the toiling masses of town and village in the whole of socialist construction.* The proletarian power now expresses itself in the economic reorganisation of society and as this purpose comes to dominate its nature inevitably changes. It becomes more concerned with higher productivity of labor than with counter-revolution—though for a while the two get mixed—and learns to use persuasion more than force. In his volume "Leninism," Stalin answers those who claim that the dictatorship of the proletariat is in fact the dictatorship of the Party over the proletariat by saying that the essence of dictatorship is force and for the Party to use force against the proletariat would be both contrary to its principles and impossible; *the workers must be convinced from their own experience that the policies of the Party are right.*

Here he was following Lenin, who said at the Tenth Congress of the Party regarding an error of the Central Committee of the Transport Workers' Union who had contemplated the use of force in an emergency, *We must convince first and keep force in reserve. At any cost we must convince first and not use force until afterwards.* Also regarding the general place of force in the dictatorship Lenin had said:

The dictatorship does not mean force alone, though it is impossible without force. It likewise betokens a higher organisation of labor than has previously existed.

The dictatorship of the proletariat . . . is not merely the exercise of force against the exploiters and does not chiefly consist in the use of force. The economic basis of this revolutionary force, the guarantee of its vitality and success, is that the proletariat represents and realises a type of social organisation of labor higher than that represented and realised by the capitalist system. That is the main point. Herein lies the source of the strength of communism; herein we find assurance of its inevitable victory.

Hence Stalin concludes: *Thus the method of persuasion must be the chief method employed by the Party in its leadership of the class.* Whenever the Party has departed from this principle in attempting to change the masses it has been compelled by the results to return to the method of educational persuasion. That was true in the campaign against alcohol, against religion, and for collectivisation. Now instead of prohibition the government makes vodka hard to get and says to the communist youth organisations, "Stop the demand and we'll close the distilleries." Similarly the Society of the Godless is encouraged to create a local demand for the closing of churches. In the matter of collectivisation, those who tried to force the pace in 1930 are now described as "over-zealous" and their conduct as a "left error."

The Sixteenth Party Congress rebuked the regional and local organisations who had "grossly infringed" the instructions of the Central Committee by attempting to collectivise completely their regions during the spring campaign of 1930, whereas the resolutions of the Committee had spoken of "two or three years or more": *This wrong and harmful attitude was bound inevitably to lead to the result that the Leninist policy toward the middle peasant began to be supplanted by a policy of administrative compulsion, inimical to Leninism through and through.* Yakoklev told the Congress: *We say straight: we are not driving anyone into the artel by force. More than that, persons who attempt to force peasants to enter the artel we regard an enemies of the Party and the Soviet government, as accomplices of the kulak.* To the Sixth Congress of Soviets the following year he said: *I repeat that we are not hurrying anyone into joining the kolhoz. We shall in the future as in the past take the severest measures against all attempts to infringe the freedom of choice as to joining the kolhoz.* He laid down the principle that the speed of entrance of individual households into the kolhozes would depend upon the help given them. So the slogan sent out in the resolutions was, *Do not persecute the individual peasants but offer them every help; in every way induce them to enter the kolhoz.* This was actually carried out. The tractor stations began to plough and harvest for the "individuals" as soon as they had finished for the collectives. A newspaper account from far-off Siberia of the local Party organisation instructing the kolhozes to help individual farmers by cleaning and disinfecting their seed and ploughing for the poor is by no means exceptional.

Molotov repeated this emphasis before the Moscow Soviets in November, 1931: *Dictatorial and compulsory methods in dealing with the working peasants are as intolerable today as in the past.* He argued that they will all come into the kolhozes *only if we patiently persist and patiently explain . . . and especially if we can really prove to them the advantage of collective labor by actually raising the productivity of the collective farmer.* Now all the leaders are basing the success of collectivisation upon the fact that nine million peasant households have become convinced of its advantages in their own experience. Says Yakoklev again:

Communists of course were long aware that large scale farming, socialist farming, was more profitable than the individual farming on a small scale. We could quote literally hundreds of Lenin's statements to that effect. But it was one thing to have a group of communists convinced of this and quite another when the peasants themselves became convinced of it.

Kalinin widens the argument for government by consent by asserting that the Soviet Government is the only government in the world which could carry out such a revolutionary measure as wholesale collectivisation because *It is the only government of workers and peasants, it enjoys the complete confidence of these classes and is based upon them.*

The story of socialist competition in all its forms shows how the force of social pressure is filling a much wider area than is, or possibly could be, occupied by state coercion. It shows also how this pressure is generated and used. Insofar as the Soviet masses are concerned, the dictatorship of the proletariat is the control of the activists over the rest of the population, expressed through the Party and those other organisations which the Party controls. It is true that a minority actually controls, but only by leading where the majority becomes convinced that it wants to go. This is the general nature of social control everywhere. The difference comes in the peculiar constitution and power of the Party and in the fact that class differences being on the way to extinction, the proportion of activists in the population is rapidly increasing, the process being accelerated by the whole system of propagandist education devised by the Party to this end. Meanwhile, as it draws in more of the former intelligentsia and also of the middle peasants, the dictatorship of the proletariat crosses those class lines that still remain in Soviet society as Lenin said it would: *The dictatorship of the proletariat is a peculiar form of class alliance between the proletariat—the vanguard of all those who labor—and the various strata of the non-proletarian laboring masses—the petty bourgeoisie, independent artisans, peasants, members of the intelligentsia and so forth. . . .*

Another characteristic of the proletarian dictatorship, differentiating it from other absolute governments, is that it contemplates, and proposes to assist, its own dissolution. Since it arises out of, and is an expression of, the class struggle, it disappears when the classless society comes in—there is nobody left to dictate to—and that is an immediate objective, well within sight. More than that, the dictatorship is not to give way to another form of state but in Communist theory the state itself is to disappear; it is to "wither away." This theory was enunciated by Engels, whose philosophic contribution to Communism as the fellow worker of Marx is being much more understood and appreciated in recent years:

With the disappearance of classes the State too will inevitably disappear. When organising production anew on the basis of a free and equal association of producers

Society will banish the whole State machine—to the museum of antiquities. . . .

When ultimately the State really becomes the representative of the whole of Society, it will make itself superfluous. From the time when, together with the class domination and the struggle for individual existence resulting from the present anarchy in production, those conflicts and excesses which arise from this struggle will all disappear, from that time there will be nobody oppressed; there will therefore be no need for any special force of oppression, no need for the state. The first act of the state, in which it really acts as a representative of the whole of society, namely the assumption of control over the means of production on behalf of society, is also its last independent act as a state. The interference of the authority of the state with social relations will then become superfluous in one field after another and finally will cease of itself. The authority of the government over persons will be replaced by the administration of things and the direction of the processes of production. The state will not be abolished; it will wither away. It is from this point of view that we must appraise the phrase "a free popular state"—a phrase which for a time had a right to be employed as a purely propaganda slogan, but which in the long run is scientifically untenable. It is also from this point of view that we must appraise the demand of the so-called anarchists that the state "should be abolished overnight."

In his work, "The State and Revolution," Lenin expounds this theory of Engels against the "opportunists" who are willing to wait for the capitalist state to wither away. Lenin quotes Engels further to establish his point that the capitalist state cannot wither away but must be destroyed by the proletariat in the course of their revolution; it is only the socialist state created by the proletarian revolution which can wither away. On the latter point he quotes from a letter which Marx wrote to Bracke, May 15, 1875, concerning the transition from capitalism to Communism:

Only in communist society, when the resistance of the capitalists has finally been broken, when the capitalists have disappeared, when there are no longer any classes (that is, when there is no difference between the members of society in respect of their social means of production), only then "does the State disappear and one can speak of freedom." Only then will be possible and will be realised a really full democracy, a democracy without any exceptions. And only then will democracy itself begin to wither away in virtue of the simple fact that freed from capitalist slavery, from the innumerable horrors, savagery, absurdities and infamies of capitalist exploitation, people will gradually become accustomed to the observation of the elementary rules of social life known for centuries, repeated for thousands of years in all sermons. They will become accustomed to their observance without force, without constraint, without subjection, without the special apparatus for compulsion which is called the state.

Lenin further argues that individual excesses in conduct, which now violate the rules of social life and require the restraint of armed forces, are chiefly caused by "the exploitation of the masses, their want and their poverty." Consequently with the removal of their chief causes, these excesses will disappear and the state will wither away for lack of something to do. But his insistence on the long and difficult process of education that is necessary to train the masses for socialism sharply distinguishes him from the anarchists with their more naïve trust in natural goodness. He himself pointed out two other differences. The anarchists want *the complete destruction of the state within twenty-four hours*. But the Marxist recognises *that this aim is only attainable after the extinction of classes by a socialist revolution and the establishment of socialism, leading to the withering away of the state*. Also the anarchists, he says, have no idea of what to put in place of the state they wish to destroy; *they even deny that the revolutionary proletariat has any necessity to make use of the state and to establish its revolutionary dictatorship*.

Lenin himself is clear that the state, he even says in one place, the capitalist state, will last for some time in the intervening period between capitalism and Communism. The state, it will be remembered, is for Communists essentially the instrument of repression and as such, they say, it will continue even after a classless society has been reached, when all the internal enemies of the proletariat have been either repressed or transformed. The theory is that it will then be needed for a time to enforce that inequality in the distribution of the means of subsistence which results from distributing them according to labor performed. Meantime the Communists propose to use the state to accomplish its own destruction. It is to assist in the withering away, to participate in its transformation into a totally different thing. Lenin argued that the Soviet state is the only one that can do this, in the "Theses and Report" he submitted to the First Congress of the Third International in 1919:

All socialists, among them and at their head Marx, placed before themselves the goal of doing away with government power. Without the realisation of this goal, true democracy, that is, freedom and equality, is unattainable. However in reality, only Soviet power—the proletarian democracy—can lead to this goal since it is now beginning to prepare the complete extinction of all government, attracting the mass organisation of the working people to permanent and unconditional participation in the conduct of the government.

The process of the withering away of the state is the negative aspect of the building of socialism. It is the replacement of both repressive and overhead government by universally shared administration of the activities of daily life and work. This has already begun, as the account of the new forms of socialist competition has shown. There is a constant interpenetration of state, economic, social, and cultural activities, involving wider participation by the masses. Krylenko, the dreaded prosecutor, the incarnation of the repressive state, remarks in his pamphlet on the trial of the Industrial Party, *Our state is already the transitional form from the state to the non-state, to the broadest democratic self-government of the toiling masses.* The present form of government is sometimes called a semi-state, Lenin spoke of it as *the transitional state, no longer a state in the ordinary sense of the term.* This half-and-half situation is reflected in the common language about the government; part of the time it is "we," part of the time "they." Even the leaders with all their insistence upon government belonging to the workers cannot avoid sometimes speaking of it as something over them, as when Stalin in his famous "Six Points" stressed what the workers were doing for the Soviet power and what it must do for them.

At the Seventeenth Conference of the Party, when

Molotov announced the abolition of classes as one of the objectives of the Second Five Year Plan (the first step in the disappearance of the state), he added, *We should under no circumstances raise in this connection the question of either the superfluity or the withering of the state. On the contrary, in the present stage it is a question rather of strengthening the proletarian state and increasing its might.* This necessity he based upon the anticipated resistance of the remaining capitalist elements to their economic extermination and also upon the hostility of the capitalist countries and the forces of imperialism to the country where socialism is being built. Meantime the Communist Party however is constantly teaching all whom it can draw into its circles for political education, to expect and work for the disappearance of the state. By its theory this waits upon the solution of the problem of distribution on some basis which does not permit of inequality, upon the finding of workable, concrete forms for the Communist ideal "to all according to their needs."

It is the definite sense of being in a transition period and of the temporary nature of present forms of organisation that sharply distinguishes life in the Soviet Union. This is different from the realisation of the experimental nature of existing forms of organisation which is characteristic of the beginning of a new era. The social inventiveness, the willingness to scrap methods, corresponds to the early attitude of American industrialists toward machinery. At the Commissariat of Education in Moscow one day I commented on one piece of information: "But another department here told me differently." "When was that?" "Two weeks ago." "Oh we've changed since then." At Odessa, just before sailing, inadvertently we ran into a new form of agricultural organisation, that had grown up in that region alongside the sovhoz and kolhoz in the past year and was already spreading to other parts of the country.

Also the Communist sense of transition is quite different from that general evolutionary viewpoint of intellectual liberalism which dismisses crises with the academic remark that every period is a period of change. The Communists have a definite analysis of the antecedents and consequents of their transition period. They know where they want it to go and are quite sure they know how to get it there. This sense of direction, this will to guide to another form of social organisation, was not present at the beginning of capitalism, which was born blind and inhibited, first by inherited characteristics and then by something that passed for a philosophy, from acquiring social consciousness.

The historic leaders of Communism—Marx, Engels, Lenin—expected the transition from capitalism to Communism to require a somewhat lengthy historical period. They describe the changes in human nature, its appetites, habits, prejudices, and opinions, necessary to realise their social ideal and remark on the time these will take. So today the Soviet leaders speak of the stubborn years required to remake the Russian worker and peasant. Also they have to move those of little faith like one of our interpreters who remarked, "Socialism is national ownership and planning. Communism is equality. Perhaps in a thousand years!"

The milestones that have been passed in the Soviet Union on the way to the Communist goal are all known to the politically intelligent section of the population—a large number, which grows larger every day. There was first the period of Conquest of Power—1917–1918; then the period of War Communism—

1918–1920, the days of civil war and intervention when goods were rationed as to a besieged city; next the period of Restoration when, under the NEP, industry and agriculture were restored to their pre-war basis; then, with the adoption of the Five Year Plan in 1927, the days of Socialist Reconstruction began. In them the whole economic organisation is being reconstructed on a socialist basis. This might more appropriately be called the time of Socialist Construction, especially after 1931, which was the third and decisive year of the first Five Year Plan, in which the majority of peasant households were definitely recorded in collective farms and so the seedbed of capitalism in the villages was broken up. By 1930, the private sector in trade was reduced to a negligible factor, so that Stalin was able to assure the Sixteenth Party Congress that Lenin's question "Who beats whom?" had for industry been definitely answered in favor of socialism. When the dominance of the socialist sector in agriculture came in 1931, it was possible for Molotov to inform the Sixth Congress of Soviets, and for that gathering formally to declare, *In our country there is no longer an issue as to the victory of socialism. The victory of socialism in the USSR is completely assured.*

The view that this development necessarily means the growth of a repressive state fails to distinguish between the attitude of the Soviet power towards its enemies and its relations with its supporting constituents. Also it derives from the historic idea and rôle of the state and does not reckon with the Communist determination to abolish both. If the leaders should be seduced by power and fall away from the true faith, there is still the fact that in this system the interests of the dominant class—the workers—are on the side of abolishing the overhead state. In other lands, ever since class society and the class state appeared, it has been the necessity of the ruling class to perpetuate the power which guarantees and protects their rights and privileges. The Socialist Soviet Republics are the first to organise for the purpose of securing the withering away of the state and to put into the hands of the millions the power to accomplish this. On this point Stalin in his "Leninism" takes up the tale which his master left unfinished:

The Soviet form of State (and no other form of State), admitting the mass organisations of the workers, and the exploited generally, to direct and unconditional participation in the management of public affairs, is able to pave the way for the gradual dying out of the State, which is an essential phase of the progress toward the stateless communist society of the future.

Thus, if present tendencies continue unchecked, the state, despite the carrying over of certain repressive functions, instead of inhibiting the initiative of the masses becomes a means for its expression, as they devise the ways and means for transforming it into another kind of government more suited to their needs and well-being. To thus change it is one aspect of the continuing revolution which Communist theory and practice encourages them to carry on.

THE SERVILE STATE?

There remains the question of whether the new form of control developed in place of the state will be that repressive bureaucracy always associated with the extension of governmental powers over wider areas of life. Does socialist society necessarily involve that abject and helpless submission to office-holders, that pettier and meaner form of absolutism, which Chesterton has wittily pictured as "The Servile State"? Again we have here a projection of the traditional form of the state and its authority before which the average citizen finds himself helpless. The main reliance of the Communist leaders in their unremitting fight against the perennial tendency toward bureaucratism is the change that their system engenders in the nature of government. The essence of the transformation from overhead government to common administration is that power is not concentrated in any controlling class but is diffused throughout the population. A socialist state in which men and women from the factories and farms are constantly inspecting, serving as volunteers in and sending new blood into, the departments of finance, education, and all the rest, is not likely to develop any undue respect for office holders nor to tolerate their growth into a new class.

The theory of democratic centralism on which all Soviet organisation is based requires the widest possible participation of the population in all the business of government, legislative, judicial, executive. Engels described the proletarian form of the state in the withering-away period as *an absolutely complete democracy.* Lenin, who regarded *a democratic republic as the best form of the state for the proletariat under capitalism,* said that *the transition from capitalism to socialism is impossible without returning in a measure to primitive democracy. How can we otherwise pass on to the discharge of all the functions of government by the majority of the population and by every individual of the population?* The concrete steps in this direction are the new forms of socialist management of industry and agriculture and of participation in state administration which have already been described. A wider aspect of it is found in the agreements in which state aid for industry and agriculture is dependent upon results. So the process of government becomes mutual.

The centralism that goes along with this democracy is at the point of executive authority and responsibility. It is democratic in two ways, first in the delegation of local powers and next in its constant subjection to workers' and peasants' inspection and criticism. This means an effective check over technicians and administrators; also of one workers' organisation over another. In both cases it is increased by interlocking membership in Party and Union. This is a different thing from the checks and balances of a rigid constitution designed to protect separate rights; it merges into positive mutual aid. It is upon this process that the Communists rely for final victory over that evil in bureaucracy, more deeply rooted than tyranny and servility, the deadly routine that stamps out all initiative. They hope to keep the people from falling into bondage to the forms they have themselves created by a continual process of infusion of new ideas and new blood and, even more fundamentally, by proclaiming a goal that leads them on continually from change to change.

Here we have to reckon with the nature and power of the Party. The Soviet state is at present a changing combination of forces. In the broad sense it is democratic because of the wide participation of the masses in an interlocking machinery of legislative and executive agencies—Labor Unions, Soviets, Kolhozes, Co-operatives. So far it resembles the group of functions and loyalties described by the Pluralists in their theory of

squad if the case is serious. Also there is nothing like the secrecy with which Tammany shrouds its doings. While Communists, like members of many other organisations, are forbidden to talk to outsiders about what goes on in executive sessions, yet the presence and participation of non-members in discussion of public business is widely sought and secured. Party conferences and congresses are carried on in the presence of the whole nation with their proceedings followed as avidly as baseball games in New York. During the last Party conference it was impossible to get papers three minutes after their arrival at the newsstand in the sanitarium where we happened to be staying. Also in the last analysis Tammany takes orders directly and indirectly from those interests from which it derives its income. Nobody gives orders to the Communist Party unless it be the voice of "the toiling masses."

Moreover the comparison with any other party is fundamentally misleading, not merely because the Communists are the only party in the country but because in its nature and purpose it is different from every other. It is operating in a situation that, mainly because of its own philosophy, methods and force of will, has passed beyond the stage of party politics. As capitalist business men properly contend, it is impossible to carry on business by a crowd of politicians who are constantly changing office. In the socialist society, government becomes the whole people's co-operative corporation and it cannot possibly be administered by a succession of vote-catching parties whose main objective is to hold office as long as possible. Under capitalist democracy the main business of parties is to perpetuate their power and the system, both governmental and financial, which is its source. In the socialist state the business of the

Party is so to guide the transition from capitalism to Communism that the state and then the Party will both become unnecessary.

A comparison which has more reality is that which likens the Communist Party to the Jesuit Order in the days when it was the power behind every throne in Europe. Communist organisation is more like that of a religious order than a political party, also they both seek larger ends than politicians. The Jesuits tortured and burned people for the good of their immortal souls, the Communists ask them to live meagerly and discipline them in "Isolated Communities" for the sake of a nobler society on earth. They both use the state to protect their own organisation as the Communists did when they banished Trotsky. The essential difference is that the Jesuits used the state to protect a religion and enhance the powers of a church while the Communists use it to realise a social ideal. So the masses can check concretely what the Communists are doing for their good on earth while they had to take on trust what the Jesuits were doing for their welfare in the world beyond. As a matter of fact no comparison of the Party with any other organisation is adequate because there is in the Soviet Union a new grouping of social forces which is not yet crystallised.

A FUNCTIONAL RELATION

The essential point is that the relation between the Party and the government is functional. It is not that of an outside or overhead organisation dictating to or controlling another in its own interests or in behalf of a third grouping. Both are seeking the same end and in a producers' society this end is all inclusive. It is then simply a question of co-ordination of functions. Thus the Soviets are described to "Beginners in Bolshevism" as the "main political organs for carrying out the general line of the Party" and they are told "The motive power of the state is the Proletarian Party." But this relationship is not a division of functions between separate organizations whose independence must be preserved, like that provided for in the Constitution of the United States. It must be viewed dynamically not mechanically, as a process of growth not a final adjustment. It is only a temporary partnership in a transition period, in the course of which the nature of both partners is expected to become completely transformed, indeed they are both to lose their identity in a larger union with the masses of the people. Meantime they interpenetrate each other through an interlocking directorate and membership and become fused by common activities. As one agricultural worker who had never heard of Adam Smith said, in describing the activities of the Commune in which he lived and the life of the surrounding villages, "and everywhere is the invisible hand of the Party."

The executives of all departments of the All-Union government are of course Party men, and the administrators of local Soviets are generally but not universally so. In all Soviet gatherings the slate of nominations for executive positions, and for the appointing bodies who fill lesser posts, is prepared by the Party fraction—that is by a meeting of all Party members who are delegates. Once made it must be supported by all of them but changes can be, and are, made by the general assembly. The same procedure is followed in all institutions, governmental, industrial, agricultural, and educational, in which the smallest unit of the Soviets elects delegates to the next larger bodies. There, and to a lesser degree in the municipal and district Soviets, the Party fraction is supposed to nominate non-members whenever they are the most capable. This holds also for the municipal and district Soviets but happens less frequently, because local office holding will have brought the best non-Party men into membership. It will be recalled that Stalin recently rebuked many of his comrades for not following more closely the principle of advancing able non-members and charged them to pay special attention to it. A teacher tells me that in the last election in his institution the first man nominated was a non-Party man, recognised as the ablest man there and so confirmed by the applause of the gathering. The majority of nominees were non-Party. When one name was read, the assembly said, "We don't know enough about him. Put him up so that we can question him."

In any stage of democracy, in any institution, it is inevitable that the most able and energetic should take the initiative and lead the rest. They usually do it by some sort of agreement or understanding in advance. In the wider sphere of Soviet affairs this is done frankly and naturally because the Party attracts that type, and it has no rivals. The Party also provides most of the leadership for the other administrative organs of the socialist state. Directors—that is general managers—of all institutions, economic and cultural, are usually Party men. The exceptions are specialists who approve the Party line and work closely with it. The local Party organisation is the determining influence in the appointment of such administrators. In appointing the director of a factory the trust—industrial corporation—would not think of disregarding either the recommendations or objections of the local Party organisation because an administrator could not possibly succeed with its co-operation. The same is true about removals and even transfers. The initiative might be taken by the higher administrative authorities but not without consultation with the local Party committee. If the initiative for the removal of an inefficient director started locally, it might begin in the Party, the Union or the Soviet, and it might come through either channel to the responsible administrative body, but in the latter two cases it would be the Party influence that would predominate. A young American-trained engineer in a responsible provincial post was wanted for research work in Moscow and desired to go. The local administration wished to hold on to him. He went to the Party Committee. Its word, conveyed to the executive, was that the Moscow job would make him more useful to the country as a whole but that he must stay at his post a year and train a competent successor.

Because its program is the successful organisation of socialist society, as the transition stage to its goal, the Party organisation assumes responsibility for the administration of all institutions. It has special educational machinery for the training of "Red Professors." They get the same three-year technical course as elsewhere but in addition, a thorough training in Communist philosophy and methods. The purpose is to have a dynamic centre in every faculty. There is at Moscow a "Red Teachers' Institute," also there and elsewhere, institutes for training "red" directors, journalists, and for other vocations. For narrower specialties, particularly in engineering, the Party selects the most promising youth, including both Party and non-Party persons, who have proved themselves trustworthy and gives them the best available technical training. The process of selection is severe. The man, or woman, must have had at least three years' experience in factory, mine, or farm, which has usually been acquired in connection with the course of study. To facilitate the choice a work record as well as a study record is kept of every student after the elementary school. There is also kept and counted the record of social—or free—work. The final test is ability on the job. The goal is a year of study abroad and for that the selection is still more strict. In the engineering profession about eighty have come up to Moscow each year to be prepared in the foreign language technicum for engineering school entrance examinations abroad. These are the pick of the land, but at the end of the year about 10 per cent will be sent back on probation to the factory. Last year one was dropped simply because he was a flirt and would give a bad impression abroad of Soviet youth; another because, while he was a brilliant student, his habits were not serious enough. Besides this emphasis upon Party standards of life there has been, all through the technical training, a stiff requirement of courses in political education, all of which are based upon loyalty to the Party and its program. The result of this whole system of preparation is that when administrators and specialists report to Party gatherings they do not come as outsiders, they are not delegates from one organisation to another, they speak as Party men or Party sympathisers, giving account of their stewardship or advice concerning the Party course. It has in the past been the custom to have non-Party administrators or specialists report or make suggestions or requests to Party bureaus or presidiums through some Party member but this is becoming less and less the case. The tendency now is to deal directly with any one who has anything to contribute to the common cause. Non-Party men are frequently invited to report and consult in

Party meetings, including even those of the Polit Bureau, the inner seat of power.

HOW DECISIONS ARE MADE

All serious questions of national policy are decided in Party circles. The final determining groups are the Central Committee, composed of 71 members and 68 candidates, meeting two or three times a year for important decisions, and in between times the Polit Bureau of 10 members, whom it elects. The Central Committee is elected by the Party Congress which meets every two years and is the supreme authority. In alternate years Party Conferences are held for purposes of discussion and clarification of policies. Their resolutions go to the Central Committee for confirmation. The general policy issues from the Central Committee and the Congress in the form of statements which are called "directives." *In the Soviet Union,* says Stalin, *in the land where the dictatorship of the proletariat is in force, no important political or organisational problem is ever decided by our Soviets and other mass organisations without directives from the Party.* In this sense, and in this sense only, does he use and allow the use of the term dictatorship in describing the work of the Party—it is *the force which guides the proletariat. . . . In this sense we may say that the dictatorship is substantially the dictatorship of its vanguard.* The more the Party and the country become engaged in the actual building of socialism, the more its directives become the setting of concrete tasks rather than the laying down of general principles. Thus the Plenary Session of the Central Committee and Control Commission of the Party, in December, 1930, set the task for collectivisation in 1931 at not less than

50 per cent of peasant households in the Union as a whole, and 100 per cent in the North Caucasus, Lower Volga, Middle Volga, and Ukraine—where the lower mark had already been well passed.

These directives are passed on to the administrative organs to be carried out, going by way of the respective People's Commissariats down through the Soviets to the local unit. At the same time they go down the Party line—including its auxiliaries the Komsomol and Pioneers—so there is an interlocking, co-operative, dual pressure toward their realisation. Also there are cross connecting links on the way down. It is thus described by one of the educational staff of the Pioneers:

We educate the children, not upon the servile commandments of subjecting themselves to leaders and parents unconditionally, but upon the concrete participation in construction and the struggle for socialism. In this we see the unity of purpose of all the three generations of the proletariat: the Pioneer, the Komsomol and the Party. In this we see the decisive link of our education when the children appear to be direct participants in the new social order. From here issues a different inter-relation between the children's organisations and the state. We receive the state program from the Commissariat Trusts and Gosplan, we on our part prepare instructions to the Soviets, work over the demands to be directed to the People's Commissariats and Labor Union organisations.

Once made, the directives of the Party cannot be criticised or amended by its members. The essence of Party discipline is that all its decisions must be loyally supported. Says the Handbook:

Members of Party organisations are bound conscientiously to fulfil the decisions and resolutions of the higher Party organs. The strictest Party discipline is the most important duty of the Party member . . . the nucleus must assist the local Party committee in its work, carrying out its directives conscientiously. . . . Before a decision we argue to our heart's content, after a decision we carry it out unanimously. Herein lies the strength of the Party.

The "internal democracy," of which the Party is proud, consists not only in freedom of criticism for all members concerning the way decisions are carried out but also in their freedom to participate, and take the initiative, in making them.

If no Party decision as yet exists with regard to any point, each Party member is entitled to argue on this point and propose his own resolutions on it to the Party. Such was the case when wholesale collectivisation came in, various proposals were made by Party members as to how to deal with the kulak.

The same thing is increasingly true for the non-Party masses. To what degree it is true for the individual depends upon the extent to which he is politically passive or active.

All decisions recorded in the resolutions of the Party, locally and nationally, are preceded by wide discussion in all nuclei and, if they are important enough, in open meetings and the press. Before a Conference or Congress a group of questions is sent to all local Party organisations for discussion. The theses—that is proposals of policy or administrative changes—of all reports are published in the papers and made the subject of discussion in labor unions, schools, and other organisations as well as in the Party gatherings. Frequently criticisms and suggestions are published or communicated to the man who makes the report. The local press and some of the youth magazines give greater attention to personal criticism and suggestion than the large central papers. Thus the range of formative public opinion and of interest in Party decisions widens. Its operation is kept of course, as in all countries, within the framework of the basic principles and methods of the established system.

A policy may start at the top as in the case of an educational program suggested by an expert, or it may start at the bottom as in the case of various forms of socialist competition. An exceptional case of another starting point for change was Gorky's intervention on behalf of the children of former bourgeoisie who were being denied access to higher education. He wrote a letter to "Izvestia" putting the case on the ground of public policy as well as the needs and rights of innocent youth. The editor took the risk of publishing it; the response was clear, and the Party made the change which ripened, with favoring circumstances, into the altered attitude toward adult intelligentsia from the old régime registered in Stalin's speech of July, 1931. It is through his speeches that important changes or developments of policy are made popular. But this is far from being an expression of the personal dictatorship that is imaginatively proclaimed in many capitalist, and in some socialist, journals. An examination of Stalin's report to the Sixteenth Congress will show that he bases all recommendations upon a gradual course of historic development, guided by the Party in a series of decisions in various gatherings, in response to public opinion; all of which he is careful to trace in detail. His conclusion on the educational question is characteristic: *Consequently the time has come for us to set about the organisation of general compulsory education. I think the Congress will act correctly if it takes quite a definite and quite categorical decision on this question.* Thus it is the will of all the activist elements in the population, as well as that of the Party, which is personalised to the remainder of the masses by Stalin's speeches.

Stalin himself is very insistent, in his Leninism, that the Soviet government—the dictatorship of the proletariat—is very much more than the issuing of directives by the Party and the operation of its machinery for getting them carried out. First he quotes Lenin:

We thus have a supple, broadly based, and extremely powerful apparatus. In point of form, considered as a whole, it is not communist; but by means of it the Party is closely linked to the class and to the masses; and thanks to it, under the leadership of the Party, a class dictatorship is realised.

Then he describes the present situation:

The dictatorship of the proletariat is the issuing of directives by the Party, plus the carrying of these directives into effect on the part of the mass organisations of the proletariat, plus their being made actual by the population at large. Obviously we are faced here with a whole series of transitions and graduations which comprise important elements of the dictatorship of the proletariat. Between the directives of the Party and their being made actual, come the will and the activities of those who carry out these directives, the will and the activities of the class, its willingness (or unwillingness) to act in accordance with the directives, its capacity (or incapacity) for acting upon them, its capacity (or incapacity) for realising them as circumstances may demand. It is hardly necessary to prove that the Party, when it has shouldered the burden of leadership, has to take into account the wills, the states of mind, the degrees of class consciousness, of those who are being led

—of the members of the class as a whole. Consequently, anyone who identifies the guiding function of the Party with the dictatorship of the proletariat is substituting the directives of the Party for the will and activities of the class.

HOW DECISIONS ARE CARRIED OUT

The measures for carrying out Party directives are worked through, not only by the responsible administrative organs but by all interested groups, who are co-ordinated for this purpose by the Party organisations and also by the influence of Party members within them. The first responsibility of all Party units in all institutions is to see that its directives are correctly and efficiently worked out. An illustration of how this is done is a meeting of the Leningrad Labor Unions on the question of improving the food supply for the workers. The Party had recently set certain tasks for the organisations concerned, trying "to develop the mass control of proletarian public opinion over all the work of collecting, producing, and distributing food supplies." First the meeting changed the number of nominations for the Presidium—presiding group—from eleven to fourteen for the purpose of adding three more workers because the list contained too many officials. Then they cut the time limit for the official speaker who was to expound the decisions of the Central Committee of the Party from an hour to forty-five minutes. They had already had sufficient discussion of these in the papers and in the unions. What they wanted now was action. It was proposed by their union committee to substitute a food supply trust for the co-operatives and to start a month's socialist competition for better methods of preparing and serving food. The speeches from the floor were concrete. There was complaint of dirty glasses and spoons in the dining rooms. *How can we keep them clean if you don't give us enough,* answered one woman worker. *Put your money into more glasses and spoons instead of into prizes for competition and we will keep them clean. Long live the decisions of the Central Committee!*

Let the delegations help as well as criticise and we'll show them what good soup is, said a cook, and proceeded to expound the relationship of good food to the intensive work demanded for the fulfilling of the Plan. Then came the union leader to sum up before they voted on the resolutions. He told them they must use their brains to make up for the lack of material demanded by heavy industry. *Even if you don't have enough glasses, you don't have to wash them in dirty water,* he said. He told them they must discover methods to make an inadequate supply go around. Every one must be made responsible for some small job. The metal workers must help get utensils. The doctors must show the dining room and kitchen workers how to be sanitary and not simply find fault. The waiters and scrubwomen *must remember that clean rooms help to educate people, making them hesitate to spit on the floor or be untidy.* So by discussion and education they came to their program.

For the execution of many measures, wide popular co-operation is secured, for instance in the liquidation of illiteracy. For others a co-ordination of agencies is effected. In the Fall of 1931, a few homeless boys appeared again upon the streets of Moscow. They followed, for its warmth, the little tank cart in which asphalt for street paving was heated. Within a few days there appeared in the paper a letter from a prominent Party man, inviting all child welfare organisations to send delegates to a conference to consider plans to get such boys all taken care of by the first of the year, and proposing a competition to this end, with prizes in the form of equipment for the winning organisations.

Behind the major measures of Soviet tactics, wide popular support is gathered by educational efforts. During the six months after Stalin's speech, setting forth the Six Points essential to the successful conduct of industry, they were assiduously studied by all kinds of groups all over the Union. Wherever we entered a political education class—in schools, in factories after hours, in an agricultural commune in the night school—the subject of discussion was "Comrade Stalin's Six Points." Everywhere in all buildings and public places they arrested the eye. They were printed in two forms, condensed for the simple and in detail for the better educated. They appeared separately in slogans accompanied by composite photograph posters showing Stalin marching in the front rank of a great host of workers of all trades. The Komsomol and Pioneer agit-brigades that come into the factory dining rooms at the noon hour to give propaganda dramatic sketches were continually emphasizing one or another of these points. Here is the condensed placard form of them:

NEW CONDITIONS AND PROBLEMS

. . . demand that we should work in a new manner. Some leaders do not see and understand etc. that a new day has come.

In this lies the cause of retarding our industry.

What are these new conditions and where do they come from?

These new conditions require at least six new demands.

1. . . . recruit labor force in an organised manner by means of contracts with collective farms, and mechanise labor.

2. . . . abolish the turnover of labor force, abolish equalisation, organise wages correctly, improve social conditions of the workers.

3. . . . liquidate depersonalisation, improve organisation of labor, place forces correctly in the enterprises.

4. . . . By all means see to it that the working class of the USSR has its own producing and technical intellectuals.

5. . . . change our relation to the engineering technical forces of the old school—show a little more care and attention to them—do not be afraid to invite them to work.

6. . . . introduce and strengthen business principles; increase socialist accumulation within the industry.

This process of educating and organising the active elements in the population for mass participation in a program is referred to as "Soviet Society forming and expressing itself." It is different from the formation of public opinion elsewhere because it involves the active participation of the masses in public business, not merely voting upon it and delegating its execution to others. The process is of course directed by the Party, including its auxiliary organisations the Komsomol and the Pioneers. The latter group energises and leads the rest of the children in the elementary schools, the former does the same thing for youth in higher education institutions, in the factories, farms, and other economic and administrative organs. At Selmash, where the Komsomol played an important part in overcoming the break in production, the secretary described it as the "belt of the machine to put through the Six Points." They had made one of them—the conservation of resources—their special objective and on free days had gathered one and one-half million poods of odd bits of metal to be remelted. They had collected eight tons in the forge shop in a period when some machines were not running because the supply was short. When housing accommodations were short they decided to erect a temporary wooden dormitory out of materials they found unused and which the Party organisation, after approving the plans, got the administration to supply.

The Party itself maintains a propaganda department for the express purpose of educating the masses concerning its directives and the measures necessary to carry them out. To the same end each local organisation in any institution that is large enough has its Agit Mass sector, while the Cultural Propaganda sector also co-operates at certain points. The general propaganda department, with its provincial and regional subdivisions, is responsible for the preparation of the slogans and posters which everywhere impress the visitor, and of the materials for exhibits which the Soviet masses, with their liking for pictorial and dramatic presentation, consume more eagerly and thoroughly than most other peoples. From the decisions of the Central Committee and the Planning bodies, the cabinet heads of this Propaganda department select the essential ideas and submit them to artists and chart makers who have been trained in special institutes for this work. They claim not to have made any special study of advertising methods or psychology but they find out by conference with their departmental representatives in local Party organisations, and by general discussion there, what the masses need to know and what they do not understand. Also they have local critical discussions of their plans and review the effectiveness of their work by a rough report of popular reactions to posters and a rough check of readers of charts at exhibits. The educational authorities train special interpreters of exhibits for children. Local participation and initiative in propaganda methods are growing fast. Their appeal is kept fresh and vital by instant use of current events. Immediately after the Japanese forces entered Manchuria in 1931, the Soviet workers and peasants everywhere were being told by dramatic posters and slogans how the Japanese imperialists were trying to find a way out of the economic crisis.

The same general procedure, intensified and made concrete in the meetings in which the workers in agriculture and industry work out their socialist competition agreements, their hozraschet and their strechny plans, makes the active elements in the masses intelligent supporters of administrative and technical procedure. As the government is transformed into the organisation of socialist construction, its business, and therefore that of the Party, becomes increasingly administrative. The local unit is informed that one of its most important tasks is the struggle for the complete fulfilment of the industrial-financial plan, with specifications of the activities involved. The General Secretary of the Komsomol says, *There was a time when we made cultural activities the corner stone of our work, interpenetrating it with politics, but now our chief task is economic, to which we give our central attention.*

As national planning proceeds, the Party becomes

occupied with measures as well as policies. Stalin told the Sixteenth Congress that *the Party should not confine itself to working out a general line of policy but should direct its application in practice from day to day —it must check the extent to which it is being applied, improve and perfect plans for economic construction, correct and anticipate mistakes.* An example of this development is found in Yakoklev's report to the same Congress, together with a warning that it must not be allowed to hamper local initiative:

The basic directions for the distribution of harvest were given by the Central Committee of the Party in the form of decisions, published in the name of the Commissariat of Agriculture and the Centre of Collective Farms . . . sell to the government in an average harvest one third to one fourth of the crop (in good harvest more.) Preserve the private ownership of winter grain sown by individuals before joining the collective farms; after subtraction of necessary minimum contributions to the common fund, distribute all the rest among the collectivised farmers, in accordance with the amount and quantity of labor done by them and their families (except for five per cent of the gross crop, which is divided among the members in accordance with the property they have contributed to the collective farm).

. . . in future instead of new instructions we must see to it that the distribution of the harvest is settled not behind the back of the collectivised farmers in some office or other, but on the basis of the direction of the Central Committee of the Party, by the collectivised farmers themselves, in their general meetings, or by the approval of the general meeting.

By 1932, this inevitable concern of the Party with measures as well as policies reached the stage recorded in a decision of the joint Plenum of the Central Committee and the Control Commission regarding the further development of municipal economy in Leningrad —housing, transport, water supply, paving, bridges, parks and playgrounds—which was expressed in a decree, jointly signed by Stalin and Molotov and addressed to all Party, Labor Union, and other organisations in that city.

On the surface, especially to those who, living in the environment of democratic capitalism, must still think of parties and government in traditional terms, this concern of the Communist Party with administrative matters looks like more concentration of power in its hands. It must be remembered however that in these matters too the Party limits itself to issuing general directives which now become concrete tasks or objectives. To fill these in and carry them out requires more and still more people as the Plan grows, and increased activity by all other organisations. Therefore this process, together with the constant drawing in of non-Party people into Party discussions, means that power becomes diffused over a wider area, both within the Party and throughout the population. It is an incitement rather than a check to the initiative of the masses. Striking exceptions can be found—cases of local Party tyranny and repression—in areas where there is no strong revolutionary spirit and tradition. The Party however deals with them rigorously when they are discovered and gradually the tendency toward distribution of power and of opportunity for initiative becomes dominant. In the Soviet Union not to be politically active is to be "backward" —a term of reproach. And there the big "political" issues are the rate of industrialisation and collectivisation.

In local institutions the process of making and carrying out decisions works according to the general pattern. Because the Party is the agency upon which the success of the Plan primarily depends, it has the final approval of all local plans. In case of disagreement between local and general planning bodies, the Central Committee of the Party speaks the last word. There are two conditions of successful administration in all local institutions —all policies must have the approval of the Party and they must be supported by the knowledge and consent of the workers. No significant technical change is made without taking pains to meet these conditions in advance. Non-Party technicians know that the way to get the workers behind their proposed improvements is through the Party machinery. This brings them into its councils and tends to establish a relation of mutual confidence.

The Party organisation approves only the general lines of administrative policy. It is done with trying to manage economic undertakings by committees, it is through with setting a Party director over a technical director. In earlier days, with the shortage of loyal technicians, it had no alternative. Today the director is either a Party man or one whose loyalty is unquestioned. So the Party demands personal executive authority and responsibility. It seeks to aid the director rather than to direct him. If he fails it will promptly remove him. The test is concrete—the fulfilling of the Plan, upon which everything depends and for which the Party takes final responsibility. At the last Party Congress Stalin was very emphatic about the necessity of one-man management:

. . . *We cannot any longer put up with our factories*

being transformed from productive organisations into parliaments. Our Party and Labor Union organisations must at length understand that without ensuring one management and strict responsibility for work done we cannot solve the problems of reconstructing industry.

For the benefit of the Communists in other lands, Molotov repeated this emphasis in his report to the Enlarged Presidium of the Executive Committee of the Comintern in February, 1930. True to the Communist philosophy that seeks to adjust the relation between opposites, he adds a word about the effect of executive authority upon workers' initiative. . . . *the Party requires the resolute application of the principle of one-man management, beginning with the workshop and ending with the highest economic authority. . . . Without it we cannot insure a rapid rationalisation of production nor consequently the lowering of the cost of production, while improving its quality. The introduction of one-man management in our factories must be reinforced by the active support of the workers organisations and must create still more favorable conditions for an increasing participation of the workers in the management of the industry. . . .*

The Party organisation in a factory may be taken as typical for all institutions. The unit is always the nucleus or circle of members who work at the same place. Therefore, in a large factory, one is organised in every brigade with a volunteer secretary to direct its activities. If the next division of the plant, the shift, is large enough the nuclei from the brigades will unite in an assembly, which will elect a bureau or cabinet to direct the work of the different sectors—Organisation, Agit Mass, Cultural Propaganda, etc. In the shop, of which the shift is a part, there will certainly be a general assembly with its bureau. The shop organisations unite in a delegated conference of the department of which they are a part, which again will have a bureau and a general committee. These again unite in a delegated regional conference with its bureau and committee and a general secretary. To the shop and department organisations, administrative and technical affairs are brought by Party members on these respective staffs. This may be done as individuals or as a "fraction," that is a group meeting, acting together but not organised into a nucleus. In like manner suggestions go back the other way.

A similar connection exists between the Party and labor unions. Thus lines run each way to and from the workers and the administration through the connecting links of both Party and Union, and the initiative may start at either end. When any change is in prospect, if the administration and the Party bureau concerned agree, it will go, according to its importance, either to the proper administrative executive organs for execution, or to a general Party, shop, department or factory meeting for discussion, consent or amendment. If there is disagreement that cannot be adjusted, it is referred to the higher Party organs for decision. In an emergency the director may, and should, act on his own responsibility. He may, but rarely does, go contrary to the decision of the local Party organisation. The test by which judgment is then rendered from higher up is whether by so doing he better fulfils the Promfinplan, that is the Industrial-Financial plan for that plant.

In one large factory the main objectives of the Party organisation were described by its executives as being the fulfilment of the Promfinplan, the development of Technical Education, the organisation of hozraschet brigades and "fighting chain brigades," improving the food supply and getting new workers for socialist construction—"Socialist workers who will work honestly." They counted 10,000 udarniks out of 17,000 workers engaged on production and 4,000 Party members. They were seeking to draw the best udarniks into Party membership. The test for admission was, *Is he meeting his quota in the Plan in both quality and quantity, attending political meetings, bringing in rationalisation suggestions, fighting bureaucracy and red tape?* The work of the Cultural sector was political education only—the union and the Komsomol attended to other aspects of culture—but in practice this turned out to be mainly instruction in improving productivity and lowering costs. The Agit Mass sector had set itself to leading the workers to fight against their faults, to analyse and locate defects in materials or management and to take measures to remove their causes. The control of the rank and file over the Party officials was emphasised. *If things go wrong we take off the leaders and elect others. If the leaders show opportunist leanings we call a general meeting of both Party and non-Party members and let the mass decide.*

All over the Union it is recognised now, as one professor put it, that the first job of the Party is to mobilise and educate the masses for the realisation of the Plan. When the administration fails, the Party—with its auxiliary, the Komsomol—steps into the breach. Down in the Baku oil fields a Party executive gives some examples:

When a new pipe line was being built the supply of pipe stopped and Azneft—the oil trust—could not get any. The workers found an old pipe line and suggested digging it up. Azneft did not take the suggestion but the Party did and pushed it through. When the same trust ran out of sulphuric acid the local Party organisation wrote to the Party organisation in Donbas where it was made, sent a chain brigade to the factory and got it. Last September the Bukta field fell down to 55 per cent production. The director said he could not get tools or transport. The Party and Union secretaries failed to mobilise the masses for action. Also the Party Committee of Bailovsky Rayon where Bukta is situated, did not fight. We changed the leadership of Bukta district, also the director, also the secretary of the Party Nucleus and of the labor union at Bukta. Now there is 89.9 per cent production there. It is due to (1) mobilisation of all the Bukta masses. (2) The help of all Baku. Each plant sent the best workers, pumps, machinery and methods of organisation. The Party committee sent two or three members to help. But one man is responsible, the new director of Bukta.

By now it is clear that the Party is not the government. Like the vital organs in the body, it is both less and more; less in extent, more in function. In one of the powerful new plays, whose theme is the war in the villages between the Party and the kulaks, the young wife of the regional Party secretary is lonely because of his absorption in the campaign. She finds relief in the company of one of his former comrades, just back from study abroad and assigned to help him. But soon this man is ordered out to the villages. "What is this Party," she asks him, "that does this to our lives?" "It is a band of steel," he answers, "that binds us all together." It is even more than that, more too than a guiding, controlling hand. It is the heart of the growing socialist society in the Soviet Union, from which vitality flows through every artery and vein to invigorate every organ of the body politic and to which it returns for new power. It is also the mind and will of the new order, interpenetrating all other organisations with its farseeing vision, its inflexible purpose.

It was only after several months of observation had led to this judgment concerning the nature of the Party's relation to the Government of the Soviet Union that I found in Stalin's "Leninism" these words of Lenin:

The Party is the directly managing vanguard of the proletariat; it is the leader. This is the sense in which the Party wields power, in which the Party governs the country. But that does not mean that the Party realises the dictatorship of the proletariat outside the limits of the state authority; that the Party governs the country independently of the Soviets, for it governs through the Soviets. But this, again, does not mean that the Party can be identified with the Soviets, or that it can be identified with the State authority. The Party is the substantial wielder of authority but it cannot be identified with the State authority.

Since Lenin wrote there has come the Plan, gathering all government within its scope, dominating and shaping all things to its ends, even the Party which brought it into being. This it does, not as an overhead scheme but as something vital, drawing all the forces and forms of life into an organic growth. The Party now must meet the same tests by which it judges the directors of all institutions and all public officials. It must demonstrate to the masses that it is the most effective instrument for securing the success of the Plan. It must show them that it can lose itself in the larger life of the new social order which the Plan seeks and is gradually bringing into being.

CHAPTER IX

THE PARTY AND THE MASSES

The official statement of the relationship between the Party and the masses appears in its shortest form in a phrase that is frequently used by its speakers when they refer to the successes realised under the Five Year Plan. They always ascribe them to the *creative initiative, the revolutionary enthusiasm of the toiling masses and* (*or under*) *the leadership of the Leninist Party.* It is drilled into the membership that the Party is not a supreme ruler but the *vanguard of the proletariat.* The initiates are taught: *So long, however, as the majority of the proletariat does not follow the Communists they cannot gain the victory.*

One distinction of the Party, when it is compared with other socialist organisations, is that it has always "based itself" directly upon the working masses—first the industrial proletariat and now, with them, the poor and middle peasants. In the days of the revolution the Bolsheviks stood for direct government by the proletariat against the Mensheviks, who wanted the workers to cooperate with the bourgeoisie in a representative form of state. Another point on which they split was Lenin's idea of keeping the Party a select activist group. Undoubtedly its strength and tenacity have come from these two points, its absolute class nature and its rigid selectivity. The tests cover personal habits as well as beliefs and social action. It is the only Party that is difficult to get into and easy to be thrown out of. It is so class conscious that when its members use the term "the class" they mean only the workers. Also the terms the workers and the masses are sometimes used synonymously. The consequence is a very different leadership for the millions than that offered by those intellectual liberals and socialists who stand always above the masses. As a striking example, at the end of 1928 the Party proposed to increase the yield of agriculture 30–35 per cent by the end of the Five Year Plan. The old agricultural experts thought this fantastic, and said it would take years. When the issue was brought down to the workers and peasants in the collectivisation program they did much more than that in less time.

The Party claims to have put power into the hands of the workers, to be the agency through which the needs and will of the masses express themselves in the person of their most vocal and active individuals. *The fundamental difference*, says Molotov, *between conditions of labor in the USSR and in capitalist countries is that in our country the power is in the hands of the workers, whereas in the capitalist countries the power is in the hands of the exploiting class.* During the revolution the Party provided the revolting proletariat with leadership, plan, organisation, and so the intelligence and will to seize the decisive moment. In this time of socialist construction it claims to be "vanguard," "teacher," "leader" of the masses. It never talks about any other kind of control, except at the point of executive authority, when the masses have made up their mind what to do. That authority is subject to mass criticism.

KEEPING CLOSE TO THE MASSES

The sense in which the Communist Party is the agent of the Soviet masses is different from that of parties in other lands, where the principle of democratic representation obtains, because of its class nature. In order that this may not be changed, whenever any addition to its limited membership is authorised the proportion of workers and peasants is specified. At present sixty per cent of the total membership must be industrial workers. This class nature of the Party gives the same cast to the government. Its cabinet—Council of Commissars—is unique in that so many of them have been industrial workers. Kalinin, the chairman, was a metal worker, so was Voroshilov, Commissar of the Red Army and Navy. A number of other trades are represented. Radzutak, Commissar of RKI, was a farm laborer. In recent months, because of the large influx into the Party of workers and peasants, there has been recruiting among the intellectuals who have proved their worth, preferably those who have come from the ranks of the proletarians. The natural way into the Party is by graduation from its auxiliary agencies among the children and youth—the Pioneers and Komsomol. Recently, according to instructions from headquarters and also as a spontaneous outcome of socialist competition, most of the new industrial members have come from the shock brigades. The practice of group applications from whole brigades has developed and is being encouraged for its effect on morale and Party prestige. The brigade that wins the banner is usually invited in without probation.

This means that replacing the revolutionary struggle by the building of socialism brings another type of membership into the Party and reinforces that element already within its ranks. The activists among the masses whom the Party seeks for its ranks are now not the mere agitators but the actual builders, the most efficient in constructive tasks. The doer is now more needed than the talker. The need for action is even moderating the Russian's notorious passion for talk. In a provincial city one afternoon we listened wearily to the report of a Party secretary to a factory meeting which was so long that the chairman tried in vain to keep many of the workers from leaving the room. We mentioned the matter that night to a group of Komsomols. They laughed. "That's old stuff," they said. "We'll get after the Party about it." In the larger centres in such meetings the union leaders are emphasising "less talk, more action" and the rank and file is beginning to turn this demand upon speakers from headquarters. In general the building of socialism is bringing to the front the socially constructive type, just as capitalistic industrialism put to the top the adventurous money-making type and his political colleague, the demagogue.

One of the basic laws of Party behavior and procedure is to "keep close to the masses." This is one purpose of its "internal democracy." Today in the factory orders are orders and, as a worker, one Party member must obey the other who is the industrial executive. But tomorrow in the Party meeting he can fearlessly criticise the policy of that executive as drastically as he wants to. For a Party leader to be "torn away from the masses" in habits, and particularly in attitudes and policies, is a major sin and an occasion for severe discipline, which members insist would reach Stalin himself if it were necessary. On this account Lunacharsky lost his place as Commissar of Education. *The Party cleaning of 1929*, Molotov told the Comintern leaders, *showed that the Party is irreconcilably against all elements which are alien to the proletariat—bureaucratic and corrupt.* About 10 per cent were expelled but of the workers only 8 per cent.

To prevent its officials from being torn away from the

masses the Party practises rotation of office, particularly in the lower posts, within the limits of efficiency. It keeps its policies close to the needs of the people and the practical possibilities of the situation by the contacts of its nuclei in all institutions. Through them the Party has several million eyes and ears constantly on the alert. Its receptivity is increased by non-Party participation in meetings where policies are discussed, in cleanings and in the examination of candidates for membership, where non-members are always invited to give testimony. These contacts are multiplied by the use of all the activities in the population in carrying out the program. Here again constant opportunities for critical discussion occur. In his "Six Points" speech Stalin urged the heads of the industrial corporations to seek them:

It is further necessary that chairmen and deputies pay more frequent visits to factories, stay and work there for longer periods, acquaint themselves more closely with the workers in the factories, and not only teach but learn from the men on the spot. To think that you can now manage by sitting in an office far from the factories is a grievous mistake. . . .

The Party also strengthens its contacts with the masses by the rapidity with which it seizes and multiplies any helpful initiative which appears among them. This it did notably in the case of socialist competition in all its forms and is doing again in its use of the *rabkors.* These are an army of worker and peasant correspondents to the Press which has sprung up as one of the expressions of revolutionary energy. Now they are being guided and trained to promote socialist construction, taught how to criticise defects intelligently and pass on examples of effective work and discipline. There is thus a process of interpenetration both ways between the

Party and the masses and this is increased by the part that the Pioneers and the Komsomols play in the schools and universities. The lines for suggestion and action run up as well as down and apparently in about the same proportion. The expert and the mass meet and fuse. The Commissar of Education makes a speech in April, 1931, before the Plenum of the Pedagogical Section of the State Scientific Council "About Certain Problems of the Polytechnical Reconstruction of the School"; in September the Central Committee of the Party issues a decree "Concerning Primary and Secondary Schools" embodying his suggestions and by December the Party and labor union organisations all over the Union are engaged in helping the teachers to work out polytechnical education.

A still more striking example of this process of interaction appears in an open letter to Stalin from the workers of Stalingrad Tractor works, translated in "Moscow News" for January 22, 1932:

Comrade Stalin: Here's what they wrote of us in the bourgeois press one and a half years ago. "In view of the breakdown of the Stalingrad Tractor Works, the Soviet Union must again buy tractors abroad and perhaps can't get them and thus the Five Year Plan will crash." Even friendly foreign specialists said "You have built an immense plant but you can't run it yourselves." The workers accepted the challenge. . . . Already Stalingrad tractor works has made over 20,000 tractors. We have freed the works from dependence on imports . . . three-fourths of the complex imported tools we have learned to make. Our neighbors, the workers of "Red October Steel Works" have learned to make high quality steel. The Stalingrad Tractor is now entirely made of Soviet materials. . . . How did we do all this? It was your speech to the First All-Union Con-

gress of Industrialists where you said "the Bolsheviks must conquer technique. They must themselves become specialists. Technical skill is all-decisive in this reconstruction period." And then in the Six Points of efficiency you showed us the way.

(*Then in detail under each of the Points they recount how they overcame their defects and won through to producing in December 1931, 2725 tractors.*)

Before the Party, and before the country, we take our pledge for the future—to reach by May 1 an output of 144 tractors daily, to make in 1932 a total of 40,000 tractors. This year must see the model tractor of quality. We pledge to build in 1932 a second factory trade school, model houses for all our workers, a House of Technique, and to make our community a model one in every respect.

(*As an honor the letter is signed by several score workers who made a special record.*)

By this interpenetrating process the mass need furnishes a constant stimulus to the Party and the Party in return awakens the inert mass. The correctness of the Party line is definitely tested by the increase of activity among the masses in carrying out Party directives, that is in realising the Plan for a new society. The underlying dynamic is the subconscious desires or the awakening elements in the mass which are seeking the light. These potential forces the Party seizes and directs. It both brings the social embryo to birth and conditions its growth, as for example in arousing the peasants to want more productivity and culture, and then creating big-scale agriculture by combining the tractor with national ownership and planning.

The mass reacts by throwing up leaders for the Party; *it promotes from its ranks more and more active and conscious builders of socialism* as Molotov told the last Party conference. Stalin reports to the Party that, *Collective farming has already produced thousands of organisers and tens of thousands of agitators for the cause from amongst the peasants themselves. We no longer use trained Bolsheviks alone. They find arguments comprehensible to the peasants which we trained Bolsheviks cannot even dream of.* Thus the system started by the Party tends to reduce that inert lump of social and political neutrals who everywhere and always hold back the wheels of progress more than the active reactionaries. Also Party discipline, and still more the ideas embodied in and behind the Plan, are proving themselves a fusing force for diverse races and nationalities more powerful than the melting pot of a common language, vote, and chance to make money.

As elsewhere the Party plants suggestions and watches their effect, sends up trial balloons in the press and if they get a bad reaction puts in the necessary counter articles. The Communist fraction in all opinion-forming organisations, particularly educational institutions, receives orders to raise questions for discussion in their preliminary stage. "Sometimes in the union," a factory foreman who had worked in the States told me, "we let them do things we know are wrong, so they will learn from experience." A camouflaged campaign may be started at the bottom when it is in reality whipped up from the top—a familiar device of politicians. It is hardly likely that the union which issued the open letter requesting the quota and card system in food supplies thought of that by itself. But to succeed, such an effort must be an honest attempt to meet a mass need or a situation that has become impossible.

Because the whole Party philosophy and ethic is based

upon the needs of the masses, it is in its practice the servant of the masses in a more real sense than are demagogues in a multiple party system which claims to be more democratic. The Party by no means follows the masses blindly. It does not worship Demos. Stalin replies to those Communists who think that the masses can spontaneously move in the right direction, that this would do away with all leadership. The Party interprets, and plans to meet, the needs of the masses by dialectical analysis based upon a definite choice of values and ends. It wants a certain kind of society, which it thinks is proved by history to be the kind needed by the masses and best adapted to give enduring satisfactions to all mankind. Toward this goal it moves inflexibly but only as the experience of the masses proves it to be right. Beginners are taught that one of the main sources of the strength of the Party is the fact *that it sees clearly the ultimate interests of its class and knows how to place them above the interests of the moment.* So the member must *work with the masses, but in advance of them, carrying the masses after him or her.* Concerning the natural action of many kolhozes in forbidding re-entrance to those peasants who had deserted, Yakoklev told the Party Congress that it might be advisable to shut the doors a few months before sowing so as not to break up the fields again; that was a question to be settled locally in accordance with conditions; but, *We must not surrender to the feelings of the collectivised farmers on this question. We must fight the tendency to close the doors of the collective farms.*

At times a temporary need may conflict with the Party's longer view of what the masses should have, endanger its leadership and cause a digression. This was the case with the NEP which Lenin called taking

"One step backward to take two forward later." Or mass initiative may crowd the pace to the point of danger as did the wholesale movement into collective farms in 1929, which led the zealots into a policy of coercion. But on the whole the Party continues in power as the leader of the masses—not in office as their representative—to the degree that it correctly interprets their enduring needs and gives adequate expression to the capacities of the masses for meeting them. Its leadership of the people corresponds quite closely to Lenin's leadership of the Party. If it is truly carried out, according to its own philosophy, it will ultimately make itself unnecessary.

It is a commonplace of history that political movements and religions are led away from their original beliefs and ideals and in the course of time change their nature completely. Against this falling away the Communist system has a measure of self-protection in the nature of its ends and methods. Its power so highly centralised on one side of it is also widely diffused at another. It can be, was meant to be, and is, used ruthlessly to disarm, and destroy if necessary, all its opponents within and without. But it cannot be so used upon the mass of the workers and peasants without destroying itself, for without them it cannot reach its goal nor indeed continue to operate. With all its enemies, it would long since have been extinguished if the vital section of the masses had not been in it.

To interpret the Soviet government as the concentration of power by a skilful and conscienceless political clique for its own advantage is to forget that while it might be so used it could not long continue to be, because of the standards of judgment and the means of making them effective which the system has put in the hands of the people. Those who see nothing but centralised control in the Soviet system are thinking only in terms of that overhead authority which has been operative ever since the days of the patriarchal family. But mixed with that, and struggling against it, is the forming social control which the evolution of democracy brings in. As this gains vitality and power, the conscious self-guidance of the masses will be substituted for that invisible hand of Providence which the early capitalists trusted to shape the social ends they were blindly rough hewing and sometimes mutilating past redemption, and also for that invisible hand of the Party which is now guiding the building of socialism.

CONNECTING ORGANISATIONS

Between the Party and the masses there is a network of connecting organisations. Stalin says that the *mechanism of the dictatorship of the proletariat* consists of *belts, levers, guiding force.* The latter is *the advanced section of the proletariat, the workers' vanguard which constitutes the veritable leader of the dictatorship. . . .* That is of course embodied in the Party. The levers and belts are *the mass organisations of the proletariat without whose aid the dictatorship cannot be realised in practice.* These are sometimes called "conveyors" between the Party and the masses but the more frequent term is "belt drive." This is more dynamic, it signifies a connection for the transmission of power. Neither of these terms however recognizes the fact that initiative and ideas are transmitted both ways.

The customary listing of these connecting organisations is Labor Unions, Soviets, Co-operatives. The Komsomol and Pioneers are considered as organic auxiliaries of the Party and it is highly significant that the membership of the latter has now been widened to include if possible all the children in the schools, a distinct modification of the class feature. To the above list there must now be added the Shock Brigades, the Kolhozes, and the Voluntary Societies, such as the *Red Cross and Crescent*—affiliating the Mahomedans; *Osoviakim*—Air and Gas Defense; *Mopra*—International Red Aid for Political Prisoners; *ODN*—Down with Illiteracy; *Drugdety*—Friends of Children; *Ozet*—Jewish Colonisation Society, to which many non-Jews belong; *Avtodor*—For Auto Roads. These, including the Anti-Religion and Anti-Alcohol societies, furnish the Party with the channels for developing its social program. Also they express and stimulate initiative among the masses by putting large numbers of people into social work. So the Party and the Labor Unions put them on their calendar of activities. For them and still more for Unions, Kolhozes, and Co-operatives, the Party takes responsibility in the manner already described for industrial plants and Soviets. It governs the country through them, not through a great overhead state machine. It directs the leadership of these organisations through interlocking membership. It refers to them matters for discussion and execution and receives suggestions and requests from them. It is a partnership relation in seeking common objectives; the Party uses them and they use the Party. So the Seventeenth Party Conference before adjournment adopted this amendment (No. 6) to the resolutions:

The conference deems it necessary to develop forthwith the activity of the Party, Soviet, Economic, Co-operative, Labor Union, and Komsomol organisations for the quickest working out of the Second Five Year

static, to see that they adapt themselves to the new tasks demanded by the successive stages in the building of socialism, to guide them in changing their form as socialism develops into the Communist society. In the case of the shock brigades, the impetus so far has been mainly from them to the Party, though it must be remembered that they have been largely inspired by the Komsomol which in turn derives its initial impulse from the Party. In 1930 Molotov told the executives of the Comintern that the Central Committee recorded a very small proportion of Communists and Komsomols in the shock brigades. He pointed to this as an "indication of how even the Party organisations lag behind the growing activity of the mass of the workers." Today the leadership for Soviets, Unions, and Party is being largely drawn from the ranks of the brigaders. Frequently these groups act as a spur to the local Party, Union, and administration. They form one of the Party's most effective weapons against bureaucracy. By a more natural process than that of the Party, they select and train for the fight for socialist construction the activist elements in the population. Often non-Party brigades will challenge Party brigades and organisations. There have been cases where the shock brigades have become independent of, and even outdistanced in efficiency in fulfilling the Plan, the local Party organisations. When this happens the local Party units are either dissolved and rebuilt from shock brigaders or put in charge of men who can work with them.

The co-operatives and the Soviets now present to the Party important questions concerning their future functions. They are the weakest links in the chain. In the case of the co-operatives the question is whether they can be developed into mass management of the food supply and the distribution of staple goods or whether, as the Leningrad Unions proposed last Fall, they should be entirely replaced by direct state distribution. Recent developments in Moscow and on a wider scale in the Odessa district, now being copied and adapted elsewhere, make it probable that a combined producing-consuming apparatus will be successfully built up. In the case of the Soviets the first question is what is to be the effect upon their future of the increasing concern of the Party machine with administrative measures. This tends to make the Soviets more of an executive organ for translating the Party administrative directives into local terms. But in the rural districts there comes in the growth of the kolhoz, which in some places was beginning to absorb or replace the administrative functions of the Soviet. This was checked by the Party decision to abolish the area Soviets and give more power to the smaller units. Also the Party instructions to the kolhozes and the tractor stations to give all possible help to the individual farmers mean that the Soviet machinery will be used for this purpose. In describing the relation between his kolhoz and the village Soviet, a chairman of the latter tells how they combined forces. The plans for the campaign of cattle delivery and spring sowing were jointly discussed and checked. In the latter case a few faults were found.

. . . they had not treated all their seed stocks, there was a shortage of fodder, not enough attention had been given to the agrarian and collective farming campaign. The village Soviet gave definite instruction in this respect to its members who were at the head of brigade sections as well as to the board of the collective farm. . . . The village Soviet directs the work of our cooperative trading organisation. . . . A general

staff for cultural work was attached to the Soviet in 1930 . . . the staff directed the work of the cultural section. . . . The Soviet and the board of the Kolhoz decided to repair all the roads in the district and build bridges.

This is from one of the most advanced of the kolhozes, so the trend is being set toward a joint relationship in which the Soviet will have the wider function and more inclusive authority. The secretary of the Party nucleus adds to the story that a *triangle was formed*, consisting of the chairman of the collective farm, the chairman of the village Soviet, and himself. After that all questions were decided jointly and *all the organisations pulled in the same direction.*

The kolhoz itself is only an intermediate stage of socialised agriculture. Some Communists have desired to direct them toward the sovhoz form of organisation and turn the whole of agriculture into food factories. Some journalists have put this down as the goal of the system. But the Sixth Congress of Soviets declared:

Any attempt to apply the organisational system of management of the Soviet farm to the collective farms is anti-Leninist . . . all attempts to identify the Soviet farms with collective farms, at the hasty creation of combined Soviet-collective farms and what is more of subordinating the collective farms to the Soviet farms are considered by the Congress as the crudest violation of the policy of the Soviets.

This policy evidently regards the agricultural commune and not the sovhoz as the ultimate type. It involves Communist organisation of social life and the kolhoz like the labor union is considered and used as an educational means to this end. On this point the resolutions say:

A general transition to the commune can only take place after passing through the artel form of kolhoz as a training school in socialised farming. . . . The kolhoz movement can rise to a higher level—the commune—only as a result of the improvement of the technical basis, the growth of collective farm cadres and the raising of the cultural level of the members of the collective farms, on the absolute condition that the peasants themselves approve of the respective changes in the statutes and that the changes are initiated from below.

With the labor union the Party has a still closer relation and a more vital concern. The distinguishing characteristic of Russian Labor Unions has always been their revolutionary political activity. It was expressed and trained in the uprising of 1905. So the Party found and used it in the revolution of 1917. Its whole tactics were developed around and from the power of the class-conscious section of the industrial proletariat. The same force is now the main dynamic for the revolutionary development of the growing socialist society in the direction of Communism. It provides much of the personnel and methods for the organising of socialist agriculture. At Leningrad and at Baku where the unions have a dramatic revolutionary history, they constantly lead in new developments. The appeal from the highly skilled workers of Tula for more efficiency in the building of socialism shows how craftsmanship is transformed into social creativity. "The labor unions are the right hand of the Party," its new members are taught. On their historic importance Lenin wrote in his "Left Wing Communism Infantile Disorders":

To govern the country and bring about a dictatorship without the closest bond with the labor unions, without their active support, without their most self denying work not only in the economic but in the military organisations, would certainly have been impossible, not only in the course of two months, but in two years.

Similarly the unions are used now in the government of all the economic enterprises. One cannot enter a large factory without the permission of the "triangle" that operates in every department. The union issues the pass, the Party countersigns it, the administration lets you in. From discipline in a brigade to changes in general policy, everything of importance starts with discussion and agreement in the proper "triangle." *On a small matter of discipline I speak to the man myself,* said an American-trained foreman, *but if it's serious we talk it over in the "triangle" for my shift because three heads are better than one. If we cannot handle it, we take it to the shift meeting.* By the same route the Party brings many matters into the union meetings to widen their program and increase the need for activity and initiative from the members.

Shvernik reported at the opening of the Labor Union Congress in Moscow March, 1932, a record of sixteen and one-half million members as against eleven million three years ago. He said that the unions are now really following the purpose of becoming a training school for Communism and were educating their members in the new incentives for work. This was the issue on which the old leaders went out, by action of the Presidium of the Central Labor Council, which is so subject to the recall process and so accessible through the annual election machinery that the action unquestionably represented the dominant element in the unions. This again represented Party spirit and plans. It was undoubtedly one of the responses to Stalin's appeal to the Sixteenth Party Congress. Answering his own question *What is the essence of Bolshevik offensive in present-day conditions?* he stressed, next to class vigilance against the capitalist elements in the country, *Mobilising the creative initiative and independent activity of the masses against the bureaucracy of our institutions and organisations which keeps in idleness the colossal reserves concealed in the heart of our social system and does not allow them to be utilised.* To this end he called for *the reconstruction of all the practical work of labor union, cooperative, Soviet and other mass organisations.*

CHAPTER X

SOCIAL SELF CONTROL

It should be clear enough by this time that insofar as the class-conscious workers of the Soviet Union are concerned they have not thrown off the yoke of the exploiters only to put their necks into one fashioned by Communist theorists. This is also true for that section of the peasants who are now trying to mechanise and socialise agriculture. Jointly they fashion the new forms of control required by a new organisation of the forces of production.

SOCIALIST LABOR DISCIPLINE

One of the most obvious of these is what is called socialist—or fraternal—labor discipline. It is exerted first by the workers themselves in their brigades and shifts; administrative authority comes in only as a last resort. It is essentially different from capitalist discipline in manner and purpose in that it puts group control upon personal behavior for the accomplishing of social ends. One evening an American engineer told us that there was no discipline in Russia either in the factories or in the schools. But a few weeks before we had accidentally dropped in upon a class of junior high school age that was efficiently conducting its own lesson because the teacher was absent. Also we knew that such group discipline is a Soviet educational objective. A few days later in the very plant where that engineer worked I stopped to listen to one of the group meetings that always occur after hours in the dining rooms. It was a shift from the forge shop and suddenly the air became tense. One of the men charged another with padding his record of parts turned out. Carefully they cross-questioned the complainant, the accused, and his helper. Quietly the foreman said he would go down and search for certain parts on which the case turned. Back in a few moments, he announced just as quietly that he had made the count and that the charge was sustained; further that it involved negligence or collusion in the office, on which they must also take action. Then they deliberated and decided the penalty. For an example, the delinquent must be tried by a Comrades' Court, and being a member of the Party his case must also be referred to that organisation. The RKI must investigate the office collusion.

The kind of overhead discipline that the American engineer was used to does not exist in Soviet industry. When disciplinary measures are initiated by foremen or other executives they are determined and carried out in co-operation with the workers and usually by them. This is true also in agriculture. A collective farmer writes:

Labor discipline on our farm is strengthened by brigade rules and socialist competition. Should a member fail to come out for his work he gets a warning the first time, the second time he gets a reprimand, the third time he is tried by his comrades.

The same kind of discipline exists in educational institutions. From their earliest years students are accustomed to meeting with their teachers, by classes and in general assembly, to discuss and jointly control their behavior. In one such meeting, which involved socialist competition between two classes, after some remarks and questions by the teacher of one class concerning methods used by the teacher of the other, the director of the institute, who was in the chair, called for the scholarship records of any cases that needed attention. These were given by elected student monitors. The worst case was that of a man who had previously been rebuked when his class accepted the teacher's challenge to finish twelve months' work in ten. The teacher had told them they had two obstacles, a girl who lacked ability and this man who was able but negligent. They had replied, *Some of us will help her to study, but he must get down to work. He can't hold back the rest of us.* He had promised to change his ways but had failed. This time the student censure increased. The director asked the delinquent for his defense. He pleaded urgent Party duties, and promised to attend better to his studies. With the warning that further fault would lead to dismissal he was allowed another chance.

The disciplinary control of the students also extends to the staff, as does that of the workers in the factories. One student told us how his class secured the dismissal of four incompetent instructors. *We couldn't waste our time and the government's money,* he said. A university director informed us how his students discussed everything and also held joint meetings with the faculty. *If they complain of the professors for inefficiency we advise those at fault to change their methods. If not, they have to go. In two years we have had only one case.* Since one-man—or woman—administration came in, the director, after listening to all criticisms, is apt to say, like one I know: *It's my job to decide and tomorrow you'll find the decision on the Bulletin Board.* If the decision is not sound then appeal goes to the higher authorities and a further process of discussion and decision ensues.

Lenin contrasted this kind of discipline with the aristocratic form by using a quotation from Aristotle:

The communist organisation of social labor is supported, and such support will be bound to grow in steady progression, by the free and class-conscious discipline of the workers themselves. Aristotle wrote, "The trades are akin to slavery. A man of honor, a man of social standing, a good citizen should learn no trade. For he will then cease to be a gentleman and the slaves will cease to be slaves. As to the management of slaves, it contains in itself nothing beautiful and nothing to excite respect. Gentlemen who can dispense with such worries shift them to their managers. For themselves they choose the pursuit of politics and philosophy."

The workers' answer is that now they too follow these pursuits, without shirking the irksome business of managing production. They extend their control to the joint discipline of personal habits that interfere with the successful conduct of the common business. A case in point is the campaign of the workers of the Amo factory in Moscow against drunkenness. If a man comes to work drunk, or stays away through drink, he is called into a meeting of his fellow workers in the shift or shop. His case is thoroughly discussed and he promises not to repeat the offence. If he does, this procedure is gone through once more. If he fails again, the Anti-Alcohol Committee sends him to an anti-alcoholic hospital for treatment for two to four weeks and his wife and family receive his wages while he is away. One man after this treatment went on a drunk with a friend for several days. His family was called in to discuss the case with the workers of his department and it was agreed to send him back to the hospital for three months, his family receiving his wages as before.

SELF CRITICISM

The widest form of Communist discipline is what is called "self criticism." It grew up naturally in the Party nucleus as review of the work. The leader, when things go wrong, asks the group to analyse the causes and starts with himself. The extreme form is the "cleaning." The whole process received a big impetus through the Trotsky episode. When he and his followers complained of lack of means of discussion, Stalin proclaimed an open season for criticism and discussion for about two weeks and "Pravda" published special-discussion editions. After that the Party put more emphasis on self criticism, since the discussion showed that there had been repression, particularly in provincial organisations. In the general "cleaning" of all Party organisations and government institutions that followed, citizens were called on, by the papers, by placards in the streets, and signs over institutions, to help by putting complaints and criticism in boxes and by participating in the hearings. The things penalised were inefficiency, bureaucracy, sabotage, dishonesty, favoritism, drunkenness, and sexual looseness.

Before the Sixteenth Party Congress, Stalin put first among the measures necessary for carrying on *Bolshevik offensive in present-day conditions*, that *the Party must develop a broad self criticism. It must concentrate the attention of the masses on the defects in our construction, the defects in our organisation and institution.*

He cited a resolution of the Fifteenth Congress to the same effect and also one by the Central Committee, June 2, 1928, calling upon all the forces of the Party and the working class to develop self criticism *from above to below and from the bottom to the top . . . without respect of persons*. The Sixteenth Congress resolved that this was not being done sufficiently: *Cases of suppression and distortion of self criticism are still to be observed. It is necessary to carry on a resolute fight against cases of this kind.* The new members of the Party are taught that *self criticism is one of the principal weapons against bureaucracy*, also that it *is a powerful weapon for the strengthening of the Party and the purging of its ranks.* It is proclaimed as one of the bases of internal democracy, since any member can freely criticise any official or measure. Also it *arouses the workers to regard the State as their own affair, develops their feeling of being masters in the country, and their sense of responsibility for disorder.*

Self criticism operates of course to improve the system but not to change its basic principles, methods, or goal. Those are held to be established beyond dispute by dialectical analysis. No one may criticise the desirability of a classless society, the necessity of the dictatorship of the proletariat, the soundness of the economics of Marx, of requiring socially useful labor from all able-bodied persons and ordering that *he who will not work neither shall he eat*. But on measures the Party is far from professing infallibility. Before its neophytes, it makes confession, . . . *we have also made mistakes of one sort or another. We are building up a new society, unprecedented in the history of humanity. Some mistakes are inevitable. We need to acknowledge them frankly and put them right.* This frank acknowledgment of mistakes was one of the characteristics of Lenin and he ground it into the Party as a basic principle.

Consequently the visitor is always asked not to praise but to point out what is wrong and in every speech and writing of Communist leaders there is a section devoted to defects and errors. Said Stalin to the managers of industry, after calling attention to the fact that output in the past year had not made the increase required by the Plan, *What was lacking? We lacked the ability to manage properly factories, mills, mines. . . . . It must be admitted to our shame that among us too, among the Bolsheviks (not merely the old intelligentsia) there are a good many people who direct by signing papers.* Said Molotov to the Seventeenth Party Conference concerning the First Five Year Plan: *We have not carried out our task as regards increasing the productivity of labor in industry. This is a big shortcoming. . . .* It is this Communist habit of washing dirty linen in public which provides such excellent and carefully selected propaganda material to their enemies.

To show how the process reaches down through the rank and file, here are extracts from two accounts of a collective farm:

The autumn sowing went better. But when we put the horses up in the stables they got very bad care. The feed gave out in the middle of the winter and the horses became so weak they could hardly stand up. Then the members of the collective farm owned up that they had been wrong and that the board was right in requesting good care for the horses. The workers demanded the punishment of those who were guilty of this lack of care and after that the horses were better fed and tended.

The other farm worker is telling how the shock regiment which he commanded went to a neighboring village and *asked the individual farmers to join the collective farm, to which they replied: "We will not join, we will follow the kulaks."*

There was a great uproar. The partisans took it as a personal offense, and I lost my temper too. We handed a black flag to the individual farmers and so brought them perforce to a meeting at Mashlykino. This was, of course, a serious blunder. When the Regional Committee of the Party heard of it, they sent orders to disband the regiment, and relieved me of my duties. We had a general meeting and acknowledged our mistake, but the regiment resolved that it was not I who was to blame, but the whole regiment. We promised to make amends for our error; the Regional Committee revoked its decision and we went on with our work.

It is evident that Bolshevik self criticism is not the individualistic introspection commonly caricatured abroad. It may have some relation to the old Russian habit of soul dissection and some affinity to psychoanalysis, but the points of contrast are more and bigger than the points of likeness. It has some of the traits of the confessional and more of those that appeared in the Methodist class meeting, where confession and group criticism were mingled. But after all, self-criticism under the Soviets is essentially a social discipline. Individuals are supposed to be criticised only in their social functions, and for a collective purpose. Criticism of persons for personal ends is called "criticism without principle." It is mostly criticism back and forth between the individual and the group. True to Communist philosophy it combines the individual and social aspects of life but gives the social precedence. The Russians have a gift for doing and taking it impersonally. All one evening in one of the activist circles of the "Proletarian Writers" we watched a girl typesetter read her story and receive criticism upon it from fellow workers and from three established writers. Only once did she object and then the popular poet who was speaking said, "We did not come here to flatter you, but to help you." After the meeting she went down the street chatting gaily with some of her severest critics.

This process should really be called social criticism. It extends constantly in scope and significance. The whole press, professional and amateur, is trained to develop it. "Moscow News," March 28, 1932, reports a new form. At the Polytechnical Museum a trial was in process. It was called by an engineering paper. The complainant was a worker in a machine plant. The defendant was the full-sized detailed drawing of a lathe. It was charged with being too complicated and not adapted to Soviet economy. Eight hundred persons were present, and there was a thorough technical discussion. The decision of the judges analysed every feature of the proposed machine and ordered the factory to proceed with its production but to reduce the output to 400 for this year, pending a thorough trial in actual work.

DIFFUSED CONTROL

In this matter of discipline and criticism, as in the making and execution of political and economic policies, the Soviet kind of democratic centralism is working out a diffused control. It is exercised through a complex of forces, whose shifting relations are bringing order out of the broken pattern of a revolutionary upheaval. It is neither mobocracy nor autocracy, democracy nor aristocracy, but a blending of the socially beneficial elements in all of these. Neither the top nor the bottom of society acts independently, neither the leaders nor the masses. Between them the lines run back and forth to meet where policies are formed and put in motion. In their execution again the lines run in and out between the centre and a group of co-ordinated, co-operating organisations. In all of them the initiative, referendum, and recall operate vitally and quite informally. Spontaneity is the characteristic of both meetings and group action, where practical affairs are concerned. In the matter of political theory and social doctrine, signs of routine and stereotyping are observable. Rotation of jobs is practised on principle and of social necessity. The highest offices constitute something of an exception, as much because the cult of hero worship still operates as for any other reason. But even this cannot protect either inefficiency or infidelity to the common interests, as the processes of criticism and workers' participation in management extend. Out of them there is emerging, with all the necessary pains of birth, a real social control.

The nature and present limits of this control are well illustrated by the behavior of the people in the matter of municipal transportation. The extremely rapid growth of the population in all cities, due to the new industries, has created an almost unbearable overcrowding on the street cars. This is regulated in part by the *militsia*—the Communists object to calling them police—who have power to fine people on the spot for entering by the front door or leaving by the back, and for getting on or off while the car is in motion. Active Communists and Komsomols assist by publicly remonstrating with offenders. Still more effective co-operation comes from the Russian quality of patience, and the rules of fair play which the universal queue—*orcherid* it is called—has developed. In some cities a militsia man stands at every stop to umpire this game of standing in line. In Moscow there are no orcherids for street cars. Victory in the struggle for entrance goes to the quick and the strong. In factory districts they will swing on to the steps of a crowded car some time before it stops and are swept along, dangerously knocking aside the front ranks of the waiting crowd. Yet when the buses first appeared in Moscow, people began voluntarily to form orcherids and now as a regular custom, at every stop, there is a line for each number of bus and the rules of the game are observed, with no militsia to enforce them. It is an extension of the social self control that is being learned in factories, farms, and offices, and also in the voluntary performance of government duties.

Back of this control and the possibility of its extension is the guiding hand of the Party and back of that is force, the same kind of force that in the last analysis sustains all other forms of society. About this fact the Communists have always been refreshingly frank. In his pamphlet answering the foreign outcry about "forced labor," Radek truly says:

We have never concealed the fact that we apply the method of compulsion to representatives of the class which has been overthrown. Thus we eliminate the kulaks as a class upon the basis of the thorough collectivisation of the peasant farms. It is a fact which we never concealed and which we consider to be a great gain to our country. But it is not our aim to cause the physical extermination of the exploiting classes.

The proletariat does not refrain from using compulsion even in regard to the more backward section of its own class, to those who are too slow in getting rid of the old habits of personal greed inherited from capitalism. Comrades' Courts, resolutions by general meetings of workers appealing to proletarian public opinion—all these are means of compulsion which we do not repudiate for a single moment. The working class building the new, better society, not for itself but for the whole of the people, for the great masses of the peasantry whose lot in the past was nothing but grinding toil, has the right to use this compulsion; because the working class uses this compulsion not in the interest of the minority but in the interests of the great majority of the people, of which it is the vanguard.

It should be added that such use of force is considered to be educational and reconstructive, according to the principles and methods of the new penology, which restrains the offender with one hand and seeks with the other to lead him to become a different being. Accordingly, the expelled kulaks are given a chance to work and after probation are received into the labor union and restored to citizenship. Some of the convicted "wreckers"—that is sabotaging engineers—who were at once sent back to the job under surveillance, have been publicly rewarded, with money prizes and with praise, for exceptionally good work.

For the crushing of actual rebellion or intervention, pure force is naturally relied on—"Force without stint or limit." It has two expressions, the army and the OGPU. The army is also the masses—made of them, thrown into their work of socialist construction on every possible occasion, used as a training school for a life of socialist activities, so that the authorities boast "The Red army is the only army in the world which knows what it fights for." This army is regarded as purely defensive and all citizens are taught so to regard it and to be prepared to co-operate with it. But the OGPU is the offensive arm of the government against counter-revolution, which means activity against socialist construction and on the lips of the extremists, opposition to prevailing policies.

The well-known aspect of this powerful organisation is its function as a secret political police and judiciary, with arbitrary powers of arrest and punishment, subject only to the right of appeal from its board of judges to the attorney-general. Frequently in serious cases the OGPU will call the attorney-general in during the earlier stages so that he approves the findings before the appeal is reached. The law regarding counter revolution, like some of our own criminal syndicalism and sedition statutes, is vague enough to catch anything. The OGPU gets instructions as to what is counter-revolutionary and anti-social from the Council of People's Commissars and this body is interlocked with the Polit Bureau of the Party. The OGPU may be ordered to investigate and clean up some literary organisation, producing a trend of thought that may become a counter-revolutionary rallying point; or the Industrial Party with its intervention plot, or the Trotsky opposition, or speculators who hoarded and produced a famine in small change. In the latter case a prohibitive law was passed afterward. There is also a special OGPU section of the army and a special transportation division, with offices in every railroad station, constantly working for efficiency in this vital artery of the socialist system, and incidentally always willing to help foreigners who have proper credentials. Absolute loyalty is demanded of the members of this organisation and the Party gives of its best men to its work. As the class struggle lessens and the area of support for the Plan widens, the OGPU—an expression of the kind of state which the Communists reject and are assisting to wither away—becomes more and more of an anomaly. Also because of its dangerous powers it is bound to become increasingly a problem. It is significant that there have recently been some changes in personnel and the definite assertion of a superior authority. A condition of the extension of social self control, according to the Communist ideal, is of course the abolition of this organisation. Sooner or later it must go, along with the kind of power that it expresses, and that will be no automatic process.

The basic control in Soviet society, as in the capitalist world, is economic. The difference is that there it is openly and directly used. Economic pressure is frankly applied to make the social program succeed and to increase the number of its supporters. It is directed through manipulation of food supply and jobs in the cities, and of tractors, seed, improved livestock, and manufactured goods in the country. The purpose and impact are more positive than negative; the faithful are rewarded and the backward are not so much punished as incited to want and to get the same things. The individual farmers are not now denied the use of tractors, improved seed, and breeding animals, but are even helped to get them. The purpose is twofold: to encourage them, by a taste of it, to desire the larger productivity that the collective use of these things brings and meantime to increase their output and so add to the All-Union resources. This appeal to the stomach, to put it crudely, helps to get the idea and the ideal accepted. Religious organisations have not been too ethereal to use it for that purpose. Then in turn the idea and the ideal become embodied in concrete historic facts.

Economic control is final in any system. Always it has the balance of power in directing the army, the police, and the politicians and in the end dictates terms to them. In the Soviet Union these different controls are unified and in process of being transmuted into social self-control, as the directing group becomes less and less the inner circle of the Party and more and more the whole number of activists throughout the population. This process accelerates as a classless society approaches, and the remnants of the middle and upper classes are drawn more and more into participation in socialist construction. When the number of activists in the population has reached the maximum that is possible through the provision of the best attainable physical inheritance, social environment and training, then the power they will have in their hands will be as near to self-control by the whole of society as it is possible to come.

SOCIAL SELF EXPRESSION

As economic and political control becomes effectively exercised by small groups of workers at their place of work, the real power in the Soviet Union, affecting also the Party which called it into being, is the force of social pressure. This is the mobilised pressure of public opinion upon the individual, working through all the organisations in and by which he lives. It is, as everybody knows, used and directed by the Party but through its influence over, rather than control of, all the opinion-forming agencies—schools, press, stage, cinema, radio, posters. If an idea starts at the top, it is introduced by the publication of a speech or an article marked "Published to Invite Discussion." Campaigns are worked up, but they succeed only to the extent that they represent the need and will of the masses.

In such cases they express the same sort of pressure that occurs in war time when the will of a people is unified, for this is what the Plan for the building of socialism has done to a very large degree. "We went early. Nobody made us. We would have felt left out if we hadn't," said a music student whose school organised a shock brigade to dig potatoes. And he was just back from the supposedly freer atmosphere of Germany where he had been sent to study. The more the ideas behind a planned economy are accepted, again as in the case of wartime propaganda, the more irresistible becomes the pressure of the mass upon the individual. Utterly ruthless it can become as when, to take a minor case, the union secretary in a newspaper office told one of the reporters that she could not get a union card unless she subscribed to a government loan—and without union membership life is hard for a worker in the Soviet Union. Also social pressure increases as the masses find out that they are going where they want to go, and not where some other people, for their own interests, want them to go.

Social self control involves control of the individual by the group. So-called progressive education, with its cult of self expression, has side-stepped this necessity for discipline. Self expression must also be self control if there is to be any society. But the self is social, and one form of its social self expression is participating in necessary social discipline. To prevent this from becoming repressive, there is the natural anarchic tendency of the individual and in the case of Soviet society, the Communist idea and ideal concerning the interdependence and interpenetration of the individual and the mass. Among those who accept it, or work with it, this system has given a great expansion to the initiative of the individual, along with a much firmer discipline than that provided by democratic society. And again within these limits it manifests a buoyancy and a purposefulness which contrast strongly with the atmosphere and attitudes of the capitalist world. Spengler's "The Decline of the West" and Krutch's "The Modern Temper" could not have been written in the Soviet Union.

Because it is the combination of self control and self expression practised in Party discipline that is being extended throughout the population, it is within Party ranks that we must look to see whether it is unduly repressing the individual. When the new member is instructed about the necessity *for iron discipline in the Party*, he is told that it *depends upon the consciousness of its members*, that is first of all upon their realisation of the importance of the utmost fulfilment of the Plan. Said one internationally known Party worker: *Everything and everybody works to one end. Once a plan is adopted, no deviation is permitted. If you cannot agree, you may resign and still be respected.* An old revolutionary objected to an inference that students would be held to lonely and arduous work after graduation more by Party discipline than by personal loyalty to the system and the ideal. When one woman head of a teachers' college was discussing with me the use and value of Party discipline in restraining the undue development of the ego and checking the love for power, she suddenly interpolated, *But you must not think that our individuality is repressed. As one studies Marxism a long time it becomes so precious and natural that to carry it out is to express ourselves.*

The question then of whether the controls being

developed by Party guidance do lead to more self expression—in the social sense—is the question of the size of the directives formed and issued by the Party and the bigness of its goal. Is the channel wide enough to allow for development of all the capacities of humanity and in due proportion?

CHAPTER XI

THE CULTURAL REVOLUTION

There are three phrases that signify the sweep of the changes in the organisation and nature of human society that are occurring in the Soviet Union—The October Revolution, The Five Year Plan, The Cultural Revolution. The first expresses the break with the past, the second the new social foundations which are being laid in the present, the third the opening up of new human resources whose possibilities reach out into the receding horizon of the future. It takes deep cutting and far reaching changes in the nature and nurture of human beings, as well as a radically different economic technique, to accomplish a real social revolution. That does not register until the political, economic, and cultural upheavals are co-ordinated in a new direction and purpose for human living.

It is a commonplace that cultural gains depend upon sufficient material resources and adequate economic technique. But there is a point beyond which this mutual dependence does not operate. The cultural revolution is more continuous than the economic. There are limits in the physical universe to the development of economic technique. But the same boundaries do not stop the expansion of human capacities. The world is "such stuff as dreams are made on" and man's capacity as social creator stretches far beyond his abilities as economic producer.

The Communists, and all who follow and support

them, are seeking consciously and collectively the widest possible extension throughout the population of all the means of culture and the fullest possible development of all human resources. The tremendous popular interest in machinery, the propaganda for the machine process in poster, placard, film, and pamphlet, the absorption of education and students in economic technique, all these express the determination to conquer the necessary means of life in order that it may be lived to the full by all. The people are told that they must remake themselves by cultural development if they are to build a new society.

In the educational process, formal or popular, economic facts and procedures are never separated from their cultural meaning. Molotov announces that economic uplift in new regions leads to the development of culture among national minorities. The pamphlet that describes the successful building of the Turk-Sib Railroad, tying together the cotton of Turkestan and the wheat and timber of Siberia, comes to its climax with the proud claim that it *also makes possible the reorganisation on socialist lines of the economy and culture of those remote regions which have escaped the stage of capitalist development. . . .*

AN INCLUSIVE CULTURE

The word "culture" is used in the Soviet Republics in its broadest sense. There it does not mean only the expression and development of æsthetic tastes and capacities, still less that these are to be enjoyed for their own sake, either by a leisure class or by some productive workers in their leisure time. Also it does not mean certain kinds of knowledge whose subject-matter is sometimes called by the classicists in education "the humanities," separated from more utilitarian studies. It includes all kinds of knowledge, general, technical, æsthetic. Also it covers those habits and attitudes ascribed to "cultivated" people. In public places many Russian people manifest a curious unawareness of the proximity of other persons. They bump into each other or you as a matter of course. They stand talking and blocking a doorway apparently oblivious to the fact that you want to pass in. When you ask intellectuals, even the new Soviet intellectuals, whether this trait is due to the crowded living and rush of post-revolutionary days or whether it goes back to physical proximity in the villages and especially in the huts, they will tell you "It is because they are uncultured." Yet the same people who have seemed unconscious of your presence outside will frequently rise and give or get you a seat in the crowded meeting because they notice you are a foreigner.

Also the term culture includes what is called "social work" in other countries. In this, as in other fields, the Soviets have no use and no need for middlemen. Professionally trained social workers they have, but of, by and for the working class and their main function is to effectively lead a multitude of volunteers, in the unions and in popular voluntary societies. Every union has its cultural sector which administers social service activities and also the intellectual, æsthetic, and recreational features of the club houses which are often called "Houses of Culture." The Sixteenth Party Congress recommended the labor union, economic and Party organisations, in connection with the shorter work day, *to develop and improve the cultural and social life of the workers, and to set about a satisfactory organisation of their free time on their off days.* This program covers also the vacations of the workers in co-operation with the Workers' Travel Bureau. Beside the Rest Homes in the scenic and health resort parts of the Union, where workers may take their vacations, there are many nearer the industrial centres where they may go for their free days.

At the present moment a special objective in the cultural program of the unions is, *Socialist methods of catering for living requirements, by organising various institutions for social amenities, creches, kindergartens, dining rooms, laundries.* . . .The purpose is twofold; to release women from what is called *the drudgery of the kitchen* or *the benumbing, petty cares of housework,* and to make more of their labor available for industry and the various tasks of socialist construction. In his pamphlet "Culture and Life in the USSR," Smidovitch estimates that three quarters of a peasant woman's time is taken up with domestic work and points out that when the village is rebuilt on socialist lines, women take part in the field work, in tending the socialised herds, in the communal kitchen, the day nursery and other social activities. In connection with the celebration of International Woman's Day, March 8, 1931, a pamphlet by G. Budny on "The Absorbing of the Woman in Cultural Work" was put out. It dealt with the plans of the Party to get the women of the villages to co-operate in recruiting members for the kolhoz and to take part in production. It emphasised the need for Red nurses, organisers of playgrounds, kindergartens, nurseries, common dining rooms, libraries, and clubs. One of the keenest observers of social progress in the Soviet Union remarked on this point, "The men here joke about the feudal attitude of the women but when these women get started they put it all over the men."

Every aspect of the physical well-being of the workers and peasants, as well as their intellectual and æsthetic emancipation, is included in the cultural program. In his statement of "Immediate Tasks," in 1931, Kuibyshev, head of Gosplan, called attention to a decision of the June Plenum of the Central Committee of the Party concerning municipal development—housing, transportation, water supply, central heating, sanitation, etc.—which declared: *The Party must squarely face this enormous problem, for it is closely linked with the problem of supplying the material and cultural requirements of the working class.* . . . All these attempts to advance the standards of life constitute the wide cultural front on which the heritage of cultural and technical backwardness bequeathed from Czardom is being overcome. It is an almost superhuman task—thus to change the habits and attitudes of these millions of "dark people" who knew not how to read or write, to use a toothbrush or a toilet. The cultural revolution now proceeding in the villages, among the mountain peoples, and throughout the semi-nomadic tribes on the semi-arid pasture lands that stretch far away toward the East, is indeed one of the epochal events in the story of man.

The Sixteenth Party Congress considered the rate of cultural progress as still quite inadequate and drew attention to the need for accelerating it. In this field "the fighting tasks of the Party in the immediate future" were declared to be the introduction of general compulsory elementary education and the liquidation of illiteracy. Since then the Central Committee has added to these two, the extension of polytechnical education and, as a corollary, there has been organized a wide campaign for adult education in technical knowledge.

But these emphases do not diminish the zeal for an earlier objective, set up in the first days of the revolution—to make accessible to all the people all the cultural treasures of the past.

THE CULTURAL PLAN

These objectives are a part of the Cultural Plan, as that section of Pyatiletka is called. It lays down the program of new schools and the rules for admission and graduation, according to the various types of students needed, so as to secure proper proportion in the trained personnel of all vocations. It also encompasses the extension of all social and cultural institutions. In these matters, the Plan is just as ambitious in its goals as it is in economic construction. For example an announcement by Gosplan in February 1932 proclaims that, among the workers in the new mining region of Karaganda, Kazakstan, 5,536,700 rubles are to be spent for educational purposes. In the first year, kindergartens are to be provided for 70 per cent of the children of that age and playgrounds for 30 per cent; universal elementary education is to be carried out. During the first six months a House of Socialist Culture is to be built to cost, with equipment, 175,000 rubles. There is to be a library of 180,000 volumes.

The Cultural Plan is carried out by a network of agencies of which the formal educational system is the centre. Its co-operating connections extend, at one end, to the public health authorities in work for children of pre-school age; at the other end, for adult education, to the chief organs for economic administration. These, in conjunction with the unions, provide the funds for the education which is carried on within the plants under their control and for the workers who are sent away to study. The students themselves co-operate with the educational authorities as volunteer teachers for those less advanced, especially the illiterate and those who have just learned to read and write. Students in universities assist in elementary education in their respective cities or nearby villages when needed. The first student meeting we attended, in Leningrad, was called to consider a report on improving the middle schools of that city which dealt with curriculum, books, lighting, and the relation of the schools to factories. Asked why they were interested in such matters, the students replied that, "the middle schools supply the material for the universities which supply leadership for the country."

Underneath this whole co-operative educational process, and interpenetrating it at every point, is the educational activity of the Party. It has its own formal system of education which parallels that of the state and receives state funds, "for services rendered in supplying leaders and managers." It contains six units: 1. Political education circles in every institution, for non-Party as well as for members. 2. District or Soviet Party schools to train active Party workers. 3. Communist Universities to train teachers for Party schools, organisers, secretaries, and leaders of various kinds, from among those workers—especially those who were active in the revolution and civil war—who formerly had no opportunities for an education. 4. Institutes for Red professors, with a three-year course in all branches. 5. Vocational Institutes—for teachers, journalists, teachers of political education to workers, Komsomol and Pioneer leaders, club workers, faculties for anti-religious institutes. The state now supports most of these students, though a few Party locals still maintain those whom they send.

The main objective and accomplishment of this Party system of education is to impart to successive generations of members the ideas and ideals of the old revolutionaries. It does this by teaching them how "to reconstruct society and to create members of the new society." This means concretely, training them to work in and through the Five Year Plan for the building of socialism, and giving them an outline of Communist society from the writings of Marx, Engels, and Lenin. This shows them the goal but gives them no millennial promise of getting there; they are experimentally to fill in the outline. The difference between this system and that provided by the state, which teaches the same disciplines and points to the same goal, is that Party institutions teach more Marxism and so produce a corps of more convinced and devoted leaders to show the way to their non-Party colleagues. Roughly speaking it is a similar relationship to that which exists between theological seminaries and parochial schools in a Roman Catholic state.

An account of Party education in a kolhoz, where the nucleus had gone to pieces for lack of it and new leaders had to be put in, gives an insight into the working of the system at the bottom. It was written jointly by the secretary and one of the members of the bureau:

A radio auditorium was fitted out to hold thirty people and to work in two shifts. The members of the Party attended radio courses at the Party school and Komsomols attended such courses at the Komsomol university. Some did not attend regularly and their cases came up before the bureau. Some active non-Party workers also attended the radio courses: they are all members of the Party now. We studied the constitution and program of the Party and discussed such questions as "The Working Class and the October Revolution" . . .

So the Party has a very important task before it, to change those farmers who only recently had each a private farm and deeply rooted instincts of private ownership into active members of the collective farm, who understand the aims and tasks of the Communist Party and help in realising them. . . .

That is why the Millerovo Regional Committee was quite right in organising a Party school for this summer. About 300 members of the Party and candidates, from the various village nuclei in our region, must go through that school in the course of the summer. There will be three months courses for propagandists and six weeks courses for Party members. The program includes studies in the theory of Marxism and Leninism.

The manager of the Cult-Prop (Cultural Propaganda) sector of the Party in one city, himself a university professor, said that it was the responsibility of his sector to tie together in common purpose and activities all the cultural organisations of his city, around the Commissariat of Education. Some of his sub-sectors were responsible for specific city-wide educational needs, like liquidating illiteracy, technical education and getting factory high schools. Thus the Party, besides interpenetrating the educational and cultural system with leaders of its own training, throws its forces into improving the state educational system and also all the agencies of mass education created and administered by its subsidiaries —the Komsomol and Pioneers, and by the Labor Unions, Co-operatives, and Collective Farms. These agencies, which are called the "Mass Communist Educational System," are considered of the highest importance in carrying through the cultural revolution. They include reading and study circles of all sorts, correspondence courses, libraries—both stationary and traveling—workers' clubs, Palaces of Culture, Red Corners, and village reading rooms. This system draws the workers of town and country at every point into active and conscious participation in the construction of socialist society and into the enjoyment of cultural life. Also it gives them training in their trade and opens the way to the higher schools and universities.

In this system the Komsomol plays a vital part, both in pushing its members to more self education and in supplying volunteer educational workers. At Selmashstroi, the organization had provided or secured most of the seven hundred volunteer teachers whom eight instructors had trained to teach the two thousand and five hundred illiterates who were found in the factory January 1, 1931; by the end of the year all were in the classes that give them the second stage of their education. When we discovered a Komsomol who was not in any class, the secretary at once read him a lecture which ended with, "What is a Komsomol if he does not learn? It is Lenin's Komsomol and his slogan is 'Learn! Learn! Learn!' " From this organisation come most of the soldiers for the Cultural Army, which has enlisted three million voluntary educational workers. One of their tactics is the "cultural raid" in which a squad goes to some place to organise literacy classes or compulsory elementary education or technical instruction. The operations of this organisation justify the claim of the educational authorities that the overcoming of the "great obstacles of our inherited backwardness" is not the business of the departments of education alone but has become the business of the workers and peasants themselves.

CULTURAL AGENCIES

The labor unions also take a large responsibility for educational affairs. It is one of their obligations to supply the hundreds of thousands of new skilled workers needed every year for socialist construction. These are prepared by factory vocational schools, in all of whose work the unions take part. They also participate in the extension of a new series of technical colleges, for they have a vital interest in the kind of technicians who are to direct the socialist economy. They assume the responsibility of "guaranteeing proper social control over the speed and quality of the preparation of technical personnel." It is arranged that not less than seventy-five per cent of students in universities shall be workers and there is an organised system of courses to prepare them at the expense of the union. Its members and their children get the preference, other qualifications being equal. The rank and file activists in the unions give some of their free time to the organisation of cultural and political education. Their Central Council assigned six thousand four hundred of them as volunteers in the Cultural Army, willing to work for the liquidation of illiteracy. In every city, labor headquarters is proud to produce its record of members enrolled in educational courses and children in factory schools.

The press must be ranked as one of the most effective educational agencies in the Soviet Union. Before the October Revolution Lenin wrote that its function was to be *not only a propagandist, but also a collective organiser of the masses*. And again in 1918: *We must transform, and we shall transform, the press from an organ of sensation, from a simple agency for reporting political news into an organ of struggle against the bourgeois lies, into a weapon of re-education of the masses, into an implement for informing the masses how to work in a new way.* Since the coming of the Plan, the Soviet papers have met this obligation to the full by the way in which they have spread a knowledge of the tasks involved, of the new ways and means that are being created to perform them, and of the achievements accomplished. It is the channel through which the new forms of socialist labor and management run to the farthest borders of the Union. The agricultural paper in the North Caucasus which selected fifteen members from the best kolhozes, instructed them and sent them to explain their methods to weaker organisations, was no exception.

Largely in consequence of such activities, the number of newspapers has grown in three years from 605 to 1406, and 1040 of these are district papers with a total circulation of 5,000,000 copies. Local factory papers now show a total circulation of 2,000,000 copies, while those put out by kolhozes and sovhozes mount up to over a million copies. Many big papers publish a number of auxiliaries on specialised subjects, like those which "Kristianskaya Gazeta," the large peasant paper, issues on "Beet and Sugar," "Flax and Hemp," and similar agricultural specialties. It also puts out two monthlies of general interest to farmers and one for the women of the villages. There is also a small monthly series which represent and appeal to all the groups and interests in a village, starting with "The Communist Guide." One of them, called "The Red Shirt," is for the art and dramatic circles and contains plays and sample programs for the village school and club. It is astonishing to see the amount of money that the active workers in the countryside spend for papers. I remember one widow with four children who was taking three papers covering different interests. In 1926 the country was spending 70 kopecks per head per year for papers. In 1930 this figure had risen to almost double—R. 1.30—and most of the increase was in the villages. It came from two causes, the spread of literacy and interest in the Plan.

Besides its educational and cultural function, journalism in the Soviet Union is ranked as an aspect of literature and like everything else has its functional philosophy. In his article on "The Soviet Press" in "VOKS" (1931), B. Persov well represents these aspects:

Research work in newspaper technique, journalistic style, journalistic genres is done by the Communist Institute of Journalism and by the Editorial Department of the Communist Academy. For Soviet authors the newspaper is not a low kind of literary work but an organic and most important variety of their own literary work . . . a Soviet newspaper must day by day illustrate the progress of socialist construction, giving scientific explanation to all the phenomena of the country's economic and cultural life. . . .

The task of self-criticism, that is, criticising concrete defects and irregularities in the execution of the plan of construction from the point of view of the construction's interest, forms to a great extent the sphere of activity of the Soviet press. These defects are never hushed up, on the contrary their roots are relentlessly revealed, their causes analysed . . . and measures for their elimination proposed.

This task of constructive criticism, with its twin—

spreading the news of successful methods—is carried out in more detail by the factory and farm papers run by the workers themselves. In his report to the Fifth Plenum of the Central Council of Labor Unions, 1930, Shvernik, its secretary, under the head of "Cultural Needs" put first the task of teaching the eight hundred thousand women entering industry that year, then:

We must reconstruct our press from the point of view of maximum service to the leading groups of industry and workers. It is necessary to organize a wide circle of workers correspondents (rabkors) around the labor union press. It is impossible to tolerate a situation in which many of the labor papers are written by professional writers. Our press must mirror all that is going on in plants and must show all shortcomings. This is possible only if we increase the ranks of voluntary workers in literature.

These *rabkors* in the factories, along with their colleagues the *selkors* in the villages, and the *milkors* in the Red Army, now number over two millions. They proudly call Gorky "the first rabkor, the first shock worker in literature." Beginning as a direct expression of mass initiative, they are now a trained and disciplined force, working all the time for socialist construction. They are the best shock workers, elected by their comrades to a position of such influence and authority that Stalin calls the rabkor "a commander of the proletarian public opinion." Their work in the villages where kulaks remain is often dangerous and some of them have lost their lives. They constitute one of the eyes of the Party as well as of the newspapers. A special magazine is published to help the peasant correspondents write effectively and they are also helped by the editorial staffs of the "travelling papers" published from trains in the agricultural regions during the sowing and harvesting campaigns. These trains carry exhibitions of technical literature and their personnel give consultations and instruction to the local correspondents.

The selection and training of rabkors and selkors now begins among the children. In 1930 child correspondents numbered 7560. The movement has passed into the collective stage. The impetus was given by "Pravda" when two years ago it invited several shock brigades in a Kharkov factory to correspond regularly to its columns. Now there are over 20,000 workers and peasants in journalist shock brigades. They have developed a new form of mass work called "raids of rabkor brigades." These are surprise visits for investigation of conditions; 1062 were made by the rabkor brigades of "Pravda" alone in 1930–31 and many more under other auspices. The brigade of the Red Triangle Rubber Factory in Leningrad did such excellent work in a campaign there for the improvement of the quality of the output that it was sent by "Izvestia" to investigate the situation in the rubber industry all over the USSR.

At the All-Union Conference of Worker and Peasant Correspondents in Moscow, February 15, 1931, the editor of "Pravda" reported a general tendency to replace individual correspondents with shock brigades and their collective investigations. The editor of the Putilov factory paper in Leningrad reported that the entire staff of the tractor assembly workshop had declared themselves worker correspondents during the hard fight to get 3900 tractors turned out in one quarter, because "the most powerful incentive to this struggle was the mass work of the press." Their methods were organised surprise visits to all parts of the plant and the concentration of information at certain points.

Burkhanov, a Tadjik from Central Asia, said that six years ago there was not a newspaper in his republic. Now there are six, besides one each for Russians, Uzbeks, and Kirjiz, with thousands of rabkors and selkors.

Stalin told the conference that the work of its constituency should not be looked upon merely as training for journalism, nor as social work, but as an important part of socialist construction. The Central Committee of the Party passed resolutions suggesting that it was time for the movement to pass from the first stage of exposing minor defects in the mechanism to looking more deeply into all the most important questions of socialist construction. A list of major tasks was given, for example, *the resolute implanting in our economic development of the principle of planning and the disciplined fulfilment of plans.* Concrete specifications were added, such as, *in coal mining they must fight for mechanising of extraction, . . . in metallurgical factories for full and rational utilisation of blast furnaces and open hearth furnaces. . . .*

Thus the press, like all the other auxiliary forces of culture which are grouped around the Commissariat of Education, becomes both a stimulant and a recipient of the initiative of the masses. It receives the impact of the Plan and gives forth its impetus. Its character is molded by the concentrated social purpose of a planned economy and it becomes a motivating force, imparting purpose to the masses and helping to mobilise and focus a common will. In this it is ably seconded by the cinema. Two thirds of the films made by Soyus-Kino, the Soviet movie organisation, are educational and informative. They are not for use in paid theatres but in workers and village clubs. They are in reality vivid textbooks showing and explaining the new industrial and agricultural processes; for instance, "How to Tan Leather," "How Combines Are Assembled." This year thirty thousand village teachers are to be trained as cinema operators. Of course most of the story films in the theatres are focussed on the tasks of socialist construction. But their makers insist that the first problem is quality, the first demand is that the pictures be *artistically and ideologically harmonious.* The call is for new producers who can show, because they have shared, *the creative life of the present in the industrial plants and collective farms, that forecasts a new life coming into being.*

No list of the cultural agencies of the Soviet Union is complete which does not mention the Red Army. Its schools, clubs, and circles run into the thousands. So do its libraries and its papers, for which it counts 70,000 milkors. In 1930 it trained 14,000 co-operative workers, 3236 kino mechanics, 5000 village reading-hut organisers, and for work in the kolhozes several score thousand other workers—labor organisers, chauffeurs, tractorists, field superintendents, cattle experts. During their field manœuvres, many soldiers find time to go to a kolhoz and talk about new methods of work. Because it is so largely recruited from the villages, it becomes, through its discharged men, a strong force for agricultural reconstruction.

SOME ACHIEVEMENTS

It is in large degree to the initiative and purpose expressed in these mass cultural agencies that the achievements accomplished under the cultural plan must be credited. While the leaders are by no means satisfied with them and take every opportunity to remind the people of their cultural backwardness, yet they constitute no mean record. They become more impressive when measured against the situation under the Czars, and when it is remembered that so much of the economic resources and human energies has had to go into building up the heavy industries. Illiteracy has been reduced from 70 per cent to 30 per cent. Even in those minor nationalities, where before there was over 90 per cent of illiteracy, among remote mountain villages and on the distant tablelands to the eastward, the educational authorities are confident that 1932 will see its end.

Compulsory elementary education up to the fourth grade has been realised in about two thirds of the Union before the date set for it by the Central Committee of the Party. In wide areas it has already been extended to the seventh grade. Some of the most striking results are to be seen in those small autonomous national republics which were allowed extra time, if the local government gave special permission, on account of their previous lack of schools. Now some of them stand near the top of the list in the number of children in school. Down in Azerbaidjan, where there were formerly no schools for the common people, the seven-grade school is everywhere. Turkish and Armenian girls, who before the revolution were not allowed out without the veil, are now to be seen in the polytechnic high school learning to operate machines, side by side with boys; and one of them has already qualified as an aviator. Here already are fifteen high schools where before there were none. Over on the other coast of the Trans-Caucasus, the smaller Republic of Abkhasia, with twenty-six nationalities, claims all children in schools. In these sub-tropical regions, agricultural and horticultural schools are in operation and when necessary students are sent away for higher training. One sovhoz in Abkhasia had two at Moscow and two at Tiflis at its expense. "This is the real revolution," said the chairman of the Trans-Caucasus State Planning Commission. "It is harder to change people's minds than to build factories."

Gosplan reports that the most rapid progress in fulfilling the Plan has been made in the training of technical personnel for industry. Everywhere the slogan is, "Improve your qualifications." The development of this movement shows how the combined forces work. Stalin gave the slogans in a speech on February 5, 1931, when he called for the mastery of technique and showed how everything depended upon it. On March 21, the Presidium of the All-Union Central Council of Labor Unions passed a resolution in which it said that, *the labor unions must organise and head up the movement of millions of toilers for mastering technique and for equipping each shock brigade with technical knowledge.* . . . On August 5, the Central Executive Committee of the Congress of Soviets adopted a resolution creating a technical publishing trust to handle technical propaganda—including radio and cinema—placing one fourth of the paper and printing resources of the State Publishing House at its disposal. Also a special technical newspaper was ordered, to popularise technical achievements and needs. Within a few weeks this appeared, being issued every third day, and was soon followed by an illustrated fortnightly review, "The Conquest of Technique." Then the Supreme Council of National Economy put Bukharin at the head of a special department to spread technical propaganda and he promptly began a popular series of handbooks. In September small groups of youth in the factories were using the eighth hour—the first after work—for special technical classes and the Komsomol was pushing this practice for all it was worth. By December the whole Union was manifestly technique-conscious and the most active workers were striving to improve their qualifications. February 4, the anniversay of Stalin's speech, was celebrated as a "Day of Technique" with mass meetings in factories and farms to survey technical achievements. It registered two new slogans: *Free the Soviet Union from Importing Machinery. By the end of the Second Five Year Plan, the USSR must take first place in Europe in Technical Development.*

On this occasion one American specialist expressed his amazement at the rapidity with which, under competent foreign instructors, men from the villages had acquired craftsmanship in the building of the new big plants. As an example he cited a few hundred young Komsomols at Nishni Novgorod who had never before handled a trowel or laid a brick. After eight months of training under American bricklayers they were able to lay from twelve hundred to fourteen hundred bricks a day, a satisfactory average for an American bricklayer, whose apprenticeship term is from three to five years. He ascribed this rapid progress to the intense desire to acquire technical skill. Back of this lies a dual motivation, promoted in skilfully controlled proportion by the Party. Most of these young workers are being filled with a creative purpose; along with this, sometimes dominating it, goes the impetus of a better standard of living.

It is noteworthy that the Soviet cultural budget, which the leaders proclaim has been totally inadequate and far below their desires, has not suffered under the necessity of building heavy industries rapidly, as it has under the necessity for economy in capitalist lands. Gosplan reports that *the budget assignment in the USSR for workers' education in the year 1931 rose in comparison with the year 1914 seven and a half times.* The appropriations for educational and cultural work in 1932 are about a fifth of the amount devoted to economic enterprises. The budget of the Commissariat of Education increases for the same year almost 50 per cent while that of the Army and Navy only 13 per cent.

This expenditure, added to in large amounts by the industrial trusts and the labor unions, covers the stipends paid to students in higher institutions and technical courses. Most of them get all their living expenses. They are being trained for public service at the expense of the state, just as future officers of the army and navy are trained by other countries. The allowance is adjusted to the family needs of married men. Many of them earn sufficient to keep themselves by their practice work, which usually takes half the time of their course. Middle and lower school teachers have recently been given a much-needed raise in salary. Also they have been put in the first food category and this means a substantial addition to their living standard. On the whole it can be said that the people of the Soviet Union have not deprived themselves of culture as they have of food and clothes, under the necessity of paying for the heavy industries that are the foundation of their socialist society. Club houses and schools have gone up with the factories. Sometimes the latter are finished first, to provide instruction for the children of the workers—and for the parents—engaged in construction. The record of the Cultural Plan shows a wider expansion of educational opportunities to undeveloped strata of the population than followed the opening up of the economic opportunities of the United States and the British colonies.

The great hunger now in the Soviet Union is for education. Almost everybody is studying, old and young. At these words two unforgettable pictures flash: a young man leaning against the wall at the entrance to a Communist University studying a textbook, his nine-year-old son sitting on the step beside him doing the same thing. The kitchen of an agricultural commune on a winter morning before daybreak—whitewashed walls, bare floors, bare tables and benches, but electric light and a modern range; as soon as the two woman cooks on duty get the breakfast started they sit down, and in a moment are absorbed in the lesson for their evening class.

Every institution—industrial, agricultural, business—has its classes after hours. The cinema industry boasts of a unique system of special schools for the training of all kinds of personnel. The theatres have creative discussion groups, combining all sorts of theatrical workers for exchange of experience and mutual criticism. There are itinerant schools for seasonal workers and classes are even carried to the fields. Writing of the Komsomol work on Pervaya Pyatiletka Kolhoz during planting season, two of its members mention this:

In the fields, during the dinner hour, we once more studied Comrade Yakoklev's speech and ninety per cent of the non-Party youth attended. This was in connection with the organisation of labor on our farm.

A cultural tent and field ambulance were open at dinner time in every brigade. Young Communists were given work in all of them. They learned in the fields and taught others the proper way of driving and man-

aging machinery; they organised courses in farming and taught by practical examples.

How this hunger for education is satisfied is shown by a note or two from the life story of a woman worker in the same kolhoz, aged thirty-seven. She had been married at sixteen to a man chosen by her parents:

I did not want to marry him, but they beat me and I agreed. After I married we were four workers in the family. We had a pair of horses and a cow. I began to have children. So I lived until 1924, when a teacher came to our village and taught the grown-ups to read and write. He called a meeting and told us that all persons between the ages of sixteen and forty could come and learn. I was too happy for words. I had three children then, but decided that I would learn in spite of everything. We went to school evenings; the teacher told me that I must ask my children to help me. I was ashamed to know less than they did and my little girl began to teach me. The other peasants laughed and joked when they saw me walking down the village street with my copy book in my hand. . . . Soon I finished the school for reading and writing and got a certificate, but the teacher said I could go on studying if I wanted to, and so I did. . . . We had also political studies at our school and for these we often remained until midnight. . . .

I began to do social work in 1924 and was elected to the village Soviet. . . . From 1924 to 1926 I was organizer of women's work. . . . In 1927 I applied for membership in the Communist Party. . . . In 1928 I was sent to Taganrog to study to be chairman of a village Soviet. . . . On my return I was very soon made chairman of the village Soviet. . . . It was difficult work at first. Many a time I cried over my papers. . . .

It became easier afterwards. . . . I used to go to the Regional Executive Committee for instructions and they would inform me about everything. . . . I spent July and August, 1929, in Moscow, taking courses of study to be chairman of a village soviet, where N. C. Krupskaya lectured. . . .

In the beginning of 1930 I was chairman of the women's work conference, where I spoke to the workers about public feeding and made the women take a leading part in that work. At the end of 1930 I was political head of our storm regiment. In May, 1931, the Regional Party Committee assigned me to work in the Region. I had to go round the village soviets and arrange women's work meetings, day nurseries and playgrounds and draw women into social work. It is hard work but that cannot be helped. . . . (The objections of husband and neighbors and how they were overcome have had to be omitted.)

Books and papers cannot be published fast enough to satisfy the hunger of the awakening masses for knowledge. The permanent secretary of the Academy of Sciences of the USSR, V. Volgin, asserts, *Never, in any class, under any social order, was there such a demand for science as there is now under the rule of the proletariat.* For the spring sowing campaign it takes an edition of over twenty-five million instruction books, and the "Peasant Newspaper" must issue a special edition of ten and a half million. More than ten times the copies of newspapers that were sold in the days of the Czar now find purchasers. More than twice the number of books issued annually in the U. S. A. are published in the USSR and the number grows with every quarter. So it is no wonder "Moscow News," in 1931, quoted Harriet S. Eddy, of the faculty of the University of

California, formerly library organiser for the state, as saying, *No country has so penetrated every part of its life with library service as the USSR has done—factories, schools, theatres, clubs, apartment houses, villages.* The cinema also comes into the record. In 1927 the Soviet Union counted itself *one of the most backward countries of the world in the number of cinematographic plants and their diffusion among the population.* Now it claims that the number of its cinematographs surpasses all other countries. *In 1932, all the cinematographs of the USSR will serve 2603 million spectators; every town citizen will visit the cinema 46.5 times a year and every village inhabitant 16.2 times.*

This aspiration of the masses for culture in all its forms was released by the revolution and the widening of opportunities that it brought. It is also a response to stimulation by the intellectuals through cultural propaganda. But they cannot set its metes and bounds by any system they may devise. Neither the wit of man nor the grip of custom has ever been able to stop the questing of his spirit or check the revolutionary capacities of his mind. So once again we see a twofold urge—coming from both the top and the bottom of society, meeting and operating throughout the whole social structure as a motive force for economic activity and for the direction of life to goals as yet unrealised, some of them not yet seen. It is to be distinguished from the similar manifestation that appeared in the middle and western sections of the United States in the last half of the last century. That was intensely animated by the individualistic desire to get on in the world. The cultural development in the Soviet Union is born of a new conception of society. It is definitely part of a forming social consciousness.

Beneath all the complexity of Soviet organisation there is an inner simplification. Under the guiding hand and iron will of the Party a pattern forms. The classless society is being woven. This effort toward social solidarity is the extension and validation of the democratic ideal of Equality and Fraternity demanded both by the nature of the machine age and the needs of its workers. It is also the climactic expression of that desire for order which has brought man from his primitive family groups to within sight of world-wide organisation.

But the Communists know well enough that solidarity is not reached merely by destroying economic classes. Economic unity is not enough. In the history of society, a ruling class preceded formal economic divisions and at times has formed itself above the economic rulers. The story of priestcraft in most countries reveals this stage, before the priesthood itself becomes economically powerful and then corrupt. The growing power of scientific experts today shows a similarity. Exclusive possession of knowledge gives privileges akin to those conferred by exclusive ownership or control of the means of production and distribution. Also the abolition of the latter does not destroy the former. Hence having removed the exploiting class, the Communists expect to make an intellectual ruling class impossible by tying all economic and cultural effort closely to the needs of the masses and by inculcating social obligations in childhood. A leader of the Teachers' Union asserts that participation in the tasks of socialist construction has removed from them all feeling of intellectual superiority. Furthermore the story of the strechny plan and shefstvo shows that as the people master technique and the processes of administration they are not to be at the mercy of experts. They become able to direct these public servants to social goals, and to check them when necessary.

But the diffusion of technical knowledge is not sufficient to secure solidarity. That depends upon more intangible factors. To be unified, society must have a common purpose and will, that is, a common judgment about the values of life. To be a genuine fellowship it must have reached a community level of culture. Without that, any attempt at social democracy, such as asking servants to eat with the family, becomes artificial and fails. To be bound together in a bond that covers the whole of life, people must stand on the same intellectual level. This does not mean that they must have the same capacities or the same tastes, but it does mean that they must have the same general interests and be capable of pursuing them together. Therefore the Communists aim at the widest possible diffusion of that power which consists in knowledge and of those satisfactions which inhere in cultural interests. This is far from meaning mental standardisation, as the case of the minor nationalities in the Soviet Union shows. Under the slogan "a culture nationalist in form and socialist in content," dozens of nationalities have acquired written languages or dialects for the first time; forty nationalities have acquired their own vernacular press and fifty-six papers are published in languages that never had one before. In each of the minor republics there has been a renaissance of literature, drama, and painting. In some of them dozens of nationalities and races are bound together in a growing unity of life and purpose while each is developing its own form of culture. This is an epitome of what is happening on a much larger scale for the USSR as a whole. The political and economic revolutions brought the common purpose and plan, the cultural revolution becomes a dynamic urge toward a much wider and deeper unity of thought and life, a unity in which there is plenty of diversity.

CHAPTER XII

CULTURE AND TOIL

The unification of society requires more than the extension of cultural opportunities of all sorts through the entire population along with the widest possible development of the capacity to use and enjoy them. It demands also an harmonious and integral adjustment of culture with necessary economic activities. In the nature of the case this has never been achieved in the class-divided society and when the testimony of the latest witness, the United States, is placed in the record there is no ground left for believing that it ever can be. Here, a serious attempt at cultural democracy now finds itself frustrated, not merely by economic conditions but because under capitalism the economic and the cultural processes run at cross purposes, are directed by contradictory principles. One seeks unity, the other makes for division; one exalts the pursuits of the mind, the joys of the spirit, the other enlarges the grosser appetites.

THE GREAT DIVISION

A significant feature of this historic situation, perpetuating and increasing those natural inequalities which are the original source of class distinctions, is the "division of labor" which Marx and Lenin attacked. By this they meant not necessary specialisation but the penalising differentiation between mental and physical work, which becomes enlarged in the differences between town and country life. Also they included the narrow specialisation in factories which reduces the worker to monotony and makes him an attachment to "the belt." When Marx outlined the highest phase of communist society he was sure that the removal of the incubus of the capitalists would be followed by such a *gigantic development of the productive forces of human society* as would in due time *reach the point of breaking away from the division of labor, of the destruction of the antagonism between brain and manual work.* This antagonistic division cultivates aristocracy, despite all proclamations of democracy, and makes labor in fact degrading, regardless of its glorification in sermons and poems. It makes culture artificial, the thinker parasitic, and the worker either a slave or a mere wage earner. Furthermore it operates to fatally divide theory and practice, making one abstract and the other the creature of precedent or the bond-servant of the market. Therefore, as many educators who are not Communists contend, this separation must be abolished if an efficient and unified society is to appear. Hence the basic aim of Soviet educational procedure is to unify culture with the necessary labor of life.

This is also one of the aims of Communist social planning. In this connection Molotov said to the Seventeenth Party Conference:

In the theses, as you know, nothing is said about wiping out the contrast between mental and physical labor in the Second Pyatiletka. This was done quite deliberately, despite the fact that there were attempts made in the press to raise this question in connection with the Second Pyatiletka. The Central Committee thought it premature and inexpedient to raise this question in the theses, because the wiping out of the contrast between mental and physical labor is the work of a far longer period than one or two Pyatiletkas. . . . In the Second Pyatiletka however, the struggle for overcoming the survivals of capitalism, not only in economics but also in the mentality of the people, should be unfolded along the entire front, in conformity with the fundamental political problems of the Party.

One of the best examples of the working of this policy is seen in the changed attitude of the Academy of Sciences of the USSR. In order to acquaint the masses with its eager wish to serve socialist construction and what it had already done to that end, in order also to change the popular but erroneous opinion that it was still an alien body in the land of Soviets, its Presidium organised in June, 1931, a special session in Moscow. Its gatherings are always open to the public but this one was organised in such a way as to be accessible to the largest possible number of workers. Its theme was, "What can Science do for the realisation of the slogan, 'To Overtake and Surpass the Capitalist Countries'?" and its nineteen reports were put in language that the common people could understand. Then during the session, groups of academicians visited a number of the leading industrial plants of Moscow to present similar reports or to discuss special subjects connected with the work of the given factory. The discussions and resolutions which followed the reports were analysed by the various institutions of the Academy and many of the problems suggested by the workers are included in its Plan for 1932. The secretary considers that:

The session has undermined the wall that divided the high-skilled workers of the Academy from the proletarian mass. It has shown the absurdity of the idea that the influence of the practical problems of life would be a detriment to the theoretical work of the Academy. The proletariat of the mills and factories where the academicians made their reports made considerable demands connected with their practical work. But it also showed its high appreciation of the value of theoretical thought and its clear understanding of the necessity of theoretical work for the solution of practical problems. Theory cannot and must not be torn away from practice. But neither must science confine itself entirely to the solution of separate problems of today, forgetting its general rôle. For the successful performance of this rôle requires a tremendous increase of theoretical knowledge.

An internationally known Communist put the matter to me more succinctly: *I used to be bothered over the question of what incentives socialism would develop to replace those of capitalist society. Now I find them in action. After all we cannot just teach communism, we must work it out.* So the leaders, just like Gandhi whose philosophy they abhor, take pride in doing some manual work. It keeps them from being mere theorists and it ties them to the masses. When I told one prominent professor, also the head of an important cultural organisation, that there were some university professors in the United States whose wives did not keep servants and who thought it only fair, and educationally useful as well, to help a little with the household duties, he proudly showed me his finger and thumb all stained from peeling potatoes. On their visits of inspection, technicians and administrators often work for awhile with the rank and file. A worker in an agricultural commune who had lived in Virginia told me that when the agronom pitched hay with the rest, if only for half an hour, it made a different feeling. Anna Louise Strong tells in "Moscow News" of seeing the President of the Seed Trust of the Soviet Union, picking beans, with the sweat running down his naked back. It is easy to smile at this but there is something vital behind it which has escaped a class-divided society in which leisure class views of life and work come to prevail. How important this is for those who would unify society may be gathered from some further remarks of my Italian-American friend from Virginia: *When the workers speak of the office staff (in the Commune) they say, "Those who sit in the office." Those who work in the office and the organisers say they work harder and longer and so need and deserve more pay. But when the blacksmith comes back after a spell of organisation work in the villages, he says, "Goddam, I've got to go to work again at the forge."*

EDUCATION AND WORK

The attempt to remove the penalising differences between mental and physical labor begins by bringing education and work together as complementary aspects of one process. In its task of developing the individual, education has a different function and goal in a society where socially useful labor is expected continuously from all who are able to contribute it than in one where success is supposed to consist in being able to escape from productive toil. Some educators define education as preparation for citizenship, but this in the Soviet Union is conditional upon socially useful labor; hence its educational system must teach people to work effectively. So the school is taken to the job in the factory, on the farm, in the ship, and to the construction enterprise no matter how far distant. In his pamphlet "The

Great Trunk Line" Z. Ostrovsky describes how it was done when the Turk-Sib railroad was being built:

The Turk-Sib was not an ordinary case of railway construction. . . . In addition to construction work . . . the Turk-Sib brought great changes in the education of the population. In a very short time there grew up in this far away steppe land a great number of schools, hostels, courses, clubs, and libraries. There was more to be done than the building of a railway. The cultural needs of the workers and their families had to be served. . . .

Almost from the first days of the construction, the youth declared persistently their desire to learn. Besides, they all understood perfectly the necessity of preparing groups of skilled workers out of the native population of Kazaks. . . . The first need was to make them literate. During the period of construction 2000 workers, mostly Kazaks, were taught the elements of reading and writing and more than 600 who had been semi-literate became fully so. By the end of 1930, 5000 literates and semi-literates were being taught. A shortage of teachers in Kazakstan made it necessary to use secondary school pupils. Buildings were scarce, sometimes earth huts were used. Supplies gave out, . . . when chalk was gone one young teacher painted a wooden board with white paint and used charcoal made by burning wood.

Sometimes mail brought syllabi a month or more late and the young instructors had to improvise.

During the last year 1100 workers received trade and technical education.

It is the same with every new plant in the distant regions. Every few days small groups of peasants come to work, often walking scores of miles. Some of them have never seen a machine before. Such a group is met and taken around by an acquaintance from the same village who builds in the daytime and in the evening learns to run a machine so that he can work in the factory when it is finished. In a few weeks these newcomers will be doing the same thing and by the end of the year they will be well on the way toward being educated persons.

Those workers, who have not had a seven-grade education and prove themselves efficient as shock workers, receive training in their specialty after their work is done. Those who prove capable of theoretic study are sent to the *rabfacs*—workers' schools—which open the way to a higher education. They may go at night or in the daytime depending upon their indispensability in the factory, their family situation, and the budget of the industry and union, which jointly bear the expense for this part of the educational system. This method selects for higher education the most efficient and devoted worker as well as the strongest intellectually. It is expected to avoid the impracticability that characterised the old Russian intellectual. Many call it Americanism because of the similarity to the rise of our self-made men, and point out its dangers. The Russian term for this special category of students means those who push themselves up. The only way to do it is through the factory, the farm, the mine, the railroad, or the ship. One meets sons of former bourgeoisie who are discouraged now, even though the universities are open to them, because they think themselves too old to start in at the factory to get a higher education.

For the children, the actual connection between study and work occurs at about the age of eleven. It has been made mentally and emotionally long before that, es-

method of application

pecially in the kolhoz elementary school or in one connected with a factory; it begins at kindergarten age in picture books that vividly tell the story of the different aspects of socialist construction. Later the child is given manual training and taken to visit factories and farms. This procedure was specified in the very important "Decree of the Central Committee CPSU (Bolshevik) Concerning Primary and Secondary Schools," published in "Izvestia," September 5, 1931, which set forth the principles of "polytechnical education" and the immediate steps for carrying them out:

Proceeding from the principle that the integral part of Communist education is polytechnical training which should give the pupil "the principles of science," acquaint the student with the theory and practice of all the chief branches of industry and carry through the close relation of teaching with productive work; it is proposed to all the Committees of Education of the Republics of the Union to establish a system of shops and workrooms at the schools, connecting this work with an attachment of the schools to industrial enterprises, Soviet farms, machine tractor stations, and collective farms on the basis of agreements. This to be done during 1931.

The connections between school and factory are cemented by means of sheftsvo agreements with the Union. In the kolhoz and sovhoz they are naturally more direct. In every place we visited these agreements were in effect. In Selmash eight out of the twelve main departments patronise some school. The drill department has an agreement with the Karl Marx School in Rostov, *Because we need workers and the Party said this was the new way to get cadres.* It covers five points:

1. Each shift is to make fifteen children acquainted

with its process of production. (They come once a week; that means thirty in a day. The operations are explained by an instructor who is a practice student from an institute. The children are attached to brigades and are under the general care of the foremen.)

2. *The department is to help with funds for school supplies. (None were available in the department or factory because everything was on hozraschet; so they got 5000 rubles out of the factory cultural fund, on the ground that it would help to get cadres.)*

3. *The department is to give lumber to make desks and benches. (They got it from extra material they found lying around, in their workers' rationalisation.)*

4. *The department is to send materials and instructors from among the engineers and skilled workers for the school workshops.*

5. *The school agrees to help in the factory cultural work, particularly in the liquidation of illiteracy.*

In this manner the labor union performs an important social function as a link between education and vocational usefulness. This connection was not established in a day. It took two years for the famous Radistchev School in Moscow to get a working agreement with the Red Mill factory. The first response was, "Why don't you stick to your books and not poke your noses into other people's business?" The barriers were broken down slowly by the school helping in the social work and cultural circles of the factory. Its activities culminated in the opening of a children's room at the factory club. Then the school children were allowed to visit the workshops to study the methods of production.

The connection between study and work in the kolhoz appears in some extracts from an account of the educational work of one of them, written jointly by the heads of the primary and secondary schools and one of the pupils.

When the second Bolshevik spring came the school children took stock of the farming tools and distributed literature on farming. . . . The Pioneers organised a brigade for collecting iron waste for the forge. They took the calves and foals under their care and looked after them. . . . All the school children worked in the fields during the weeding campaign. . . .

The whole school took part in the second collective farm sowing campaign. . . . All the 138 pupils helped to sort and treat seeds. Our school workshop undertook repairs of farming tools.

The school children also did cultural work among the collective farm workers in the fields, talking to the workers, reading the newspapers aloud to them or explaining the instructions of the organisations in charge of things. . . . In the campaign for general literacy, the pupils of the school taught 215 adults to read and write. . . .

The next step in the combination of study and work, and the second part of the polytechnical system of education, is the direct connection of secondary schools and higher education with the productive economic processes. The unifying method that runs through all such institutions is first, the political education that explains the Plan and outlines its underlying principles and goal and next, the division of time alternately between classroom study and practice work that was started in engineering education by the University of Cincinnati. This runs from alternate days for high school students to periods of three months each for graduate students, preparing to teach.

The whole polytechnical system is co-ordinated in

the "Educational Combinats" that may be seen in the new large industrial plants, with their large faculties and modern school buildings which the young and the mature use together with a unifying purpose. They include a network of courses running from the elementary school for children and literacy classes for adults, to a technical college. They make it possible for a worker to become an engineer without leaving his work, or for a boy or girl in the same manner to become a technician or to prepare for the university. They bind the active members of the community together, not simply in the common pursuit of knowledge but also in the clarifying and realisation of the common ends for which education is sought. This is workers' education, not as a separate thing created perforce by and for a neglected group, but the education of a working community trying to share all the burdens and all the satisfactions of life.

The nature of the polytechnical education that is expressed in these Combinats is well revealed in one of the units of the FZU or factory secondary school. This is a combination of some features of our high schools and trade schols with some others of communist devising. Classes run both day and evening. Some students are earning their way, others are paid by the trust to study. Parents may send their children to an outside school if they prefer. The technical practice work is done the first year in school shops and the second year in the factory. The basic courses are in mathematics, physics, chemistry, history, social science or political education, and German. The requirement of social science means more than book knowledge. Graduates must be conscious of their relation to society and be socially active.

The system has obviously taken the project method and enlarged its scope. That method became popular in Soviet educational circles during the days of NEP. Then it was used, as it is elsewhere, to train children to function creatively within the limits of the existing environment. Now it connects the children with the actual construction of socialism, that is, with the attempt radically to change the environment. The program of a model country school of the earlier period shows the children doing the same sort of things that they do in many other countries—nature studies, seed plots, etc. Today in the country schools, they are working actively in the process of collectivisation. A sample agreement for socialist competition between a kolhoz and a school binds the latter, beside certain specifications for the improvement of studies to:

. . . *help push through compulsory education and liquidate illiteracy among twenty adults. Organise brigades for social activities and produce at least four plays during the year. Organise not less than fifteen anti-religious corners in the houses of pupils. Organise in the village reading room a corner of complete collectivisation. Clean up the houses of collective farmers from parasites. . . . Liquidate illiteracy in the kolhoz. . . . Attract into the kolhoz all the poor and middle peasants.*

In one of the advanced polytechnical schools in Moscow the older students planned during one winter an electric plant for a village, secured an appropriation, and the next summer set it up. They also cleaned and repaired an abandoned artesian well. This transformation of the project method is another result of the coming of the Plan. That all-encompassing framework of the people's life is itself a great educational project, unfolding the capacities of the multitudes through creative tasks and giving to life meaning and unity.

This connection of education with productive labor does not mean that education is subordinated to industry or agriculture. It is a different thing for children in school workshops to make bolts or nuts for factory or kolhoz than it would be to make them for a private manufacturer in the competitive profit system. When the process is one of direct, conscious participation in social creativity, altogether different educational values appear. It is true that at times school children become an auxiliary labor force but there is no element of exploitation involved. On the other hand polytechnical education escapes the danger of making childhood and youth a period of economic idleness, a point that the employers have always scored against capitalist restrictions on child labor. Also it neither charges the whole cost of education to the productive labor of adults nor creates a parasitic official class, living off the state. Most of these Soviet students, even when they are paid a stipend, more than pay their way by their practice work and their other activities. Student labor is an important item in Soviet economy. All of the harvest of Verblud, the great experimental farm, was cut by the students.

In the Soviet Union education and business have a common purpose and goal. The great new plants are not merely factories, they are also educational institutions, with classes overflowing from the schools into the offices, with group meetings of all sorts in the dining-rooms. It must be remembered that technical education is only one integral part of the Cultural Plan, that the Cultural Plan and the Economic Plan unite to make a social economy, and that in Communist theory labor itself has a direct cultural meaning and value. Therefore when the technical institutes of the universities were recently attached to the respective trusts operating in the field for which they train personnel, it did not mean that education became dependent on business. It meant that the trusts became responsible for the finances of the institutes and that there will be co-operation in working out educational policies. But the educational authority will be where the Central Committee put it in the case of the primary and secondary schools:

It is necessary to carry out the association of teaching with productive work upon such a basis that all of the social, productive work of the pupils be subjected to the teaching and educational goals of the school.

Soviet educators do not like to have the polytechnical system described as vocational because that word commonly implies preparation for personal jobs or private professions, and also a narrow specialisation which they are seeking to avoid. They insist that their system has both a social purpose and a cultural scope. They point out that a foreign language is required, literature taught, and that classes in art, music, and dancing can be found even in some technical schools. Also those who have artistic talents, an aptitude for languages, or the desire for the scholarly life can, by competitive examinations, go with scholarships directly from the elementary school to the institutions that train especially for these pursuits. Then there are some schools for these special subjects, which those desiring can attend by paying fees. But from none of them can a person graduate without having taken courses in social science and done social work or having worked at least six months in a factory or collective farm. This latter requirement can usually be met by practice work while in training. We happen to know one young man with an exceptional voice, a machinist, who has for some time been studying, and will soon go to Italy, at the expense of the factory for which he has been working. Such an happening is not infrequent and is always a matter of pride to both workers and administration in the plant concerned.

The Central Committee in its decree on the schools insisted that:

The Soviet school has for its purpose to prepare all-sidedly developed members of a Communist society. It gives the children an incomparably wider social-political outlook and general development than the pre-revolutionary bourgeois school. . . . (But its purpose is not being sufficiently realised.)

The Central Committee considers that the cardinal defect of the school at the given moment consists in the fact that the school does not give a sufficient volume of knowledge on general subjects and does not sufficiently solve the problem of preparing for the technicums and the higher schools. The children have not sufficiently mastered the basic sciences (physics, chemistry, mathematics, the native language, geography, etc.), for these reasons the polytechnical school has frequently got a formal character and does not prepare the children to be all-sidedly developed constructors of Socialism, which relates theory to practice and masters the technique.

Any effort to tear away the polytechnisation of the school from the systematic and thorough mastering of the sciences, particularly physics, chemistry, and mathematics, the teaching of wnich must be based upon strictly definite and thorough developed programs and be carried out according to strictly outlined schedules, is a gross corruption of the idea of the polytechnical school. "To become a Communist is possible only when one has enriched one's memory by the knowledge of all those treasures which have been developed by humanity."

The Committee laid down as the basis of all further work in the schools the instructions given by Lenin in 1920 in critical notes on his wife's plan for polytechnical education. The first two, out of three, are: *1. To avoid early specialisation and to prepare instructions related to this. 2. To increase the general cultural courses in all professional and technical schools.* The general aim of the schools is to train *conscious builders of socialism* and in this endeavor the factory and the farm are used, because socialist society depends upon the machine and all must know how to use and direct it as an instrument to enable all the people to secure the highest possible culture. Therefore instead of the fear of the machine that oppresses our humanists there arises a new sense of co-operation with it. It is neither the master nor the servant of man but a fellow worker using and expressing in its mechanism, for a common purpose, the same infinite energy that animates his person.

That this union of education with productive toil is the way to break down the traditional distinction between mental and physical labor was foreseen by Marx and Lenin. The former is effectively quoted by a Pioneer educational leader in support of the polytechnical school:

From the factory system, has grown the embryo of the education of the future which for all children of a given age will combine productive work with study and gymnastics. This will be not only a method for the increase of productivity but the sole method for creating all-sidedly developed people.

Then follows an equally apt quotation from Lenin, whose demand during the years of the revolution was to *unite every step of education with the workers' and peasants' labors.* He said further in his speech to the Third Congress of the Komsomol:

We cannot imagine the ideal future society without the unity of teaching and the productive work of the new generation. Neither teaching and education without productive work nor productive work without a parallel teaching and education could be raised to that height which is required by contemporary technique and the condition of scientific knowledge.

The effective union of education and work is made possible by the shortest workday in the industrial world. This enables young people to pay for their education by socially useful labor and also permits the worker to take advantage of the educational opportunities offered at his place of work. Furthermore there is a constant determination to keep the speed and intensity of factory work within such limits that they will not deprive the worker of the energy necessary to study. To the same end, monotony is controlled by the method of rotation of work. To avoid the robot-making tendency of "the belt," a Moscow shirt factory, for example, with fifty or more jobs in making a shirt, has installed a system to rotate the workers from one job to another every ten days. This in itself is regarded as a form of polytechnical education.

THE ARTS IN FACTORIES AND SCHOOLS

The workers themselves have taken a hand in lessening the differences between manual and mental workers. This is one obvious effect of the different forms of participation in managerial and technical functions they have devised—their hozraschet, inventions, rationalisation, and sheftsvos over governmental departments. Also the old wall of division between the cultural life and the life of the toilers has been further broken down by the numerous literary and art circles among the workers. In agriculture and transportation, as well as in industry, these circles provide not only a channel for amateur activity in the new mass forms of art but also a centre for constant discussion of all the problems of the cultural revolution. Recently they have done much to promote technical knowledge and train shock workers. But these efforts have not diminished that intense appreciation of the æsthetic aspects of life which was so manifest when the revolution threw open the art galleries, theatres, museums, and libraries to the multitudes. Last year the attendance of workers at theatres in Moscow showed a large increase. In what other country do the unions of different factories habitually buy out theatres for an evening, or carry on constantly within their ranks competent critical discussions of literature and art? When the workers of the Stalingrad Tractor plant made their report to Stalin on how they had repaired the breach in their production they were also able to say that they had raised and realised the slogan, *A plant of modern technique must become a plant of foremost cultural and political work.* An All-Union contest of pianists to choose the Soviet representatives at the International Chopin Festival at Warsaw was judged by a jury composed of workers and members of organisations of science as well as of art. A dramatic and musical All-Union Olympiad is now held to which all the republics send their best bands, choruses, and dramatic companies.

In a number of "VOKS," devoted to the art life of the

Soviet Union, the writers speak much of *Mass self-activity in art.* By this they meant that:

Differing from an ideal interest in spectacles, from a consumer's attitude toward art, the interest of the many million workers and peasant masses is characterised by an exceptional creative impetus of the masses, by a yearning to participate actively in the various kinds of art . . . at present a process of creating new forms of art is going on under the influence of the growing spontaneous activity of the masses themselves. In these new forms the formerly passive spectator becomes an active participator in creation.

The mass forms of art include: *processions and demonstrations, theatralised meetings and mass actions, political carnival and agitational storming. . . .* Here is an example of mass action: *The Moscow Park of Culture and Rest organises a great mass staging, consecrated to the Sixteenth Party Congress. The staging takes place in the squares situated on the bank of the Moskva. The course of its action includes a demonstration of protest against the papal campaign and all the spectators take part in the demonstration. Further part is taken by representatives of shock-work factories and kolhozes who report to the Congress on their accomplishments. The staging assumed the character of a grandiose mass action.*

The remotest workers are not beyond the reach of the rising wave of artistic activity. Opera singers are taken to the big farms for the festival of spring sowing to lighten the long planning meetings and the intense labor. The lumber industry has spent three million rubles for the cultural needs of the forest workers. To them go itinerant libraries, cinemas, and theatrical troupes, including a "living newspaper" to present current events in dramatic form. In the spring when they are driving logs down the streams, they find "boats of culture," provided with books and musical instruments, ready to accompany them down the larger rivers.

These extensive æsthetic activities, especially because they are creative and not simply appreciative, more than make up for the fact that it has been financially impossible to put the arts into the school program to the extent that the educational authorities desire. There is however a Cultural Section in Narcompross—People's Commissariat of Education—which promotes mass art activities among children. It publishes a monthly magazine, called "Art for the Children," designed for students in the grades and in factory and farm courses, which seeks not only to spread the principles and methods of art but also to make it one aspect of socialist construction and of polytechnical education. There are also several other publications to help the children entertain and express themselves, including one to aid the teachers in suggesting material to the children for their wall newspapers and the dramatic performances which they give in the schools, clubs, and factories. The Komsomol also co-operates with a similar periodical for the Pioneers. They all focus of course on the Five Year Plan, but that is as wide as society itself.

This section is appropriately enough under the leadership of Krupskaya, the widow of Lenin, who has long been a champion of both polytechnical education and the widest cultural development for the masses. It was formed in response to a popular demand for leadership in artistic education for children which followed a performance by 10,000 children at the All-Union Cultural Stadium in 1921. Its educational principles are expressed in its publication, "The Children's Theatre," which has been included in the educational program since 1918, both within the schools and as a special dramatic organisation. There are now about fifty special theatres for children operating and this number will be brought up to two hundred by the completion of the Plan. So Narcompross explains why it sponsors the theatre as a part of the system of Soviet education:

. . . *because the child unlike adults thinks in images and assimilates them under emotional impressions. The child from eight to twelve is according to its mode of thinking much closer to the artist than to the scholar. School education is based almost exclusively on logical thinking and gives very little food to the emotions and to thought in images. This latter is entirely too early suppressed and replaced by abstract thought without color, tone, and emotional tint. And this forever makes personality poor and colorless. The culture of the senses is just as much a necessary element of education as the culture of thought. Therefore art must be an inseparable element of education.*

To secure the co-operation of all interested groups in working out these principles, the Cultural Section of Narcompross organised in 1921 the Central House of Artistic Education in Moscow. The joint objective is to have every child learn to sing, to play some instrument, to do simple modelling, and to design a poster. At present fifty per cent of the schools of Moscow have music in their program and the plan is to have one hour each of music, painting, and modelling in the five-day week. The Central House has the power of censorship over all plays, radio numbers, and films planned for children and also over circuses, which are organised and used for educational as well as amusement purposes. It selects the subjects for the films, judges them before distribution and studies the effects upon children. Always an effort is made to get the children to express themselves, by arranging the program so that the audience has to take part. In the Children's Theatre the actors will frequently ask questions of the children, and get their criticism. Special kino theatres now are being built for children, and in the clubhouses they have their own performances at separate hours.

The usual combination of mass initiative, technical guidance, and government action is seen in the fact that the above activities were in due course followed by a decree of the Council of People's Commissars of the RSFSR. Observing the growth of *the artistic self-activity of the toiling masses (200,000 art circles in the RSFSR alone)*, and also the *turning of art toward participation in problems of socialist construction and the cultural revolution, the Council proposes to Narcompross, in order to secure the training of the necessary art workers, to reorganise the system of art education upon the following principles:*

a. Elementary art education must be made a part of the general system of training and educational work of the polytechnical school. b. The Art technicums must prepare instructors for mass self activity, also teachers for the art courses in the polytechnical schools and producers of the various art specialities (actors, orchestra personnel, painters, etc.). c. The higher art schools and rabfacs must prepare teachers for the art technicums, also artists, play producers, composers, and stage performers, also administrative personnel for art establishments. d. Courses and studios of the type of the factory school must be attached to art production establishments for training property managers, costume designers, illuminators, stage mechanics, etc.

Then follow instructions about reorganising self-supporting art schools and attaching them to art-producing establishments; about organising scientific research in art, increasing courses for teachers of art, introducing part-time practice work in all art schools, and changing the control figures of the Cultural Plan for 1932 to provide for these extensions of art education.

(A recent decree orders plans drawn for academies of art in all chief cities.)

PROLETARIAN ART

This educational work in the arts among children dovetails into that being done with adults by the various Proletarian Associations of Writers, Musicians, and Painters. These organisations have common principles, methods and aims. Consequently they keep in contact with each other. Their central principle is naturally best expressed by the writers. They conceive literary work as a form of social—that is political—activity, which makes it socially as well as æsthetically creative. Also they conceive it to be one of the weapons of the class struggle, a tool for the making of the new society. They believe that literature should help in finding ways and means to change people. Therefore they seek to unite the writer and the worker, exactly as theory and practice are united in the new education, and thus contribute in their turn something to breaking down the division between mental and physical labor. This they do by sending writers to the factories, mines, farms, and places of new construction for their material, and by helping the shock workers to express themselves in writing. One of their slogans is, "Literary production must become the task of the whole Proletariat."

The Associations of Proletarian Writers draw their new members from the factories and farms; ninety-three per cent of the members of the Moscow Association are workers. They hold lectures, seminars, and meetings for joint criticism to improve the literary skill of their members. Prominent writers all over the Union meet frequently with circles of factory and farm workers to help in a critical discussion of something written by one of the members. Also it works the other way. Authors present their outlines before circles of workers for their criticism and suggestions. The State Publishing House has adopted this method and holds frequent critical evenings at which its publishing plans, editors, and authors get the reaction of other groups of workers. This practice is prevalent even among the smaller nationalities, whose literary renaissance since the crushing hand of Czardom was removed is more proletarian than nationalistic, both in form and content.

The contacts between writers and workers proceed from sharing literary endeavors to the actual sharing of life—*I consider*, said the late revolutionary poet Mayakovsky, *that we must at least work with the industrial workers or if we can't do that, we must find another way of participating in all the daily life of the workshop.* This process becomes more natural as workers become writers. The workers themselves spurred the professional writers on to get at closer grips with socialist reality. The general meeting of the Lenin factory in Moscow, on August 2, 1930, demanded:

That the writers put an end to the squabbles between cliques and unite in the struggle for building socialism under the slogan "Into the Thick of the Working Class, Into the Mills and Factories."

That proletarian writers read their completed and

uncompleted works and plans before proletarian audiences and take into consideration their comments.

That the organisation and development of literary circles in factories and the reinforcement of factory newspapers be considered one of the chief tasks of proletarian writers.

We express full readiness to take patronage over the Federation of Unions of Soviet Writers (FOSP).

The executive bureau of this society called for thirty volunteer writers, the next day fifty appeared and were sent to work on factory papers. The Lenin factory called for further plans. So the secretariat resolved to conclude an agreement with the factory to do, among other things, the following:

By co-operation between their factory circles and a group of writers, to write a Red Book on the history of the factory.

To attach writers on a voluntary basis to definite groups of shock brigaders.

To study and reduce to general principles the experience of writers in socialist construction—through conference and exhibitions. . . .

To instruct the "Literary Newspaper" to strengthen and extend its connection with factories.

Shortly thereafter the workers of the Kalinin factory decided to take sheftsvo over RAPP—the Association of Proletarian Writers for the RSFSR. A little later that Association challenged the All-Ukrainian Association to socialist competition in drawing shock brigaders into literature; a procedure which had been called for by the Central Council of Labor Unions. In the course of that campaign two shock workers, who had been in the Red Profintern factory for forty-three and thirty-four years respectively, undertook to write its history, *inas-*

much as we have worked in this factory all our lives and are well acquainted with its history. The workers of another factory wrote in:

We are reconstructing the work of our literary circle on new principles. We have had enough of "literary-astronomical poems" about the stars and moon. Our problem is to establish such a literary circle as will combine literary study with the life of the factory and with our social and political work.

The Association of Proletarian Musicians reports a similar development. In 1929 it began to turn from a small group into a mass movement. A great number of workers' musical groups joined its ranks, many of the older composers *put their creative work at the service of the cultural revolution, of the struggle for socialism,* and new proletarian composers began to appear. Its local groups, who name the musical rabkors for its press and for the factory papers, publish special wall papers on musical problems and organise collective visits to concerts and operas—with critical discussions later, are now acquiring a majority of foremost shock workers in their membership. These groups also organise mass singing of proletarian songs at every opportunity. The Association finds its *hardest task is to undermine the most harmful influence of jazz—a false stimulant to the emotions. It has mechanised the minds of the people as church music has dulled them with its opiate,* and *reflects the decaying psychology of the bourgeois world.* The Association is determined to *clean the last remnant of bourgeois sentimentality from our songs.* It wants no more writing about *burning hearts.* Proletarian music must be the music of everyday life and work. Tunes must be inspiring and the songs must *teach the workers, especially the youth, why we need engines and tractors and what the tractor means to socialist construction.* Its statement of creative principles contends, *At the base of the composer's work must be introduced the new forms of socialist organisation of labor such as socialist competition and shock work.*

The Proletarian Musicians use some of the classical music of the "bright period" of the rising capitalist world, when it was fighting music. This means specifically Beethoven, some of Bach, Moussorgsky, and selections from others. In folk music they reject that which reflects the sentiments of petty bourgeois farmers or a subject labor class. According to one critic, the foremost proletarian poet, Demian Bednyo, uses the folk song form to express the moods and deeds of the masses as they awake into and fight for a new existence. The mass use of music begun in behalf of the nationalist spirit is being transmuted to wider and higher uses. In gramophone records, the collective musical activity of over a hundred tribes is being recorded as an expression of the beginnings of song creation, of the initial linking of music with a collective economy. Symphonic orchestras in a number of provincial towns are carrying on the musical education of the masses by accompanying every concert with oral explanations and the publication of essays. In Voronezh, an industrial centre of one hundred fifty thousand where there had never been a symphonic orchestra before the revolution, the musicians recently decided to organise one themselves. They agreed with the Regional Cinema Administration to hold rehearsals on their free day and to play at concerts without extra pay. The administration on its part paid for a conductor and for some extra musicians needed to complete the organisation. Though soloists were purposely not invited, the concerts drew overcrowded audiences and yielded a socialist profit. Similarly new life is coming into the operatic world and the musically interested people all over the country are looking for *the birth of a real Soviet opera.* K. Korchmarev voices the expectation in his article in "VOKS" on "The Musical Balance of 1931":

We will now demand from a musical theatre the production of operas which are capable of exciting the spectator from the working class by their present-day subjects and by a music corresponding to these subjects in its intensity. From the symphonic music organisations we will require symphonies reflecting those great experiences and changes which are now going on in the consciousness of many millions of people in our country.

Another unusual symphonic activity is that of the orchestra of the Central House of the Red Army in Moscow which is composed of seventy-five musicians who are doing military service. It gives frequent symphonic concerts, with explanatory talks, in barracks, camps, and Red Army clubs. Last summer it travelled to remote camps and barracks in districts where a symphonic orchestra had never been heard before. Its appearance assumed the form of a music festival and in some places it was necessary to organise a special concert for the workers who desired to hear a symphony for the first time.

The drama naturally provides the widest form of expression for proletarian art. There are theatres which confine themselves to themes taken from the field of socialist construction. The largest number of all the cultural circles in the workers' clubs and villages are those that cultivate dramatic expression. Everywhere itinerant theatres are subsidised by unions, co-operatives, and state organisations. Little Theatre troupes also go out from the Central Red Army House. They are trained by professionals, for the Actors' Union has taken sheftsvo over the army. The "Red Shirts" and the "Agit Brigades" are small dramatic groups, the one professional, the other amateur, that carry on propaganda for socialist construction and satirise anti-social conduct. From the Central House of Artistic Education in Moscow instructional theatrical companies go out to help the amateurs in the smaller places, and a journal called "The Village Theatre" does the same thing in print. One thing they specially do is to teach the peasants to "make artistic Red weddings to replace the former drunken orgies and their coarse and vulgar traditions."

The advance guard of the proletarian movement in the theatre is TRAM—Young Workers' Theatre. Some Komsomols began it in 1922 at the House of Communist Education in Leningrad. It has had three periods: mass performances in public squares and theatres, portraying historic events; "living newspapers," depicting topics of the day; plays built on themes of socialist construction. In 1931, the "Third Decisive Year of the Five Year Plan," TRAM concentrated its work on the fulfilment of the political and economic tasks involved. Its brigades are active *at the most burning spots of construction . . . are fighting on collective and Soviet farm fields for sowing, for harvesting, for the growth of collectivisation.* Besides giving its own performances, the movement is aiding the children's theatre, and has organised among its own youth circles, Plastic Art and Musical auxiliaries, co-operating with the older proletarian associations. Also it has organised short-term courses, correspondence courses, a special section of the faculty of the Theatrical College, and two technical schools for the training of its personnel. *The TRAM artists are in the first place shock workers, fighting for the carrying out of the industrial and financial plan not only by means of art, but also in their immediate work at the machines.* One of its leaders declares that *having reformed itself in a Bolshevist way*, that is by directing its energies to promoting present socialist construction, it *must raise, in its new stage, its artistic quality to the highest degree.*

The cinema is not left outside the scope of the proletarian art movement. There are Associations of Revolutionary Cinematograph Workers—ARRK. Their main activity is the "creative discussion" which has centred practically on the question of transforming the film from a means of entertainment to an agency for mass education. The association claims that when it began work the cinema economists conceived the film as only an entertaining artistic production. *The production of educational films occupied a relatively small place in the system of cinema production. As regards the cinematographication of the school for instance, we lagged behind even many of the bourgeois countries.* The Moscow ARRK organised a series of conferences on films for the use of the schools and for the free time of the children. As a result:

. . . . *We now have a sharp change in the entire cinema policy. The centre of gravity of the whole film production has been transferred to the creation of mass-education films. The bulk of the financial, material and human resources are placed here. Of the 500 big units included in the production plan for 1932, 400 are devoted to the different sections of the educational film. . . . With a similar energy we undertook the cinematographication of the Soviet school. On January 1,*

1931, only 860 Soviet schools were supplied with cinema-projectors. On January 1, 1932, their number was brought to 3,718 units. On January 1, 1933, 8,718 Soviet schools will be cinematographised. If we consider on the other hand that besides the 120 new commercial cinema-theatres in towns (showing almost exclusively artistic picture productions) which we will build in 1932, there will be created in that same year 1,050 club and 15,000 village cinema plants (showing chiefly educational films) we will understand the scope and scale of the new movement.

The painters are not by any means in the rear of the procession of proletarian art workers. The Federation of Art Societies has the common aim to uphold as artists the ideas of the revolution and the propaganda for socialist construction. One of its members is the Association of Revolutionary Artists and another the younger Association of Proletarian Painters—IZORAM. Its members have relations with the workers and with economic production similar to those described in the case of the writers and musicians. One of its writers agitates for new ways and means to get a wider circulation for pictures. *At present*, he says, *the picture exists for reproduction . . . it must reach the masses through the colored magazine cover and the picture post card.* A group of publications continually extends the boundaries of the art world. "Soviet Art" carries current news of the art world and discussion of the relation of art to the masses, urging them to create their own forms, and not to imitate foreign designs. "For the Proletarian Art" is especially strong on the relation of the Communist philosophy to art. One number, discussing the problem of the cultural legacy, takes the ground that bourgeois art is to be overcome by surpassing, not by ignoring it, and that its vital elements must be selected and built upon, exactly as socialist construction does with capitalist economic forms. "Art for the Masses in the Village" is a supplement to a paper called "Learning" which gives directions for improving village theatres and theatrical societies and does similar work in drawing and painting. One critic commenting on a recent exhibition of paintings remarks that it gives convincing proof of the radical change which the revolution has accomplished in converting art *from an æsthetic factor for the beautification of life into a factor of organisation.* To illustrate that, when art students and organisations in Moscow held a conference on decorating the city for the celebration of the October Revolution, before they discussed plans they listened to an address on the state of the country and the world.

(Since the above was written the Proletarian Art Societies have been liquidated by government decree and the workers in all the arts have been united in one Union of Art Workers, with various sections, connected with the Central Labor Council. This was done for three reasons: 1. All art workers have sufficiently absorbed the Soviet point of view. 2. A caste movement in the art world is to be avoided. 3. Overlapping of organisations is to be prevented. Thus the principles of Proletarian Art are extended, but the censorious, repressive spirit is banned.)

The museums too have been drawn into the stream that is carrying the cultural life to the masses. The art and natural history museums are systematically visited by, and explained to, school children and workers from industry and agriculture on a scale more comprehensive than can be found elsewhere. The museums of revolution send lecturers to the factories and organise corners of revolutionary history in the clubs. Also travelling museums are organised and sent on tour, even to the remotest places, where their coming is an event. They publish the results of their work in albums and on post cards and scatter this graphic propaganda all over the country, reaching places where their travelling exhibits have not yet penetrated. Their aim is *to elucidate to the masses their revolutionary past and to teach them to build their socialist future.*

Communist writers recognise that, as a result of the industrial revolution, the bourgeoisie in a short period *created a new epoch in science technique, literature, poetry, music, and the arts. But it was the product of a limited class, reinforced by a narrow social stratum of intellectuals and is limited in scope.* Now the social revolution, as it moves on to a classless society, is gradually drawing all the resources of the population into scientific and artistic creation. Thus the arts, for the first time since the early days of human organisation, are once again developed on their own natural roots in the life and labor of society, from which they were cut off by the rise of the class-divided society. They need depend no longer upon patron, or middleman but only upon the masses from which they come and to whom they rightfully belong. They need no longer suffer, as the movies and the radio have, from the ignorant and callous hands of the profit seeker.

That the multitudes seeking their goal of the good life for all, in using the arts for their present need as well as for their enjoyment, will not mutilate them as much as commercialism has done, is evident at every turn in the Soviet Union. That proletarian art, on its way to be a community art, has a new quality as well as a greater quantity also appears. In an article expounding his theory on socialist theatres, Alexander Tairov, answering the charge made by bourgeois critics that the quality of theatrical productions had to be lowered in response to the change in the class composition of Soviet audience, declared: *On the contrary, because of the influx of workers to the theatres we are compelled to raise the calibre of our performances. The working class audience is more sensitive and responsive to æstheticism and places higher obligations on theatre workers.* Stokowski, the famous conductor of the Philadelphia Symphony Orchestra, said a similar thing after serving as guest conductor in Moscow. A more direct glimpse of the Soviet worker's artistic capacities is afforded by a resolution of the workers and office employees of the Electro factory in Moscow concerning Selvanksy's poem, "The Electrofactory Newspaper."

. . . *Its political actuality, its high artistic value and its sharp innovations make him an honorable shock worker . . . in regard to further prospects, the whole series of the factory's problems, in particular the rebuilding of human material, has not been put by him, and if put, could not have been solved by this medium. We expect . . . more deepened kinds of work devoted to the analysit of the new mankind, the Bolshevist worker, the Komsomol shock worker, the active working woman.*

It is evident that the development of such capacities of appreciation and expression among the workers is a force making for both the unification of culture and a united society, because it increases the community of interest.

CHAPTER XIII

THE UNIFICATION OF CULTURE

Since capitalism replaced feudalism the world of culture has been divided against itself as well as against the economic sphere, in which the pursuit of profit runs counter to the cultural pursuit of truth, beauty, and goodness. Various interrelated conflicts exist: between classical and technical education—one deriving from the landowning, aristocratic, and the other from the trading, democratic mode of life; between philosophy and science—a difference of method and aim since philosophy became separated from practical needs and science became subordinated to moneymaking; between æsthetics and social utility—the use of the arts by commercialism causing a revolt that raises a dilettante standard of art for art's sake. But when exploitation has been ended the main cause of these divisions has been removed. When economic organisation is guided by a social purpose neither art nor science nor philosophy need fear it nor be separated from it. They can join it in a common pursuit of the same goal. When this happens culture itself begins to be unified.

THE EFFECTS OF A COMMON PURPOSE

One of the first evidences of this unification is the closing of the gap between leisure and work which began with the rise of the landowners and was fully established with the appearance of a leisure class. Capitalism did something to extend the area of both work and leisure, but except for the fortunate few whose work has a cultural aspect and a social purpose, its only solution of the problem was to put necessary work into one part of the day and cultural pursuits into the other. Then as the pursuits of leisure time became also subject to the spirit of money-making, the main bond between these separated aspects of life is that they share a common debasement; the multitudes pass from the monotony of "the belt" to the sensationalism of the standardised press and movie, or the cheap advertising programs of the radio.

But when the necessary labor of life is intellectualised by an understanding and mastery of scientific technique, and spiritualised by the conscious acceptance of a social purpose and goal, then the arts belong not only to leisure time but also to the working hours. So they come naturally into the factories, mines, and farms, as both the expression of, and the stimulus to, the social aims of toil. This use of them incites the pursuit of their other aspects after working hours, whose activities are also colored and determined by the general social purpose. There remain also for leisure time the recreational aspects of culture—particularly sports and the enjoyment of nature. In a society dominated by a conscious effort for the development to the full of all its people these also become contributory to that end, and they are not defiled by commercialism. One of the most striking things now to be observed on the streets of Soviet cities is the recent increase in the number of stores devoted to the selling of sporting goods. A similar growth of interest in nature is also appearing. Last Fall squads of children and young people were constantly to be seen planting trees.

The control of culture by a social purpose must not

be confused with its control by special interests for purposes of propaganda. The use of painting in posters which entice persons to buy a particular brand of cigarettes and in those which seek to enlist them in the activities of the Five Year Plan develops an entirely different set of values, both in the painters and in the beholders. The purpose that increasingly dominates Soviet culture was initiated by a small company but now it comes naturally out of the all-engrossing building of socialism, just as in the Middle Ages it came out of religion. This development is well illustrated by the case of the press. It is a controlled, propaganda press, as is every other press in the world. But today the control is not so much that of a group in power, or of a doctrine, as it is the imperative of a social plan and purpose. It can be closed to, and used against, the enemies of the controlling group in the Party, only as long as it appears that these people are also the enemies of the kind and tempo of socialist construction which the activist, and therefore dominant, section of the population really wants.

For the faith within the Communists, that they can avoid the historic fate of all social movements and keep their socialist construction from setting into rigid institutional forms, controlled by sectarian interests seeking to perpetuate mere dogma, they give several reasons: the fact that their philosophy requires continual movement; the inclusive nature of their purpose; the wide and extending non-professional participation in administration, education, and the arts. The main course of development for education and the arts will always be determined by the source from which they derive sustenance, whether it be religion, the money-makers, or the masses. The hope that the latter situation will give wider scope for creativity and be less bound by tradition rests on the inclusiveness and the mutuality of the motivating purpose, and also upon the fact that the number of innovators will naturally increase as artistic ability spreads through the population.

The purpose that so frankly dominates Soviet education and is coming to control the arts is twofold. Its dual nature is well expressed in the opening sentences of the report of A. Severyanova to the Ninth Congress of the Komsomol on "Two Worlds and Two Systems of Education":

We created a system of public education constructed about the industrial enterprises and the collective farms as centers of the social, economic, and cultural life of the country, a system which absorbs the children from an early age into socialist construction and the class struggle.

As the class struggle wanes and the classless society matures, only the positive aspect of this twofold purpose remains. It dominates the proletarian art workers. As A. Greck puts it, they seek to produce art which will act *upon the beholder not only through his æsthetic emotions, but will also agitate and infect him with the spirit of the new construction and the enthusiasm making itself felt in all parts of socialist construction and so plainly shown in the work of the shock brigades and in socialist competition.* This of course is done naturally as the shock brigaders themselves find expression in some form of art.

In answer to the old question of whether its devotion to social utility, even in the highest and freest form, does not diminish the æsthetic function of art, the Soviet art workers answer that they are determined it shall not. In his article on "Art in the Five Year

Plan of Cultural Construction," B. Ettinhof, Assistant Chief of the Art Sector in the People's Commissariat for Education of the RSFSR, asks:

But what are the main aims we put before art, what must all our workers of art strive at, according to our plan? Must they help by their work their audience in theatres, concert halls, art exhibitions, etc., to develop æsthetic tastes? Must they acquaint it with the classic works of world masters, with the best masterpieces of artistic genius? Must their aim be public entertainment, creating pleasant rest for people tired by work, or must they strive to raise by art the cultural level of the toiling masses?

We must answer in the affirmative to all these questions. Yes, every form of art, each one by its own means, must serve all these aims. And in the main, art must with every powerful means of mass influence that is inherent to it, aid in raising the mass consciousness, in organising the mass will, mind, and enthusiasm for the great social reforms, the socialist construction, going on in our country, for internationalist socialist education. Such are the main aims of art according to the Five Year Plan.

In this use of the arts for an inclusive social purpose another union is achieved; æsthetics and ethics not only stand now upon a common ground, they also have a common aim. What this does to art values is in the end a matter of taste rather than a subject for debate, but tastes too are affected by social pressure. A generation whose art has been molded by a social purpose will have other tastes than one which has received it from the hands of the money-makers. There are of course abiding values and standards, confirmed by a sufficient succession of experience. How these are likely to be affected when shock workers turn writers may be seen in the following condensed extract from a sketch done by two of them—"Coke, Men, and Firebricks," by V. Panferov and V. Ilienkov. It appeared with others of similar origin in "Literature of the World Revolution," No. 5, 1931, and the editors apologised for defects of style but thought that notwithstanding the sketches were worth printing:

. . . Five hundred and eighty-six bricks are required for lining a coke furnace. . . . The lining bricks are of all kinds, conical, pyramidal, cubic, spiral, hooked. You have to know the place of each of these bricks. You have to know how to spread on the cement in the right way, spread it so that there shall not be a single fault, for very soon the furnace develops a thousand degrees centigrade and at that temperature gas will find a way out through the very smallest crack. And then there must be absolute accuracy. Neither a centimeter more nor a centimeter less. Everything must fit like the wheels in a watch. That is why there is always an instructor superintending the lining work. Even when there is only the very smallest defect he makes the masons do the whole row again.

That's accurate work for you.

And every time a mason puts in a new brick he wrinkles his forehead, or in the case of Zhilin, strokes his coarse whiskers. . . .

Zhilin has the air of a forlorn starling. He came to the site of Kuznetstroi quite a short time ago. Over there where he came from, amongst the scattered Siberian villages, he was looked upon as a past-master in his trade. For about twenty years he had put in broad-based Russian stoves, and his linings were famed like the trade-mark of a good firm. . . . Oh Zhilin had a good opinion of himself, too, out there in the country. . . .

But here at the work of lining the coke-furnace they took him off the second day. When the group of fire-brick workers in which he was had finished their shift, the line of bricks was ten centimeters out, the instructor had three whole rows of lining bricks taken out and where Zhilin had been working under one of the bricks a small wooden splinter was found in the cement, as a result of which the bricks lay unevenly and the edges were out of alignment. This was the reason why the work of the whole group was ten centimeters out. . . .

"The splinter would be bound to burn away at the high temperature and the gas would make its way out" they explained to him.

Zhilin did not believe them and an argument followed. Then they asked him: "But where did that splinter come from?"

"What do you think, I used it to mash up the cement, of course!"

And they took him off the work and made him carry bricks. They put him with people who had never handled a mason's trowel in their lives and Zhilin protested. . . . But nobody listened to him. It was no concern to them. The furnace had to be finished in time, indeed it had to be finished before time, according to the instructions that the masons had recently received and so every one was straining every muscle and using his last ounce of skill.

"How can we find time to think about Zhilin?"

And Zhilin's spirits fell. In the end he felt as though he had got old. Got old suddenly and unexpectedly, withered up like the green of the trees withers up in a hard frost that comes prematurely.

(Then the brigadier—Shidek—took pains to teach him.)

". . . That fellow," he says to us, "was taken off the work by the foreign experts. He used to shout as he spread his mortar, refused to recognise the brigade, wouldn't do anything that didn't suit him; but we got him into the brigade eventually. I put him between two master masons as a pupil. They took a lot of trouble with him and now all the muzhik has evaporated from him. He has become an expert, but not a private, independent expert." Shidek smiled. "He has joined the labor union. Have you seen? He's quite an asset to the union. That's the stuff. What do you say?" . . .

He is a man who is usually calm and self possessed. Something must have put him out that he is fidgety, and frowns and runs about from one place to another. Today he has again been beaten by Obolemski's brigade. . . . Obolemski, that young slip of a Komsomol who smiled shyly and hid his eyes whenever you spoke to him, but yesterday had laid 2.2 tons per man.

They said this was a world record. Just imagine!—laying 2.2 tons per man and then smiling. . . .

That is why Shidek is so agitated today.

"Damn it all," he mutters. "What are we going to do about it?"

"The experts? . . . They are ready to work ten hours instead of eight. More, they suggest dividing the brigades into two shifts and they themselves will work sixteen hours a day. One could work twenty hours a day. One could break one's back at the work. But is that what the country wants? Is that what you call the joy of construction?" . . .

Then on the first of June, Shidek came to his workers with glistening eyes.

"Well, how are things going?" he asked the experts.

"Well enough but it's a tough job, these bricks are a match for us all right."

"A tough job. There's no tougher job than building socialism, but we're building it," Shidek answered.

He had learnt Obolenski's method of lining and had perfected it. Instead of having the cement spread on each brick in turn he had it spread over ten bricks together, and he placed the experts at the ends of the rows, and wedged in four of the learners between them. Then he noticed another thing. The bricklayers were often held up by the people who brought them their bricks. . . .

Shidek came to an agreement with these people according to which they would get paid in proportion to the tonnage of bricks laid in a day. This gave them an interest in the progress of the work. But not only this, he divided his brigade into two shifts, took one section of the furnace and transferred his brigade to cost accounting.

"We'll fight like devils," the whole brigade threw themselves at their work.

"Go at it!" Shidek shouted, climbing up to the top, and he started to listen to the sound of the mallets. The noise made by his brigade had become elastic and had lost its grating sound. It had become soft and sometimes quieted down to a sound like the rustling of birds such as you hear in the woods when the grass is dry under foot. . . .

Shidek again looked in the direction of Obolenski's brigade and saw Obolenski himself coming towards him.

"Well, you see we're catching you," Shidek said.

"Yes . . . good," Obolenski answered, smiling and blushing slightly.

. . . Night.

. . . and from a distance, Kuznetstroi looks like a huge floating dock rolling at anchor. . . .

Here we are again at the furnace lining and here are Shidek and Obolenski again before us.

What is it that is moving them, what is it that prevents them from sleeping at night?

"It wasn't for rubles that we came here (rubles we can pick up anywhere and we don't refuse them if they come our way) but we came here because we wanted to show ourselves what we Komsomols are made of," Obolenski answers.

"I don't know," Shidek answers at first, then after a moment adds, "it's something in my bones I suppose, but I feel I must be altering things, creating something, so that our people may say afterwards, Shidek and his brigade are great workers."

Our class is busy creating.

We are living in an age of great endeavor.

TOWN AND COUNTRY

The union of culture with toil that is occurring in the Soviet Union also promises to close another historic gap, that between the life of city and country. It is a division of culture as well as of labor, recorded in the terms "clodhopper" and "hayseed," and immortalised in the fable of the town and country mouse. Long before the days of Horace the aristocracy sought to combine the delights of town and country life, to enjoy both realms of culture—nature and nurture. But these artificial attempts, resting always on a body of subject and deprived workers, could not escape the decadence that has been the final lot of every aristocratic society. For a time the opening of America promised a different result. Men and women of culture went to the wilderness and founded universities, and free land enabled the children of peasants to graduate from them. The result was some educated, working farmers whose qualities are recorded in the verses of Robert Frost and Vachel Lindsay. But that type passed with the coming of the machine age which promised, with its electrification and its agricultural colleges, to lighten the burdens of rural toil and to urbanise the countryside. What it actually did, under the control of finance, was to cut the roots of rural culture, incite industry and agriculture to economic war against each other, and cause the collapse of farming before it brought the economic crisis to the cities. What now remains of the country-life movement except some museum exhibits of a lost hope?

Now come the Communists, renewing the attempt to unite town and country on the grand scale that is possible only in a continental land. Having removed the exploiters—landlords in country and profit-makers in town, with no barriers of property ownership, facing with resolute determination the ingrained prejudices and superstitions of the peasants, they are using the machine to its fullest capacity in big-scale agriculture. They are tying together the two basic forms of production—industry and agriculture—in due proportion by their social economic planning. These facts, along with the extension of the new socialist forms of labor and management to the farms, constitute the economic base from which are to be removed the contrasts between city and country which Marx and Lenin both set down as one of the basic aims of Communism, along with its twin, the removal of the differences between mental and physical work. No part of the program is more vital or better understood than this. The Fifth All-Union Congress of Soviets reiterated it:

The polytechnical school should serve in the hands of the Soviets as one of the means for the abolition of class divisions in society, for the elimination of the contradictions between city and village, and for the elimination of the estrangement between manual and mental labor.

Ask any company of Komsomol students whether they are willing to serve in their profession in the villages and in their reply, catching the implication of hardship, they will be sure to say, "but you know we are going to remove the differences between city and country life."

In pursuit of this purpose interdependent industries and agricultural sections are drawn together in a network of relations involving a continuous exchange of personnel; the rural population is organised on the same pattern as the new industrial regions; barrack-like apartment buildings with communal kitchens and dining rooms are built in the country, instead of the garden cities that will some day take their place. The enthusiasts plan highways lined with continuously connected centres of industry and agriculture, enjoying common cultural opportunities. Meantime, the initiative of the masses makes real the plans of the thinkers by an increasing number of contacts and interchanges. In the agreements between kolhoz and factory each agrees to send workers to help the other in its rush seasons, and this constant flow of labor back and forth naturally develops a common mind. This process is extended by the new policy of recruiting factory labor by joint planning and contracts with the kolhozes instead of haphazard migration of individuals. A large plant like Selmashstroi has a sub-sector in the bureau of its labor union on "Work with Villages." It sends sowing, harvesting, and repair brigades, others for cultural work and organisation of labor, and office workers go to teach accounting. There are joint meetings between different factory departments and the kolhozes over which they have sheftsvo, for inspection and criticism of each other's work. Just before the October Revolution celebration, everybody in the plant gave a free day's work to buy an extra tractor for the district under its patronage.

The factories also supply the countryside with permanent workers. In the Novo-Annensk district in the Lower Volga country there are 106 workers, a number of them occupying responsible Party and Soviet posts, who have come from the AMO automobile works in Moscow. To the state farms which are under the special care of the factory, 30 highly skilled workers have been sent, along with considerable machinery, including 6 trucks. The factory organised 26 creches for the sowing campaign, for which the Komsomol members made 500 cots out of scrapped metal. Also a cinema automobile was given, the district was equipped with radio and telephone by the time of the spring sowing, and an editing staff was sent to organise a permanent kolhoz paper. This practice has developed from the first campaign for this purpose, which sent 25,000 workers from the factories to help organise the mass movement into collective farms in 1930. That company will be forever famous in Soviet history. They were selected from 70,000 volunteers who responded to the call and

55 per cent of them had more than ten years experience in industry and were real organisers. The departure of one unit of 200 from Moscow for the farms of the North Caucasus was signalised by a demonstration of 30,000 people. Many of them have remained in the villages as permanent leaders. Selmash has 20 who send in periodical reports of their work and the factory pays to their families the difference between their present salaries and their former wages.

The Komsomol is also an important factor in binding town and country together in a community of effort and life. Everywhere its brigades go out to the villages for all kinds of activities. As a typical instance, from the small town of Sukum on the Black Sea coast, last spring when tobacco planting was behind the schedule, storm brigades were at once rushed out to work in the fields for a week. The same thing was done for the tea plantations. In such cases the factories and other institutions pay the wages of these youths while they are gone. It is also a constant practice for students to work in the villages, both during emergencies and in vacations. In every company of students with whom we met, the percentage who had done this was always high. At the Leningrad University, out of a group of eleven graduate students preparing to teach different subjects, six had spent the previous summer working in collective farms. At the other end of the Union, in Baku, during the third week in December, we could not meet with the upper class men in one institute because they had all gone until January 10, to help kolhozes put their accounts in order. The unions of the educational workers, the medical workers, and the office workers, consider themselves under special obligation to supply voluntary technical service to the villages. The Central Technical School of Theatre Art in Moscow sends all its students, after the first year of study, to sovhoz and kolhoz regions for two months of practical work. The actors go in small brigades to give simple plays, the stage-managers organise mass games, songs, and dances, and take part in the cultural-political work of the village reading room and the sovhoz club.

These volunteer cultural contacts add to those arranged by the authorities in the constant exchange of group visits between city and country. Adults are taken to see the new processes in industry and agriculture, the country children go to the art galleries, museums, concerts, and theatres; the city children are made acquainted with nature and also help in the fields. Thus a community of culture is growing around an economic life that is being knit together in a unified process. The Commissar of Agriculture reports correctly that the bond between the factory worker and the peasant grows daily stronger. But something more is happening. Last winter in Moscow, one of the best known writers remarked that the word "peasant" is no longer liked in the villages because it carries an implication of backwardness. The people of the countryside now want to be called agricultural workers. Their whole mentality, their entire outlook on life, is changing along with their modes of work. While the planners draw the blue prints for a still closer union of industry and agriculture in decentralised units that will enable both sets of workers to share the same cultural advantages, by their agreements between factory and farm, their mutual assistance and criticism, the inter-change of social work and life between their active youth, the workers and peasants themselves are rapidly weaving back and forth a common pattern of life.

The extension of common cultural appreciations and activities throughout the population, their co-ordination with the machine process through polytechnical education and in the Plan, the ideals inherent in the Communist philosophy, all operate finally to remove altogether the ancient distinction between the intellectuals and the workers. Now the workers become cultured and the intellectuals join the proletariat, in psychology and in activities. But in the younger generation, born to the new manner, there are only different types of workers, pursuing a common goal with common methods. These, along with a sufficiently common training, provide a community of interest, even between specialists. Hence the halo of the intellectual goes into the discard along with that of the saint. Also the present prestige of the "worker" becomes artificial and disappears along with his very real special privileges which, according to report, have led some people to be as anxious now to show a proletarian family tree as they were before to exhibit a record of patrician descent. Meantime among the older generation the signs of a real social democracy may be observed, especially at those sanatoria and rest houses where some engineers, managers, professors, and army officers may be seen sitting at the same tables to eat or to play chess, on neighboring chairs at the cinema and concert in the clubroom, and waiting their turn for medical treatment with workers from factories and farms.

What is equally important is that the fact and taint of parasitism are removed from the artist. If he is released from direct activity in economic production it is because he is, by the judgment of the economic producers and at their expense, contributing more to their lives and to the process of production than if he were otherwise engaged. Likewise concerning all those socially useful activities not directly connected with economic production, and for all forms of recreation, there arise common standards, so that they are more and more pursued in forms equally beneficial to the individual and to society. In these ways a unified culture, at one with all its own parts and also with the economic process, becomes a powerful force for social unity. It helps to overcome the remnants of class distinction and to draw its roots.

According to Communist teaching, the outcome of the class struggle is to be a consciously directed worldwide social order. The revolt against the oppressors and exploiters carries with it more than the necessity of the oppressed and exploited to find freedom and justice. The class-divided society is historically an anti-social trend, thwarting the urge toward solidarity that has been working from the days of the primitive kinship group, against the terrific handicaps of nationalism and race prejudice, toward the organic society. So far the operations of this urge have been mostly subconscious, through the processes of diffusion of culture, social imitation, and industrialisation. "Consciousness of kind," as Giddings calls it, awareness of common needs and capacities, has had a slow and difficult development. The barriers that have been thrown across its path now prevent mankind from using co-operatively the new resources which science has made available for human progress, and divert it toward the use of those new powers for mutual destruction. It is now sufficiently clear that no formal union of states, in whose nature there lie deep the very divisions which have heretofore prevented the extension of man's tendency toward mutual aid, can release the race from its present incapacity to achieve unity.

The Communists seek a further goal. While the academic sociologists elsewhere are debating whether there can be a social organism, the Soviet workers—with brain and hand—are beginning to make the organic society, co-ordinating its several members in a functional relation, guiding it consciously toward chosen ends, animating it with an inflexible will. While in other lands there spreads the consciousness of decline, the feeling of frustration, the temper of futility, the masses in the Soviet Union are becoming conscious of the renewing of life and the turning of a new page in history. Theirs is the buoyant spirit of youth and they expect their work to grow, with co-operative efforts in other lands, into a world society directed by a consciousness and will as wide as the human race. To this end they are trying to unite the blind urge of humanity toward unity with its conscious aspirations and ideals for solidarity, in one great stream of motivation.

CHAPTER XIV

THE REVOLUTIONARY IDEAL

The driving forces that are changing economic incentives, developing the initiative of the masses and achieving the cultural revolution in the Soviet Union work through and are directed by the Communist Party. It is therefore necessary to enquire into the motivation of that organisation and to see how it is being transmitted to the rest of the population.

THE PULL OF THE FUTURE

The immediate end around which the Party crystallised was the seizure of the Russian state in the name of the proletariat. In the background was the attraction of a social ideal. Behind its revolutionary activities was the desire to release the masses from the oppression of both Czardom and capitalism, and also the pull of the future possibilities of mankind. The Communists cannot be called Utopians because their ideal society is not static and they proclaim a scientific method for realising it. Also they define it only in terms of general values, leaving their specific form to historic development.

When Soviet educators are asked what they teach about the nature and form of the Communist society which is to be reached after the long transition period of socialism, they usually reply that its outlines have been given by Marx, Engels, and Lenin. So the vision of the future that is given to Soviet youth is authoritative and consistent. The Pioneers are told that the abolition of classes is to be accomplished, that material resources will one day be so abundant and so equally distributed that all will be free to develop their cultural capacities. It is always in terms of this kind of freedom that Soviet youth answers the question about what kind of society it is working for.

New members of the Party are taught in addition, in the Handbook, that *All people will be members of a single fraternity of labor. . . . Labor will become a natural human requirement. People will work without any compulsion.* On this point Lenin is quoted: *Communist labor is gratis labor for the good of society, labor performed not as the fulfilment of a definite obligation, not to earn the right to certain provisions, not according to rates legally established in advance—it is voluntary labor . . . contributed without any thought of reward . . . from a habit of working for the common weal. . . .*

There will be *such vast resources that every one will be able to get everything he or she requires quite irrespective of work.* All other forms of compulsion will go with the disappearance of the classes. *Gone will be the armies, the prisons, and all that.* New freedom will appear.

The enormous spread of industrialisation and the lack of all unproductive expenditure will allow of the maximum reduction of hours. The citizen will be able to devote his leisure to social work and the arts and sciences. The extreme specialisation which now makes people so one-sided and narrow will disappear. . . . All will have the opportunity of doing brain work and per-

fecting their knowledge. The last traces of inequality will disappear.

An epoch of unprecedented human progress in the sphere of technical discoveries and inventions, in the sphere of art and science, will set in. Religion, like all other superstition and prejudices, will be done with once and for all. Humanity will become physically and mentally stronger.

The economists naturally emphasise the technical aspects of the Communist ideal for society. Lapidus and Ostrovityanov, representative professors in the Communist Academy, look forward to the highest possible development of economic planning. The necessary equilibrium between production and consumption will be achieved by the conscious direction of all society. Distribution will be entirely according to need. On this point they also quote Lenin, who in turn is expounding Marx:

"The narrow horizon of bourgeois law" which compels one to calculate, with the pitilessness of a Shylock, whether one has not worked half an hour more than another, this narrow horizon will then be left behind. There will then be no need for any exact calculation by society of the quantity of products to be distributed to each of its members; each will take freely "according to his needs."

The economists add that Lenin does not mean that the time has come to undertake the realisation of this ideal, he is merely making a scientific prophecy. In similar vein they themselves remark that it is not possible *to change over at the moment to the calculation of cost price not in money but in labor hours*, but when Soviet production reaches its highest stage *money and credit will entirely disappear and commerce will be trans-*

formed into a technical organisation for socialist distribution. The latter term should of course be "Communist."

Marx and Lenin also look forward to moral changes in human nature as the result of a change in economic environment. Personal excesses of conduct are to "wither away" with the gradual removal of their social causes. It is thus that the state is to disappear. Here Lenin thus expounds Engels:

We set ourselves, as our final aim, the destruction of the state, that is of every organised and systematic violence, every form of violence against man in general. We do not expect the advent of an order of society in which the principle of the submission of the minority to the majority will not be observed. But, striving for socialism, we are convinced that it will develop further into Communism, and side by side with this there will vanish all need for force, for the subjection of one man to another, since people will grow accustomed to observing the elementary conditions of social existence without force and without subjection.

THE PUSH OF THE PAST

Those who are familiar with the story of Utopias will recognise that the Communist leaders in their outline of the future society are using elements which appear in some form or other in practically all of them. They are affirming values whose inherent motivating power is strengthened by a long and wide succession of ethical judgments, including some by persons whom it is the fashion of Communists to denounce, for instance Jesus and Gandhi. But the Communists do not give these values the authority of moral absolutes. Instead, they put behind them the power of historic necessity. They analyse history as a succession of class struggles which finally brings the workers to power to make the classless society in which alone freedom and justice for all can be realised. But this is not fatalism. It requires in each nation that the workers have the intelligence, and the will to seize the historic moment and guide the course of destiny. It has been the function of the intellectuals in the Communist movement thus to put the push of the past into the consciousness of the masses whose present needs impel them to make a new society.

The workers have played their part in the shaping of the Communist ideal. By successive revolts, they have shown the thinkers what was needed and have moved them to share their lot. By the seizure of the means of education at every opportunity, they sustain the judgment of the cultured concerning the desirability of intellectual and æsthetic development. With every extension of literacy and the franchise this affirmation grows stronger. The further the opportunity to cultivate the good life extends, the nearer to unanimity is the judgment concerning the values in which it consists, the greater is the determination that it should be available to all. The democratic revolutions make the social revolution imperative.

A MOVING GOAL

The ultimate fate of the Utopias of the past has been to get themselves postponed into the dim and distant future. They then provide an apocalyptic hope as compensation for present failure and justification for adjustment to a world that ought to be rebelled against. Against such contentment the Communists think they have saved future generations because their ideal is in terms of values that are capable of infinite development and require continuous struggle. They do not permit themselves to regard any social forms they are now developing as final. The only thing they are attempting to fix beyond the power of change is the general direction of advance. Whoever would understand what they are doing must never forget that they are writing a moving chronicle, so that he who reads it must also run.

It is upon the dynamic nature of their social ideal, as well as upon the increasing participation of the population in all forms of administration, that the Communists rely to enable them to break the historic rule that all revolutionary movements crystallise into authoritative institutions which forbid change. There is another penalty of age, for parties as well as for men. It is the tendency to be content with winning one fight. The harder the battle the easier it is to rest content with one's labors. Also the machine age, because of its laboratory concern with the immediate, tends to withdraw men's eyes from the distant goal for human living. The only means of escape from these disastrous tendencies is the vision of a moving goal, whose pursuit requires a continuous revolutionary process in human nature. The Communist ideal affirms the former, its basic philosophy requires the latter.

CHAPTER XV

THE SUPPORTING PHILOSOPHY

The Communist philosophy is called dialectical materialism. It is their own product and their philosophy of history, with its familiar doctrines of class struggle and economic determinism, is but one of its aspects. All students, above the elementary school, are required to study it in varying degrees. In the first seven grades they get some of it indirectly in their political education—or social science—classes. Any company of university or technical students, when the talk turns to student life in the visitor's country, is sure to ask if the students there are interested in dialectical materialism.

TWO SCHOOLS

The best-known living exponent of dialectical materialism is Bukharin. His volume "Historic Materialism" presents the narrow, rigid, economic determinism whose appearance led Marx to give thanks that he was not a Marxist, and Engels later to demonstrate that it did not represent their joint views. Bukharin was removed from high office because of his policies for the peasant situation and the rate of industrialisation, and his philosophic viewpoint is now called the "mechanistic heresy" and strenuously fought. For instance, a symposium of "Economics of Labor" prepared at the Communist Academy finds the mechanistic heresy expressed in a *purely quantitative theory and practice of rationalisation now appearing in some quarters, based on the idea of getting out what is put in.* Also in a report to the Academy on Economics of Labor as a Subject of Instruction in the Higher Schools, P. Marcus criticises a mechanistic approach on the part of some Soviet economists which ignores the changing relations in production that are the decisive factor in the organisation of labor. Another aspect of the mechanistic heresy is exposed in a critique of the films of Eisenstein by Anisimov, which charges that remarkable producer with allowing his work to become permeated with *the ideology of the technical intelligentsia* of other countries, on whom the following judgment is rendered:

We know that the ideology of the technical intellectuals is permeated with technical fetishism, which plays a specific rôle in the formation of their world outlook. Here we always meet with a tendency towards fetishism, the technical covering of reality, a tendency to take it for the whole, that implies a misunderstanding of the real content of the social process.

Similarly the Proletarian Musicians declare that, *The theme of the new socialist relations to work cannot be developed with the aid of the naturalistic approach of the bourgeois urban music which expresses the mechanistic sensing of the universe by the bourgeois artist who fetishises productive processes as such.*

Writers of the younger school occasionally speak of the mechanistic view as "vulgar materialism." Its essential thesis is that mind and matter are the same thing, that mind is but a function of matter. Its opponents, however, maintain that while consciousness and matter are inseparably united, nevertheless mind is a distinct quality of matter. Also they say there is something outside consciousness which is not a mere mental projection but is real, and consciousness reflects it more or less correctly. Lenin put this thesis in a much-quoted sentence in his reply to the idealists concerning the nature of reality and how it might be known. He answered that he knew what reality was because he found the same laws working in his mind that were also working in human society, in the atom, and in the stars. Here the process of life is viewed as creative and calling for the purposeful activity of man. Hence the exponents of this school of dialectical materialism are continually attacking what they call the "creeping empiricism" of the mechanistic evolutionists. Finding great joy in battle, like all youthful movements, they also wage a vigorous offensive against the behaviorists and their assumption of an unbroken continuity of cause and effect.

Engels, who contributed the most to its formulation, said that dialectical materialism focusses its attention not upon things themselves but upon the relations between things. Holding that life is always and altogether in motion, that the relations between all things are constantly changing, it seeks to discover the laws of these changing relationships, including those between man and his environment, in order that he may direct the process of human society even as he is able to control the forces of nature when once he understands the laws of their movement. This attitude is well illustrated in a paragraph from a long resolution on "The Creative Principles of Proletarian Music" adopted by the First Conference of the Russian Association of Proletarian Musicians:

The art method of the proletarian composer must proceed from the opening up of the real contradictory social facts and by a clear concept as to the final goal of the working-class movement. Such approach removes the insoluble contradiction of the narrow middle-class man between that which is and that which should be or that which is hoped for. From the point of view of dialectical materialism there is movement in every thing which exists, that is, in actuality, which solves its contradictions and includes the elements of its reconstruction or transformation. This creative method while it is realistic at its base by no means is passive or has the imprint of passivity, "of a neutral objectivism." On the contrary it calls for an active direction and a class-conscious relation to the themes on the part of the artist.

Marx once remarked that philosophy ended with Hegel, meaning philosophy as a process of making abstract mental formulæ. After that, by his instrumentality, came dialectical materialism which seeks both to explain life and to change it. In the latter function it becomes materialist dialectics, sometimes called the organic-historical method. In this phrase, the word organic implies that the new is always conditioned by the old and that, therefore, all present relationships and the connections between them and the past must constantly be reviewed if the right road into the future is to be found. This method, which is still in its infancy, is now being applied to every branch of knowledge. In the study of the operations of the mind, it is formulating a theory of knowledge which rejects metaphysics as harmful. In the study of nature it has developed an hypothesis concerning the character of evolution that separates it from both the mechanists and the vitalists. In the study of man and his doings, it subdivides into economic and historic materialism—the latter including the phenomena of religion and ethics—and becomes both chart and compass for the course of social evolution, particularly for making the transition from capitalism to Communism.

Dialectical materialism is then a very practical philosophy. It changed that mental discipline from a means of escape out of the dirt and danger of the social struggle into a tool for the remaking of society. Philosophy has before now served as an instrument of the state but the Communists are putting it to a different use. They are employing it to forecast and hasten the abolition of the state. Its first task was to formulate a revolutionary theory without which Lenin said *there cannot be a revolutionary movement.* This it did in terms which require a continuing revolution against all official privilege and power. In his "Leninism," Stalin affirms that *revolutionary theory is a synthesis of the experience of the working-class movement throughout all lands—the generalised experience.* This is the first time in history that the working class have had a philosophy. It is now avowedly used for their class purposes. But one of its hypotheses is that their interests coincide with and depend upon the affirmation and realisation of universal values. It holds they can find for themselves and their children the emancipation they seek only by creating the classless society. That it works in this direction is manifest in that previously quoted section of Stalin's industrial-management speech which had to do with changed relations between the workers and the intellectuals: *It would be wrong and dialectially incorrect to continue our former policy when conditions have changed.*

A Society of Militant Dialectical Materialists exists in the Soviet Union, one of whose functions is to increase the effectiveness of this philosophy in giving direction to current affairs. Its adherents also claim that materialist dialectics is a method for transmuting theory into fact as well as for turning the facts of experience into successfully working generalisations. Molotov made this point in his report to the Executive Committee of the Comintern—Communist International—in 1930:

Marx wrote: "The weapon of criticism cannot of course replace criticism by weapons. Most force must be overthrown by force equally material but even theory becomes a material force directly it takes hold of the masses." These last words of Marx are particularly appropriate to what is now going on in USSR. From the time that not only in the working class but also amongst the millions of peasantry there began to take place the definite turn of tide toward socialism, the ideas of Communism "become a material force." These ideas penetrating deeper and deeper into the masses become transformed into the real facts of socialist construction, the volume of which is becoming truly gigantic.

One of the most significant things in the Soviet educational world is the interest of technical students in philosophy, an extension of a Russian characteristic. A friend, who teaches English to some of the more advanced, says that for the conversational discussion period they almost invariably select some philosophical or ethical question. When a group of students in another technical institute in a different part of the country were asked why a certain professor was the most influential man on the faculty, they said it was because he related dialectical materialism to all his teaching. When we asked that professor what practical use this philosophy was in engineering, *It teaches us to examine everything in all its relations*, was the immediate reply.

Elsewhere, another young engineer amplified the matter: *If I have to select the type of tractor for a certain region I must consider more than its mechanical qualities. I must take into account all the economic and social factors in that district before I make my decision.* So for technicians to consider things in all their relations means specifically to take into account those social considerations which heretofore have been too largely ignored by science—even by politics and economics which are accustomed in the academic world to consider themselves as scientific disciplines. Among Komsomol groups, the first answer to the question, of what practical use is dialectical materialism, is likely to be, *It helps us to find our way and especially to see who are our enemies.* They speak in terms of the class struggle and the political battle over the making of the program for the building of socialism, the fields in which so far the Communist philosophy has found its largest practical use.

THE GUIDING PRINCIPLES

In attempting to shape social progress, materialist dialectics has so far used three principles. The first is, that quantity tends to become transformed into quality and quality into quantity; that is, a sufficient increase in quantity at a given point in society usually introduces a new quality and the quality in turn occasions an increase in quantity. These interacting processes may be seen in the growth of a crowd into a mob which is bent on a lynching or a revolutionary outbreak. On a wider scale, they are manifest in the extension of literacy or the franchise, or in the social and economic changes that follow the massing of the workers in factories. At least there is enough data behind this hypothesis of the relationship between quantitative and qualitative changes in society to show the inadequacy of the method of quantitative analysis of social phenomena, now so prevalent in academic circles in the capitalist world. In "The State and Revolution" Lenin cites an instance. He is commenting on Marx's account of the Paris Commune, which had related that:

"*The police, until then merely an instrument of the government, was immediately stripped of all its political functions, and turned into the responsible and at any time replaceable organ of the Commune. . . .*"

(*So to Marx the Commune seems to have replaced the broken machinery of the state by a fuller democracy.*) Lenin adds: *Here we see precisely a case of the "transformation of quantity into quality." Democracy carried out with the fullest completeness and consistency is transformed from capitalist democracy into proletarian democracy; from the state (that is a special force for the suppression of a particular class) to something which is no longer really a form of the state.*

The second guiding principle of materialist dialectics was called by Engels, who formulated its laws, "the law of the interpenetration of opposites." As expounded and used by Lenin, it means that things move in a unity of opposites which are continually struggling against each other until a breaking point is reached, as in the conflict between the masses and the classes. At the historic point of change, it becomes apparent which elements of the old need to be destroyed, which retained and developed in another direction in a new synthesis, as the Communists are now doing with certain parts of capitalist economic technique, after completely abolishing its basic principle of private ownership of the means of production. This and other contradictions in the Soviet Union, especially the conjunction of freedom and repression, cannot be understood unless one remembers the communist philosophy about mutually interpenetrating opposites and how their movement may be guided. At the beginning of the transition period between capitalism and Communism the proportion and relation of many opposites is continually changing and it is the business of the Communist Party to keep them moving, and in the right direction.

The third guiding principle of materialist dialectics is the negation of negation, that is, the victory achieved by the leading opposite is the basis for a new synthesis in which many of the elements are repeated on a higher plane until finally the victor is itself negated. The crowning example is found in modern social movements. Capitalism negated feudalism only to be itself negated by socialism which in turn will be negated by Communism. This is obviously a development, in more detail, of Hegel's familiar trilogy—thesis, antithesis, synthesis. This he formulated by analysis of the workings of the mind in the history of philosophy but, because of his idealistic bent, turned his conclusions into pure abstractions, making his historical data mere footnotes. This was what Marx meant by saying that he found dialectics in Hegel standing on its head. He put it on its feet by applying the method, as Hegel had begun to do in his philosophy of history, to the study of human society, and particularly to the relations between the classes.

Lenin used the dialectical method with a master hand in the strategy of the Bolshevik Revolution and in laying the foundations of socialist society in the Soviet

Union. The Soviet system itself, with its centralism and its democracy, expresses the dialectical unity of opposites. The place of Lenin in Communist philosophy is a controversial issue. Like everything else in the Communist world it is fought under a slogan, which in this case is, "Lenin *versus* Plekhanov." The older school limits Lenin's contribution to putting into practice Marxian principles as they were developed by Plekhanov, the leading Russian Communist philosopher before Lenin's appearance, with whom he carried on a long and victorious controversy. The younger school, which is now in power, holds that Lenin represents a new theoretical stage in the development of dialectical materialism. His particular contribution is the unfolding of the law of the unity of interpenetrating opposites, which he considered the heart of dialectics and subject to unlimited development. But, as Stalin says in his "Leninism," Lenin also *undertook the great task of generalising, on behalf of materialistic philosophy, the main achievements of science since the days of Engels, and of comprehensively criticising the anti-materialistic trends of certain Marxists.*

There is in Moscow a Lenin Institute devoted to editing his works and other documents relating to his period. As its work proceeds, Lenin's standing as a philosopher becomes clearer. Two quotations from widely separated quarters will show how generally his method has become accepted. The first is from the symposium of the "Economics of Labor" prepared by the Communist Academy:

Briefly the nucleus of dialectics is reduced to the study of the unity of opposites. This latter presupposes the study of each phenomenon in itself and in its relation to other phenomena. Each phenomenon must be studied in its manifold developments with its inner contradictions and on the basis of their movement and their inner conflict. Thus each phenomenon is viewed as the unity of opposites. Dialectics presupposes a unity of analysis and synthesis, that is the investigation of separate parts of the aspects of phenomena taken separately and the summing up and combining of these separate parts revealing not only the qualitative but the quantitative differences of the whole from the characteristics of its separate parts.

As an example of these transitions, Lenin pointed out the struggle of the content with the form and the inverse changing of the form by the content, that is the transition of quantity into quality. On the basis of revealing these contacts and transitions is opened the endless process of the new study of phenomena.

The second quotation is from an editorial on "The Philosophy of Literary Art" in the "Magazine of the Russian Association of Proletarian Writers," 1931, No. 2. It follows a brief outline of the tasks which are to be undertaken by proletarian literature:

This means to master Lenin's theory of the creative method and the application of dialectics as understood by Lenin, viz., the splitting of the unity and the struggle of the opposites on the basis of the leading opposite which is the essence of materialistic dialectics.

The struggle for the Leninite stage implies the necessity of acquiring one of the basic deciding peculiarities of Leninism, namely the Leninist concreteness, the ability to analyse all questions in terms of the peculiarities of the precise concrete historical moment, of the specific concrete stage of the class struggle.

To develop further the philosophic theory of Lenin as he developed the theory of Marx and Engels, and

CHAPTER XVI

THE DIALECTICAL METHOD

While he has a guiding theory, the Communist philosopher derives his formula for social action from an analysis of the facts in the given situation, but always in relation to their historic background. On the basis of this analysis, he then projects the situation from its actual status to all its possible directions and makes a choice between them.

A STIMULUS TO SOCIAL CREATIVITY

It is thus evident that the use of this method develops social creativity. The dialectical analyst does not simply judge which of the opposites in the given situation has come to prevail and then follow it. He decides when the time is ripe for human energy to force to dominance the factor he desires to come to power. The Communists desire a classless society. They conclude by historic analysis that it can only be realised by the working class. Hence they help them to power for this purpose, not merely to give them the victory over the capitalists. It is in such union of choice of values with selection of measures that the mind and will become socially creative. The latter alone is only opportunism; the former is sterile idealism.

It is evident that the subjective factors of courage and decisiveness play a large part in the successful use of dialectical analysis. In 1917, Lenin constantly held back his party from making a premature attempt to seize power until the strategic moment arrived. He stressed the will to victory and quarrelled with the Mensheviks because of their drifting. Similarly his followers today denounce any deterministic dependence on the dialectical method as being quite foreign to its nature. In the monthly, "For the Proletarian Art," an article on the "Problem of the Cultural Legacy," discussing what vital elements to select from it, points out that the dialectical method is not the *mechanical selection of dominant or majority elements* as is being done by some Marxists elsewhere; on the contrary it *selects from the concrete situation by analysis, the creative, revolutionary, world transforming elements and joining with them, helps them on to victory.*

Similarly in his article "The Creative Scissors" A. Afinogenov insists that the method of placing opposites mechanically over against one another and assuming that one will destroy the other is not the dialectical method. By this method the opposites are removed to a higher plane where they appear in another unity, involving different relationships between them and immediately developing new contradictions. The union of capitalistic and socialistic elements at the present time in the Soviet Union is again the best large-scale example. An excellent smaller example in that scene is the changing status of the family. The mechanistic dialecticians were going to destroy it altogether. Now it appears that it has certain qualities that are both indestructible and needed, therefore these qualities are being transposed into a form of family life adapted to the machine age.

It might be said that materialist dialectics is an attempt to unite the scientific method with philosophy.

Indeed the Communists like to call it a science. By that term, the feeling of certainty is increased. Marx gave them the lead by saying that philosophy must become *a philosophic science.* New members of the Party are told that *The teaching of Marx and Lenin—Marxo-Leninism—is for the proletariat the most important science. The Party program is based upon this science.* The phrase *scientific Marxian analysis* is also quite common. For example, in its decree concerning primary and secondary schools, the Central Committee of the Party resolves that *All Commissariats of Education should make a scientific Marxian analysis of present programs.* . . . It is this attempted guidance of the opposites in history and life that gives an entirely different significance to the contradictions appearing in the Soviet Union than belongs to the contradictions of capitalism. The former are the recognised and controlled characteristics of a transition period which is being guided toward its goal, the latter have become destructive cleavages in a society no longer able to manage its affairs.

IN ECONOMICS AND GOVERNMENT

After the mechanists were put out of high office in 1929, it appeared that the philosophical leadership at the Communist Academy did not sufficiently represent the actual work of the Party. It was not dealing with concrete problems and seemed to be nearer to Hegelian idealism than to Leninism. The result was a change in the staff. The new leadership has seminars working on the application of the dialectical method to collectivisation, to the natural sciences and other practical needs.

It also analyses material from all the scientific institutes and from the Central Committee of the Party, in order to make generalisations wherever possible.

The economists have made the dialectical method quite prominent in their work. How they use it may be seen in the Communist Academy Symposium on the "Economics of Labor":

In beginning the study of economics of labor we make it our chief aim to learn to apply the fighting theoretical weapon of Marxo-Leninism in the class struggle for the conquest and penetration of socialist organisation of labor.

The study of theory must *reveal the laws of constructive socialism in a given concrete situation,* must show the student how critically to overcome all the anti-proletarian approaches to the labor question and how to aid correct planning and social regulating of the organisation of labor.

The method is dialectic materialism. It compels us to view everything we study historically in the process of its changes, to gauge its movements from the point of its conception to its dying off, to observe it all-sidedly, in its multiplicity and its unity, with all its contradictions, as the phenomena of separate productive relations. We must guard against the danger of mechanistic materialism but equally against the Menshevik idealistic heresy. . . .

Due to the application of these principles of dialectics we can establish the relation of the basis to the superstructure, we may study the contradictory development of productive forces and relations in production. On the basis of the dialectic method we can study the historically conditioned economic categories which express definite relations in production.

In the matter of economic incentives the dialectical method works out a union of the personal and the collective interest which are so separated in capitalist motivation. This was done theoretically by Marx, Engels, and Lenin. Concretely it is being realised in the present situation: for the unregenerate, in a skilful mixture of higher wages and the appeal of the Plan; for those of the true faith, in an equally effective expansion of personal influence and power in proportion to devotion to the common cause.

In the forming of government policies, the dialectical method naturally plays a leading rôle. All important decrees have a philosophical preamble. Elsewhere if a philosophic mind happens to get into political office, as in the cases of Balfour and Poincaré, its writings are an excursion from administrative and legislative duties. The latter are affected by them only indirectly. In the Soviet Union every policy is thoroughly scrutinised and evaluated by the prevailing philosophic method before the various gatherings of the Party and the Comintern. The NEP and the Five Year Plan were both worked out, and indeed fought out, this way. The Soviet foreign policy manifestly rests on a skilful use of the interpenerating contradictions between the capitalist powers and again between them and the Soviets. Thus Plato's ideal of a government by philosophers is realised in a form far different from that control by an intellectual ruling class which he desired.

The recent Party disputes over deviations to the right or to the left have combined philosophical and practical differences. The Stalin group now contends that Trotsky and the Leftists, Bukharin and the Right Opportunists, both failed in their dialectical analysis of the peasant situation; also Tomski in the matter of the labor unions and their function. At the Sixteenth Party Congress, Stalin illustrated the political use of the dialectical method in his report when he was discussing "Deviations on the Question of Nationalities." He defined these as two, toward Great Russian jingoism and toward local nationalism. He then contended that the apparent contradiction involved in the stimulation of national cultures during the dictatorship of the proletariat by those who desired in the future to achieve their amalgamation into one common culture with one common tongue, was in fact a demonstration of *the dialectical quality of the Leninist way of treating the question of national culture.* (*They are being encouraged to*) *develop and expand, revealing all their potential qualities, in order to create the necessary conditions* (*for their later fusion*), *when the proletariat is victorious throughout the world and Socialism becomes an everyday matter.* This appears contradictory. So does the Bolshevik position regarding the state.

The highest possible development of the power of the state with the object of preparing the conditions for the dying away of the state. Yes it is contradictory;—but this contradiction is a living thing and completely reflects Marxist dialectics.

Or for example take Lenin's attitude towards the right of nationalities to self determination, up to and including separation—sometimes expressed in the simple formula "Separation for amalgamation"—it smacks even of the paradoxical. And yet this contradictory formula reflects that vital truth of Marxist dialectics which makes it possible for the Bolsheviks to storm the most impregnable fortresses in the sphere of the national question. . . . Whoever has failed to understand this peculiarity and contradictoriness of our historical times, whoever has failed to understand this dialectical character of the historical process is lost to Marxism. The unfortunate thing for our deviators is that they don't understand and don't want to understand Marxist dialectics.

Naturally a method to which is ascribed the authority of certainty gives great power to those who control the machinery for its interpretation and application, along with the right of excommunication. To claim infallibility is a continually besetting sin for those who enjoy the support of a confident doctrine. It is so easy to rationalise one's own policy as the correct dialectical line and to damn any opposition with the epithet "opportunism." Also there arises the perennial tendency toward traditionalism, to prove the correctness of the administrative line by the mere repetition of Lenin's words. Citations from him, properly selected, can be used on either side of the argument over differentiation or equalisation of income. Against these dangers, the dialectical method carries some protective characteristics. Its ultimate sanction is the need of the masses. Its tests are concrete. The approval necessary for the continuance of Communist administration is not votes but action. In all reports and speeches the increasing activity of the masses in the new socialist forms of labor and management, in the organisation of collective farms, in volunteer services in promoting the cultural revolution, is always cited as proof of the correctness of the Party line.

The best continuous view of the workings of the dialectical method in a government policy is provided by the peasant problem, on which everything else turns. Lenin once said, *So long as we live in a petty peasant country, there will be a firmer economic base for capitalism in Russia than for communism. This must never be forgotten.* His analysis of the different economic interests behind the apparent homogeneity of the peasant mass led him to the tactic of dividing it against itself and uniting the preponderant elements in alliance with the city proletariat. The approach to this lay through NEP one of whose slogans was *smytchka,* meaning alliance, between workers and peasants. To win the latter was one of the reasons for temporarily restoring the private market. Beyond that, Lenin urged the *successful promotion of camradely collective farming* as the only way for the working class to *convince the great peasant masses of their integrity and make them into staunch and reliable allies.* His analysis and program went further. He said, *There are two souls living within the peasant: one soul is that of the toiler, the other soul is that of the speculator, the petty trader.* As toiler the peasant is attracted toward socialism, as speculative grain-seller he is attracted toward capitalism. So Lenin wanted to hang on to and develop the toiler soul and to eliminate the other by changing its economic environment. One of these things is now being done in the collective farms, the other in the liquidation of the kulaks. Lenin was against forcing the pace: *Influence can only be brought to bear gradually and cautiously, through successful practical examples upon the millions of small peasant households.*

In extending this line of policy, the Party proceeded to squeeze the kulak out of the market by developing great mechanised state farms that raised and sold grain cheaper, and to attract the middle peasant into alliance with the poor peasant in the collective farms, with the economic advantage of tractors, better seed, and credits for buildings and livestock. When the middle peasants began to come into the collective farms in great numbers, when state farms and collective farms together were able to produce sufficient grain to make up for the loss of kulak production, it was judged the time to "liquidate the kulaks as a class." This decision came after a decisive struggle within the Party. The Lefts led by Trotsky had wanted to advance against the kulaks earlier. But their policy, said Stalin to the Sixteenth Party Congress, would have thrown the middle peasants into the arms of the kulaks and given them domination because there was not collective production to replace theirs. The revolt of Trotsky, however, compelled the Party to make the thorough dialectical analysis of the peasant situation with which Stalin supported his claim to the Congress, that the Party had "correctly chosen the moment in passing to a resolute offensive along the whole front in the second half of 1929." This included speeding up the tempo of the industrial section of the Five Year Plan in order to supply the needs of the rapidly increasing collective farms.

The Right Opportunists, led by Bukharin, had wanted to slow up the whole movement. They thought the kulak could be educated into socialism and they advocated raising the price of bread as a step in this direction. Then they would have tried to educate him in co-operation and make him a part of the economic machinery of the state. The philosophers said that this policy of Bukharin was the practical expression of his mechanistic philosophy which calls for a continuity of events without breaks, whereas dialectical materialism presupposes not only the interpenetration of opposites but also the necessity of splitting them apart when the historic moment is ripe. Stalin asked what guarantee Bukharin had that the kulak would not make use of his improved position to utilize the poor peasant as a labor force and so create a capitalist state within a state. Before the Party he contended that the policy of the Rights would have "left us stranded and given domination to the kulaks" by delaying collectivisation and slowing up industrial development, thus producing a crisis and a shortage of grain. Consequently the Congress decided that the Rights are kulak agents in the ranks of the Party and all who share their views must leave it.

When the offensive was started, its success was endangered by the zeal of those who, contrary to the instructions of the Central Committee, tried to push through the whole campaign in one spring, and in some cases used coercion, and in others set up communes instead of collective farms. The result was to incite the spirit of revolt among the peasants in certain regions which, if it could have been used by its enemies, would have been a serious menace to the safety of the Soviet Union. The situation was changed by Stalin's famous speech "Dizziness from Success." But this forcing of the pace really delayed the collectivisation movement, as the peasants who had been coerced, or had come in without preparation or conviction, soon left the collective farms; some never to return and others only after much evidence of their superiority. Why then did this movement get so far before it was stopped? Some observers think that the information that came to headquarters was inadequate; others that Rykov, then Chairman of the Council of People's Commissars, was not working wholeheartedly with Stalin, others that the leaders were opportunistically waiting to see if the forced pace would succeed. In either case, disaster came near and the situation was only retrieved by an authoritative repudiation of compulsion and a consistent use since then of the educational method. The result has been a genuine growth of collectivisation, so that Molotov was enabled to report to the Seventeenth Party Conference as the second result of the Five Year Plan—the first being the growth of industrial construction:

A fundamental change has taken place in agriculture . . . the collective and state farms. This represents a complete change of mind in the masses of small and middle peasants in favor of socialism. This . . . solves the most essential and most difficult problem of the proletarian revolution and is of world historical significance.

When the dialectical method is thus used in making the policies of government and in giving direction to society, it provides a connection between the past, the present, and the future which at some points is similar to that afforded by trust in the guiding hand of Providence. There is the same sense of certainty of direction; the difference is that for the dialecticians it proceeds from a process of reason which can be checked, instead of coming from a faith whose object is beyond scientific analysis. The responsibility laid on human beings is also different. For the Communist the future does not depend at all upon the will of God but upon the correct analysis of the present in the light of the past and the will to act accordingly. He is confident that man can, by selecting, rearranging, and developing certain factors of history, move forward toward the world of his desire. The only limitations he acknowledges are the blind, uncontrolled forces in nature and the accidental in history. That this is not Utopianism but scientific prophecy and creative action is the Communist claim. But part of its strength undoubtedly comes from Utopian elements—its faith in man as the conscious culmination of the cosmic process, as both a part of nature and its master; and more particularly, its faith in the invincibility of the proletarian mass as the creators of the best possible form of society.

IN SCIENCE

In the field of science the use of the dialectical method at once gives rise to an interpretation of its nature and function in terms of the class struggle. From the Soviet point of view there is no such thing as pure science, standing objectively above the battle of life. Its neutrality in the contest of politics and the struggle of social forces is only a pose which it is impossible to maintain. It never is and never can be the private concern of individuals, interested only in scientific discovery. Its general direction, like that of art, will always be determined by the social-economic environment which generates and nourishes it. Therefore the Soviet scientists, in every international gathering in which they appear, always attack the position of "science for science's sake." Among such offensives in the papers of the Soviet delegates to the Second International Congress of the History of Science and Technology in 1931, there stands out this phrase of B. Zavadovzky: . . . *scientific theories express not only the actual state and level of knowledge attained by science but also the ideological justification of the economic interests of warring groups and classes.*

This viewpoint was naturally the point of division at the Seventh International Psychotechnical Conference held in Moscow, also in the summer of 1931, since this branch of science applies psychology to the management of industry and particularly to the human relations involved. Some of the delegates from other countries, despite the fact that the direction and limits of their work as investigators in factories were obviously set by the firms which employed them and by the general nature of the capitalist system, contended vigorously for objective science. Others, and the Soviet delegation was not alone in this, took the dialectical view, and the general secretary of the International Psychological Association, the outstanding French authority in the field, explained in detail why he considered it the only genuine scientific point of view. The basic difference between the two views was analysed by Professor I. Spielrein to consist in the fact that the bourgeois approach was based on the premise that the peculiarities of human nature are biologically determined while the Soviet approach, resting on the dialectical understanding of the motive powers of human society, stressed the part of the social environment in determining human characteristics and the mutability of all those psychic differences which are determined by heredity.

In one instance the main idea is selection, in the other education. In one instance the affirmation that science stands outside of classes and seeks eternal unchanging truth, seeing its goal in service to humanity; in the other the stressing of the class character of science, of the party character of the truth it seeks to discover.

The latter phrase refers of course not to the nature of a scientific discovery, but to the uses to which it is put. Is it to serve the classes or the masses? At this point the dialecticians enter the lists in the longstanding argument over the relation between theoretical and applied science. Here is the culmination of their attempt to remove the distinction between theory and practice. They admit the extremely complicated nature of the question but they contend that the rigid definitions of formal logic do not allow for the actual fact of the continual passing of one into the other or for the relativity of the conceptions of the concrete and the abstract. They point out that the relations between theory and practice change with the historic situation and that their planned socialist economy is both calling for the largest possible development of scientific research and continually throwing up new problems for research scientists to work upon. For instance, Professor Colman maintains that only a planned economy can present problems that demand the *complex participation of various branches of mathematics, for example, calculation of probability combined with differential geometry, or calculation of variation and the theory of numbers.*

It is thus the Communist contention that when they insist on science performing a social function, instead of limiting it to a purely utilitarian rôle, they are giving the greatest possible stimulus to the development of new theories and the widest possible field for their application. They contrast the limitation of inventions under capitalism, and the contraction of opportunities for scientific training and research by the present world depression, with the increase of scientific training and research, and the growth of inventiveness, in the Soviet Union. They point to a larger interest in scientific theory on the part of the masses than appears elsewhere. They contend that the influx of new men and women from the working class into the ranks of the sciences generates scientific creativity.

It is at this point that Soviet leaders raise their claim for the creation of a new type of culture as well as a new economic system, a new life as well as a new philosophy. It is life organised for the first time on the basis of science, it is a culture in which theoretical thought and the experience of the workers are united, that they are trying to develop. They expect to unify science behind their social purpose by the penetration into all its disciplines of a single method—the method of dialectical materialism. They are confident of achieving a social synthesis through a common culture created by the masses themselves. The All-Union Scientific Research Planning Conference in an address to *all proletarians throughout the world, honest scientists of all countries and the heroic builders of the Soviet Union* prophesies that: *All applied sciences will go hand in hand with the valiant fighters . . . to overtake and outstrip the advanced capitalist countries within the coming decade, to emerge as the world center of a new powerful, socialist technique of proletarian culture, revolutionary science and socialist labor.*

A perusal of the reports of Soviet delegates at international scientific conferences shows that they also sound the evangelistic note. They are manifestly desirous of converting their fellow scientists to the dialectical method. They are advocating the reconstruction of science itself by the use of this tool. They believe that it can overcome the contradictions within science itself—for instance between determinism and chance—because they think that these only reflect the contradictions in capitalism which are now causing its disintegration.

The Soviet papers at the International Congress of the History of Science at London in the summer of 1931 dealt with the use of the dialectical method only in general terms, interspersed with affirmations of faith. It will *destroy the old traditions of metaphysical methodology that now hamper science.* (*Only by investigations from this standpoint*) *shall we be able to work out the problem of the conditions in which the opposing factors of a law melt into each other, . . .* says

Professor Colman the mathematician. After a technical analysis of six gulfs now existing in the field of mathematics he insists there is only one way out, *conscious, planned reconstruction on the basis of materialist dialectics*. A plan can only be drawn up by collective work and only in a country where the national economy and science are planned and the total experience can be coordinated. The foundations must be supplied by a dialectical study of the history of mathematics, comparing its development in different social epochs. A volume of this sort is now in preparation.

Whatever may or may not be the future value for particular sciences of the dialectical method there remains the significant fact that it is making of science in general the same demand that it makes of philosophy—to change the world as well as explain it, and to do this consciously in the direction of a scientifically approved social goal. As B. Hessen puts it:

The great historical significance of the method created by Marx lies in the fact that knowledge is not regarded as a passive, contemplative acceptance of reality, but as a means to effect its active reconstruction. For the proletariat, science is a means and instrument of this reconstruction. That is why we are not afraid to expose the "earthy origin" of science, and its close relations with the methods of production of material existence. Only such a conception of science can be its real liberator from those fetters with which it is inevitably burdened in class bourgeois society.

IN THE ARTS

In fulfilment of its unifying function in the world of culture the dialectic method is rapidly penetrating all the arts. As S. Romov points out in reviewing the art exhibitions season of 1931, *Soviet artists and bourgeois artists are separated not by differences of stylistic schools but by two different world conceptions. With us in the USSR, the chief determining feature of art is its social purpose and its saturation with ideas.* The ideas are of course the teachings of Marx and Lenin, and the social purpose is the building of socialism as the way to a Communist society. Whether it be in literature, theatre, painting, or music, the proletarian artist is one who views life from the standpoint of dialectical materialism and actually participates in the reconstruction of society according to its methods.

At the present moment this means first of all that he and his art enlist for active service in the class struggle. In its resolution on "The Creative Principles of Proletarian Music" adopted at its first conference, the Russian Association of Proletarian Musicians declared:

The Association regards the creative work of the proletarian composers as an implement of the class struggle of the proletariat. Proletarian music reflects the rich many sided psychology of the proletariat which is historically advanced and (dialectically conceiving and understanding the world of class) must penetrate by its deepest roots into the very substratum of the worker and peasant masses, unite their emotions, their thought and their will, and raise the masses for further struggle and construction.

They expound this theme by finding the origins of proletarian music in the class struggle. Also the dangers and contradictions of its first period, they ascribe to the fact that *the composers were not organically related to the working class and did not sufficiently grasp the method of dialectical materialism.* In the winter of

1931–2 in Moscow there was held a series of discussions concerning the creative method in the proletarian literary movement. A. Selwanovski reported on proletarian poetry:

. . . *An acute class struggle is going on; the wiping out of the remaining roots of capitalism is in progress; a new type of productive relationships is being born, and with this a new type of thinking, feeling and morality. Yet in proletarian poetry, petty bourgeois influences still dominate to a considerable extent . . . the classes which are being dislodged and eliminated are carrying on a bitter struggle in the sphere of art, especially poetry. . . .*

He outlined this struggle as a battle of styles, and described some of the tendencies that hinder the development of the dialectical method in poetry.

The dialectical method, according to the resolution on Creative Method adopted by the Plenum of the Federation of Workers in Special Arts, also demands "a critical re-evaluation and an overcoming of all inherited stylistic achievements." This re-evaluation however is not to be carried on in a "laboratory experimental manner but in practice," it is to be related to the actual problems of the reconstructive period. The problem of the cultural legacy is to be overcome by surpassing not by ignoring, by selecting and developing the elements that are close to the thought and life of the proletariat. The same course holds for the classical technique in music, according to the resolution of the Proletarian Musicians, which proclaims:

Simultaneously with the participation of the proletarian composer in the construction work and the struggle of the working class and an intense study of Marxo-Leninism, it is equally necessary critically to study the legacy of the past, the mastering of which is one of the conditions which determines the development of a new proletarian musical style. First of all the study of Moussorgsky and Beethoven must be continued. But the chief emphasis must be made at this present moment in mastering the Beethoven creative method.

Concerning this problem of the creative method dialectical discussion makes some significant claims. The proletarian musicians maintain that proletarian music inevitably creates a great variety of genres which none of the others (stylistic formations) ever possess. The old methods are impotent to develop the new themes:

The theme of internationalism cannot be developed by the method of abstract symbolism which ignores the complete forms of the class struggle of the international proletariat, which solves this problem upon the plane of mystical cosmism (or relation to the cosmos) and the middle class idealistic cosmopolitanism.

The theme of socialist reconstruction of the village, the breaking up and the re-education of the psychology of the millions of peasants cannot be interpreted by the method of passive stylisation of the images of the peasant musical thought which has grown on the basis of a natural economy (i.e., simple, mutual exchange). Neither by the method of individualistic impressionism which proceeds from the primary biological origins, that is from the dominance of natural over social and class elements in the environment.

Compositions are beginning to appear which indicate a new form of symphonism. It is not purely instrumental but choral music, says D. Gachev, *the substance of which is a dialectical development passing through contradictions, and unfolding consecutively great musical action.* An example is "The Raising of a Railway Car" from Davidenko's unfinished opera, "1919." It gives a picture of the struggle of a human mass to overcome obstacles by collective labor.

In architecture the new forms in Soviet cities are attempts to express the Marxian definition of architectural art as "a dialectical unity of technics and ideology." On this basis the Communist architects are trying on the one hand to overcome that extreme functionalism which finally *denies that architecture is an art and transforms a building into a machine* and on the other that extreme formalism which *considers architecture as an abstract form isolated from life and subject to the "eternal" laws of beauty.*

No section of art is without some manifestation of dialectical influence. The museum workers announce a new thing in museum work, the complex exposition, *based on a chronological foundation and on the class principle.* The latter has been applied by means of *a parallel exposition of chronological, contemporary life-conditions of different classes.* The Associations of Revolutionary Cinema Workers *want the artist not to confine himself to a mechanistic demonstration of the facts of our reality but also to reveal its deep inner contradictions. . . . An artist must make his relation to reality apparent in his picture.*

In the theatre, the young Communist actor studies his part dialectically, seeking to bring out the conflicts and struggles which lie at the bottom of the dramatic problem of the play. Reviewing the results of the Moscow season of 1930–31, P. Markov finds that the Soviet stage has passed from its first period of portraying the dramatic events of the new age into the generalisation of its social experience. *A single fact told in a performance becomes a condensed reflection of a great problem.*

But in the worst performances all that appears is a photographic copy of current happenings. The theatres however have opened a fight against this *primitive naturalism* and the battle is nearly won. *It gives way to an analysis of reality in the light of dialectical materialism, in its development, in its passionate and violent fight, in the richness of colors and figures, in the psychologic penetration without embellishing masks, . . . in the aspiration broadly and boldly to reveal the fundamental laws governing our time.*

In like manner the proletarian writers announce that dialectical realism must finish forever with the naturalistic, photographic method of description. It must draw living men and women with all the inner contradictions they still possess as a hangover from a past not yet completely banished. In proletarian writing psychological analysis is never an aim in itself, as it often is with bourgeois writers, *trying to save themselves from the contradictions of reality by escaping into some metaphysical hothouse of the "soul."* When it is used to portray the changing mentality of the participants in the class struggle and the continuing revolution, it becomes a factor in the reshaping of their minds. The accurate portrayal of this emerging new man requires an understanding of Lenin's teaching concerning the relation of the general and the separate, which in this case are the mass and the individual. *This means that the opposites (the separate opposed to the general) are the same: the separate does not exist otherwise than in that relation which leads to the general. The general exists only in the separate, through the separate. Each separate (in one way or another) is the general. Each general is a part (or an aspect or the essence) of the separate. . . .*

Eisenstein, the film producer, is criticised for not thus

analysing the relations between the mass and the individual. *The masses are taken arithmetically . . . as a simple sum of separate items. The artist thinks quantitatively . . . he cannot understand that the sum of hundreds and thousands of men produces a whole greater than its parts, that out of the added quantities a new quality arises.*

In his article, "The Creative Scissors," Afinogenov contends, after describing in detail what the dialectical method demands in the creation of an "image," that creative work is as unlimited as dialectics itself. He maintains that dialectical materialism is not a levelling process or an attempt to squeeze everything into the same forms but a creative method which contains unlimited possibilities of variety, with infinite shadings in its portrayal of actuality.

The climax of the influence of the dialectical method in the arts, however, is its demand that the artist shall become creative socially as well as æsthetically. Working class literature must itself become one of the immediate factors in the remoulding of men's minds. Music must select themes, and unfold them in ways which will *organise the consciousness of the proletarian towards his final goal as the constructor of the communist society.* A favorite phrase of Afinogenov is *changing actuality by means of art.* In the theatre this means changing in a corresponding manner the thoughts and emotions of the people to whom the theatre appeals. *Thus the production not only reflects actuality but in itself becomes a factor which changes it. The creative image thus becomes the criterion and indicator of the movement of actuality. In this manner the artist (author, actor, producer) ceases to be a superficial entertainer but includes himself in the system of the social life through the cre-*

ative transfiguration of this life in the images of the artistic production.

In similar vein the monthly journal of the workers in spacial arts calls upon them to become active participants *in the socialist remaking of the psycho-ideology of the working masses.* The monthly journal of the proletarian artists is more specific. It finds the dialectical problem of the painter in the current struggle between the old and the new modes of life, between individualist and collectivist morals and psychology. This demands an emphasis on the creative will. The dialectical method requires art to proceed from actuality itself and to change it by advancing those processes and tendencies which lead to the revolutionary socialist transformation of the whole of life. Thus the effect of Communist philosophy upon art and the artist is to give them a larger purpose and a deeper motivation.

A REVOLUTIONARY PHILOSOPHY

It is apparent from even this cursory glance at the nature and workings of dialectical materialism that it is not simply a philosophy of revolution but a revolutionary philosophy. It continually demands change and provides a method for moving life from one plane to another. It departs altogether from the academic tradition of pure thought, just as it does from pure science and pure art. It uses the reflective thinking which follows after action to lead to more action. It calls for a continual series of action-thought-action, constantly breaking and uniting these opposites to achieve new forms of human living. This essential and distinguishing characteristic of their system is relied upon by Communists to prevent it from succumbing to the fatal tendency of every school of thought to become a stereotype. They insist that its capacity to keep mankind from stagnation is its great virtue. They maintain that it cannot produce a monotonous world because by its nature its categories of thought must be as varied as life itself, they cannot be limited to those it has so far formulated and used.

It is inevitable that the tendency to rely upon authority should already appear in Communist circles. It is natural that students should say, "when we are in doubt we go to the words of Lenin," and that professors can be found who speak of Marxism as though it were a final, unchangeable, metaphysical truth. Such attitudes are regarded by active dialecticians as holdovers from the former authoritarian world which will be overcome in due time. They themselves say that a true Marxist cannot use the proof text method, nor stand upon the letter of the law, because Marxism is not Marx but a method that distinguished him from the metaphysicians because it provides for constant movement. In the controversy with the mechanists it was asserted that to quote the text of Marx on issues concerning which the facts were not accessible to him was anti-Marxism. If, however this type of Communist is asked whether any one is free today to improve on Lenin as Lenin improved on Marx he objects to the form of the question. He contends that what happened was that Lenin concreted Marx for his generation, a process required by the dialectical method. "Leninism" he says, "is Marxism in our epoch. We adapt it to our needs." This is exactly what the followers of Jesus, Buddha, and Mahomet are now doing. But the Marxo-Leninists would object to being put in that category. They emphatically are not revisionists but extenders of the Marxian line whose nature is, they insist, that it requires continual extension. It is in this sense, allowing for some concession to the cult of hero worship and to the inevitable authority of a commanding figure, that Stalin used the magnetic phrase "Under the Banner of Lenin" in the peroration of his report to the Sixteenth Party Congress before a series of brief sentences reciting past successes and impending triumphs.

There is a point, however, at which the dialecticians proclaim and submit themselves to a final authority in their thinking. They regard the essence of the dialectical method as unchangeable. It takes different forms in different historic situations, it develops various working principles, but as a principle of method it is final. Yet paradoxically this is not finality because it requires always the movement of all things, which is its basic hypothesis. Therefore it does not check the initiative of the mind, without which society stagnates, but continually incites it. That it halts at questioning the method itself seems to the dialecticians only common sense. "You do not waste your time questioning the axioms of geometry; they are sufficiently demonstrated," is their answer when this point is raised. They regard their attitude as scientific not dogmatic. They contrast it with the paralysing scepticism and tentativeness of liberalism as that degree of certainty which is necessary to action and to human progress. They hold that the dialectical process is demonstrated in nature, in history and in the workings of the mind, and that by it man is enabled to control all three of these to his chosen end.

There remains the question of whether the Party, which is the guardian and administrator of this powerful and reliable method, will not thereby become an end in itself. History is full of cases in which a priesthood guarding a sacred truth has become the ruling power and finally more mighty than the truth itself, which it has then corrupted and destroyed. The Communist leaders recognise this danger and try to avert it by continually recruiting from the masses. But they rely more on teaching the masses to think and act according to the dialectical method, for that will make the Party ultimately unnecessary. In the Communist society where people will be sufficiently intelligent to choose wisely, and socially minded enough to act for the common weal, its leadership will not be needed. Stalin recognises this in his "Leninism":

It follows from this that as soon as class has been abolished, as soon as the dictatorship of the proletariat has been done away with, the Party likewise will have fulfilled its function and can be allowed to disappear.

This calls to mind a passage at the end of the Bible that forecasts a society in which there will be no church because none is needed, but today one does not see much recognition among ecclesiastical organisations of the desirability of such a situation, nor much active working for the end of institutional religion. But the Communists do not rely upon faithfulness to the original vision for breaking the death grip of custom. They depend upon the extension throughout the masses of those capacities which both enable and require the abolition of all overhead powers. They are doing consciously what the church did unknowingly in Western Europe when it began to spread knowledge, to the ultimate destruction of its own authority.

CHAPTER XVII

THE TRANSFER OF MOTIVATION

If the historic scene is to be kept moving in the direction of the Bolshevik social goal, the motivation of the Party—its revolutionary vision together with the philosophy which supplies it with rational support and concrete means for realisation—must be diffused throughout the population. The number of activists must be continually increased. This is being accomplished in several ways.

BY EDUCATION

The educational system is dialectically devised for the purpose of developing people who will be not only builders of socialism but also makers of the Communist society. In his book, "The New Education in the Soviet Republics," which is available in English, Professor A. P. Pinkevitch declares the intention of Communist educators to make class-conscious warriors for socialism, who will be able to fight and to create *in the interests of the proletariat and consequently, in the final analysis, in the interest of the whole of humanity. . . . The aim is, so to speak, the indoctrination of the youth in the proletarian philosophy . . . all that trains a truly socialistic morality will occupy the first place.* This general purpose is officially stated in the first clause of the preamble to the decree of the Central Committee of the Party concerning primary and secondary schools: *Following the path of realising the program of the*

Communist Party according to which "the school must be, not only the conductor of principles of Communism in general, but also the conductor of the ideological organised educational influence of the proletariat upon the semi-proletarian and non-proletarian strata of the toiling mass, with the purpose of educating a generation fit to establish complete Communism," the proletarian state has attained enormous success in the cause of spreading the school system and reconstructing the school.

From their earliest years in the nursery school and the kindergarten children are trained to be socially minded and so to act. This is not done by preaching principles but indirectly. They must help each other put on and fasten their clothes. They must learn how to hold meetings. They are taken to the factory and told what it all means. They are not considered separate from adult society, but members of it with rights and duties. Their picture books present life in its collective aspect; they teach them group games or portray the tasks of socialist construction with children assisting. For instance, out of a group of books selected for their illustrations, one for nursery age shows children learning traffic regulation; one for kindergarten age pictures the children getting up a play to celebrate International Youth Day. The new First Reader for country schools opens with "Go to work little kindergartners to build up socialism" and, after showing them how it is being done, ends with a forecast of world revolution whose slogan is, "We workers of the whole world jointly struggle against the capitalism of the whole world under the banner of the Comintern." The companion book for city schools opens with "Let us organise our life and work" and closes with "Enemies cannot destroy our banner. We are building socialism in the USSR and we are able to defend it." This is followed by a picture of the Soviet flag and the slogan "Long Live the World Revolution."

The children are early introduced to current history. When the Sixteenth Congress of the Party was in session its meaning was taught in a fresh-air colony to children who were from three to nine years of age, in the following manner. To the youngest the phrase "The big men of the Party are meeting in Moscow" was repeated for several days; for the four-year-olds a sentence was added—"to make life better for people in the villages"; for each year of age another sentence was added until the nine-year-olds knew the elements of collectivisation. Teachers say that they can pick out children who have not been through the collective training of the kindergarten ("mothers' pets" they call them) by their egoism and possessiveness. They correct these tendencies by games requiring mutual aid, by seating a selfish child beside an unselfish one and by reasoning with the delinquents. Self-government begins with the lowest grades, but children are elected not to office but to leadership in the social work required of all. This begins with improving conditions in the school, for instance the collective meal. It goes on to helping a child who has become vagrant because both parents are working, or to visiting the poorer children who are helped out of a common fund for which all parents are assessed proportionately to their wages. If a drunken father is found, the children themselves take the case to the labor union at the factory.

In the third grade brigades are formed for social duties and for study. This method runs through the whole educational system. It unites groups of four or five students for collective work in the classroom or study. Sometimes strong and weak students are mixed and the average grouped together; sometimes the average are mixed in some brigades with the strong and in others with the weak. Some higher institutions have found this retards the strong too much and they now, by student action, put weak, average, and strong in brigades by themselves. No matter how the grouping is done, the effect is the same in the development of the practice of mutual aid, of collective thinking and action. One Russian-American professional man who had gone back to help the land of his birth remarked that he noticed in his own child and her companions a distinct change from the egoistic to the social incentive as compared with the days of his youth. "Now they put society first," he said, "they help each other to study instead of some trying to get ahead of others." Also he observed more solidarity between the pupils and the administration.

It is also manifest that the children feel themselves part of the socialist system. In the apartment house in which we stayed in Moscow, a boy of nine appeared at a meeting of the house committee and made a good speech, requesting a room to be set aside in the basement where the children could work and play. In his report on the work of the Pioneers to a textile factory conference of over a thousand workers, a boy of eleven told how some drunkards broke down the fence of an old orchard which had been given the children for their collective farm. They had complained to the factory administration who referred the matter to the educational authorities. "Nothing was done about it until we children persuaded the workers to repair it." The ten-year-old daughter of one family with whom we became acquainted was helping in the factory day-nursery after school and could describe its whole operations.

The work of the schools in developing social attitudes among children is ably seconded by the Young Pioneers' organisation. It penetrates all the lower grades and develops the capacity for self government and for social duties. Its aims are set forth by Krupskaya in familiar Communist terms, as though the children were adults—"no classes, no oppression, no exploitation, a full and happy life for all." The Pioneer leaders, always Komsomols, explain to the children the difference between capitalism and socialism; why they must defend and strengthen the growing socialist society; why and how the abolition of classes will come and material conditions will some day be equal so that the cultural capacities of all can be unfolded. The Pioneer books and papers portray again the tasks of socialist building and the children taking part in them. One of them tells the story of the Sixteenth Congress of the Party, its reports and resolutions, with photographs. It is done partly in rhyme and, by way of contrast, a sketch of Fascism in other countries is added. The practical result of all this is correctly summarised by Radek:

Every day, every hour, the child hears how we are creating a new society by great efforts, hears that the man who works, the man who helps carry out the Five Year Plan is a real man, but whoever does not help in this great cause is an enemy and a parasite.

. . . . as we lay the foundations of socialism, the children's socialist society is growing from below . . . is the authority which helps to overcome anti-social phenomena among children.

The social-mindedness that is early developed in Soviet children is soon crystallized into the spirit and purpose of the Party. To this end all schools, institutes, universities, and supplementary educational agencies teach history, social science, and economics from the revolutionary and class point of view. These courses are compulsory for all students even though their specialty is some form of engineering or one of the arts. Always the instruction is organised around the concrete data of socialist construction and world events. In discussing the problem of developing the feeling of international solidarity among the Pioneers, one of their leaders says: *A strike in Mansfeld or in Passaic, any great revolutionary event, must excite our youngsters, must stimulate in them the feeling of joy for the victory of the workers and the feeling of sadness in case of their defeat.* In the factories the newspaper "Pravda" is often the textbook for the political education courses organised by the Party, with whom the labor union combines in the effort to enroll as many workers as possible, making attendance one of the requirements for election to the rank of udarnik. In the schools, the terms "political education" and "social science" are used interchangeably; the general technical description being "social-political education." This part of the curriculum is naturally a special concern of the Party. In its decree on the primary and secondary schools the Central Committee, stressing the necessity of opposing *every effort to inject the children of the Soviet school with elements of an anti-proletarian ideology,* proposed to the Party organisations *to strengthen the leadership of the school and to take under their direct observation the organisation of the teaching of social-political disciplines in the seven-year schools, the pedagogical technicums and the pedagogical higher schools.*

In the earliest years of childhood social-political attitudes are formed indirectly, but by plan, in the kindergarten in addition to being imbibed increasingly from the atmosphere of the home. In the seven-grade school social-political education becomes more definite but is still more indirect than formal, being developed by activities auxiliary to the curriculum, not by specific courses. Its scope is revealed by the table of contents of the research report of I. I. Rufin on that subject. There are chapters on Education in Atheism, Internationalism, Collectivism, Revolutionary Activism, Social-Political education as a problem of Socialist Competition, Co-operation of School and Adult Population in the Establishment of Social-Political Education. The editorial introduction by one of the staff of the Moscow Research Institute of Scientific Pedagogy urges the teacher to remember that social-political education is the participation of the children in the solution of the political problems of the proletariat. The first chapter expands this definition:

Above all must be emphasised the class principle. Bourgeois pedagogics bases education outside of politics. This is a fraud. Social education will cease to be political only with the realisation of the Communist order when there shall be no class division in society.

In the seventh grade, that is for children of fourteen and fifteen, formal instruction in social-political education begins. In the secondary school, the subject breaks up into History of the Party, Five Year Plan, Building Socialism, The Transition to Communism. "A Working Plan in Social Science for the Seventh Year" that was seen by chance in action in a classroom in a small school in Moscow has for its first theme "Capitalism." An introductory talk by the teacher gives the class-struggle interpretation of history, describes class oppression in the capitalist order, declares the goal of the workers to be a classless society and the Soviet social order to be a "transitional stage called socialism." Then come three sub-themes and under each a list of questions to be discussed, with the hours assigned to them, an outline of methods of study and a list of references. These are the themes:

1. (*a*) *The principles and action of the law of value which determines the prices of goods and controls production in capitalist society.*

(*b*) *The shrewd mechanism of exploitation of workers by the bourgeoisie. The methods by which the labor of the working class is acquired by the capitalist. How labor is purchased and sold under capitalism. In what consists the power of capitalism over the workers and in what is the essence of their complete subjugation under capitalism.*

(*Then comes an outline of home work.*)

For 1. (*a*) *Prepare a graph of general change of social production under capitalism and interpret it in groups.*

(*b*) *Draw a graph of the impoverishment of the working class under capitalism and interpret it in class.*

(*c*) *Prepare a diagram of the level of wages of the worker in various countries and interpret it in the class.*

2. *Concentration and control of capital by means of corporations, trusts, etc.*

3. *Class stratification and exploitation in rural Russia.* (*Taken from Lenin.*) (*Showed process same here as in England; farm laborers drifted to cities and became proletariat.*)

In the educational Combinat in the factories about 15 per cent of the technical courses for workers is given to political education and political economy. The former covers the history of revolutions, the class struggle, and current events; the latter deals with problems of production with special emphasis on the difference between capitalist and socialist economy.

In addition to this formal instruction, the Red teachers and professors interpenetrate the whole educational system just as the Party interpenetrates all the activities of the masses. They have been specially trained to impart to the younger generation the motivation of the old revolutionaries by teaching them how and in what direction to reconstruct society and how to create the members of the new social order. Through the whole system runs the influence of dialectical materialism. Its educational function is to keep the present situation related to the future goal and to see that correct methods are used for its realisation. An instance of its effectiveness, casually met, was the resolution of a graduating class of the Polygraphic Institute in Moscow promising themselves to put into art the best technical work with a Marxist content and to set up proletarian art in place of the bourgeois variety. Incidentally they recommend that one of their number be not graduated because she had danced the fox-trot and was under the influence of anti-Soviet elements. Another they formally censured for being socially inactive, although she pleaded that she had met the formal requirements for social work.

Supplementing the educational system, the propaganda of press, posters, radio, and film continually evokes devotion to socialist building and world revolution. The social morality incited by the cinema is of course the opposite to that stimulated for the most part by films in capitalist countries. For Soviet movie audiences the aristocrat and capitalist are always the villains and the proletarian and Communist always the saviours, both in personal situations and for the world; for them not personal success but sacrificial devotion to the common cause is the ideal, collective efforts not personal exploits are glorified. All the forms of culture work incessantly to the same end—literature, art, music, drama. As in the golden days of the mediæval church they were focussed on the religious ideal and view of the world, so now they are directed toward the building of socialism and the development of a Communist society.

BY EXAMPLE AND CONTAGION

The Party also expects that its motivation will be diffused throughout the population by contagion from the example of its members. One of the basic differences between the Communist Party and other political organisations is that it takes hold of the whole life of its members, whereas they exclude matters of religion and personal conduct. To be a Communist means more than following a political-economic program, it means embracing a philosophy of life and conduct. It also involves submission to a discipline which requires one to be anti-religious in attitude and puritanical in behavior. In the latter respect it patterns after the monastic orders and the early Protestant sects rather than previous political parties. But its discipline is more enforceable than theirs. In the early days it rested upon the power to expel plus the difficulty of forming any rival organisation. Now it is also backed by control of economic resources and state machinery. The combination of a rigorous use of the power of expulsion with a compelling social ideal and arduous concrete tasks operates to attract and maintain a membership drawn from the highest types in the population.

The new member is told that the masses place special demands upon him, that they will judge the Party by his conduct and therefore he must be an example always—in work, in study, in his way of life, in the new socialist discipline. *The whole shop has got to see that Communists have higher labor-productivity, that they work better, that their output is better quality.* Krupskaya once described "What a Communist Should be Like":

First of all a Communist is a social person, with strongly developed social instincts who desires that all people should live well and be happy. . . .

Second, a Communist must understand what is happening about him in the world. . . . He must clearly picture whither society is developing. Communism must appear to him not only a desirable regime but exactly that regime to which humanity is going, where the happiness of some will not be based on the slavery of others and where there will be no compulsion except strongly developed social instincts. And the Communists must clear the road, as you clear a path in the wilderness, to hasten its coming.

Third, a Communist must know how to organise creatively. Suppose he is a medical worker, for instance. He must first know medicine, then the history of medicine in Russia and in other lands, then the communist approach to the problem of medicine, which means: how to organise and agitate wide masses of the population to create from the ranks of the toilers a powerful sanitary organisation in the cause of health.

Fourth, his personal life must be submitted to and guided by the interests of Communism. No matter how much he regrets giving up the comforts and ties of home, he must if necessary cast all aside, and go into danger wherever assigned. No matter how difficult the problem he must try to carry it out. He fights with everything that harms the cause of Communism. Nothing can leave him indifferent. Body and soul he must be devoted to the interests of the toiling masses and of Communism.

Stalin also has given us the two outstanding characteristics of the active Communist worker:

. . . Leninism is a school where the study of the theory and practice of Leninism produces a special type of Party and State official, a special kind of style in public work. What are the characteristics of this style? what its peculiarities?

There are two: (a) revolutionary zeal, inspired by the Russian spirit; and (b) businesslike practicality, inspired by the American spirit. The combination of these two in Party and State work constitute what we call "style" in our activities.

This definition is evidently an adaptation of a phrase of Lenin's which was further expounded by A. Severyanova in her report to the Komsomol Congress in 1931 on "Two Worlds and Two Systems of Education":

When we speak about the type of man we need we must take as a principle the following thesis of Lenin: "Calculation of forces, sobriety and fierce passions."

Among ordinary folk dreams are put over against facts, passion against sobriety and calculation of forces against revolutionary enthusiasm. Whereas the basic principles of communist education of the masses, the style of Bolshevik work, is based on the fact that alongside of concrete affairs there goes forward the revolutionary dream, and the sober practicalism of the or-

ganiser marches together with the enthusiasm of the revolutionist. . . .

Against the cheap emotionalism of bourgeois writers and poets we . . . advance an emotion which is infinitely higher, namely the emotion of the masterbuilder of the new life. . . . In this our education there is sobriety and fierce passion, there is love and hate, there is pride and glory and a dream. At the basis of all these emotions are the interests of the class, the struggle of the proletariat. This is our basic morals.

From this it should not be concluded that we destroy the common feelings of love, competition, pride, and dreams peculiar to every man. . . . We make them over in the process of struggle. We refine competition into emulation, we purge it of envy . . . we purge the healthy proletarian pride . . . from vainglory and snobbishness; we purge glory of careerism and selfseeking. . . .

The personal characteristics which the Communists are trying to develop provide not only examples but also leadership. In the crises of the struggle for the building of socialism the example and the contagious spirit of leaders are the factors that save the situation. In the last analysis industrial society depends upon the loyalty of the man with special knowledge. In emergencies the expert holds the key to the situation. This is one reason for the popularising of technical knowledge. It widens the base from which the technically gifted, the natural leaders in a scientific age, can rise, just as the area of selection for administrative posts, for the professions and the arts, was widened from the aristocracy to the middle class by the Industrial Revolution. In the promotion of technicians, loyalty to the common cause, as well as capacity, is a determining factor. Practically all of the group of young engineers who last year, after rigid selection from all over the country, gained the high reward of being sent abroad for further study, were either heroes of the civil war or had proved themselves true and tried in Komsomol and shock brigade activities.

The function of Communist leadership is twofold, both for the Party and for the individuals whom it puts into positions of prominence. They are to provide the masses with intellectual direction and a permeating dynamic. It is the combination of these qualities that is distinctively characteristic. The human expression of the attempted union of theory and practice is a blend of scholar and man of action, and the Communists expect to make this the general type. It is a truism that the necessity for outstanding leadership, and likewise the possibility of it, decreases as the level of intelligence rises. The cultural revolution accelerates this process. It is further speeded up by success in achieving the classless society, in which power is to be so widely distributed that social revolution becomes unnecessary. In the revolutionary situation the turn of events depends upon the leader. His initiative sets off the dynamite. In the constructive period, with its complexity of operations, group leadership is required. But in the Communist system there is always place for the unusual individual to acquire influence corresponding to his qualities, provided his devotion to the cause and capacity to co-operate are equally prominent.

In the dialectical view the mass and the leader are opposites which can interpenetrate for social progress as long as the leader recognises that the interests of the mass must predominate. Leaders must come out of the mass, be created by it and remain organically related to it. They voice the sub-conscious needs of the mass, see first the goal they must reach; in them the mass finds expression and focusses its will. The leaders' ability to sense correctly the present needs of the masses in relation to their ultimate goal is tested by the reaction of the activist groups in the population. Sometimes they must secure support for plans that require renouncing immediate needs in favor of the longer goal, as in the case of tightening belts to build heavy industries. Sometimes they must lead a retreat and yet be able to turn it into victory by keeping the vision of the ultimate goal always in view. This was the difficult requirement in the case of the NEP and in the present emphasis upon differential incomes.

To succeed, the Communist leaders must be able to transfer to the activist elements among the masses not only the vision of a goal and the revolutionary will to reach it no matter what the cost, but also something of their own capacity to understand and increasingly to use the intellectual method by which they chart their course. This is the explanation of the leadership of Marx and Lenin. Marx, in conjunction with Engels, combined an exceptional capacity for critical analysis and philosophic generalisation with emotional reaction to human values, and a willingness to sacrifice comfort and risk liberty for them and for his convictions. To these, in the decisive historical moment, Lenin added the courage and will to translate dialectical judgment into action. Practically unconscious of himself as an individual, he was absolutely sure of the ideas he had absorbed and the method he was using, confident that history and nature were behind him. This confidence he imparted to others, so that to the masses he becomes inevitably another symbol of authority, but to thinkers who accept his philosophy an inspiration and a guide to its further use for the same ends.

Similarly to impart to the people a sense of the certainty of the dialectical method and the invincibility of the Communist ideal is the need of the present leaders. They have the difficult task, according to their own philosophy, of deciding between interpenetrating opposites that continually change their position, such as their need for peace and their desire for the world revolution. This means practically that they have to keep the people intelligent and enthusiastic supporters of a course that cannot be sailed straight to its haven but on which one must constantly tack. As they overcome these difficulties and the contradictions in their situation grow less, the practical use for dialectical guidance will also diminish. Then, if it is to live, their philosophy must needs turn its attention to those inner contradictions in life itself, in the nature of the universe, with which religion at its best has been concerned. These, in its scornful rejection of religion, Communist philosophy has heretofore ignored as inconsequential or, in its engrossing concern with immediate practical needs, has denounced as dangerously diverting. But it may be presumed that these issues will sooner or later claim their due attention, for it would be contrary to the nature of the dialectical process for it to become static. If it is true to itself it must lead always to higher levels of life, to the answering of all questions, the solving of all contradictions.

THROUGH THE SOCIALISED INDIVIDUAL

The central point at which the dynamic, generated in and by the Party, is switched out into the population is the relationship between the individual and society. The Communist is not deceived by the myth of the separate individual which has muddied the thinking of the Western nations. His dialectical analysis shows him the individual and society in an interpenetrating relationship, with their relative positions changing according to the historic situation. The pure individual he recognises as an intellectual abstraction. The fact of solitariness is a psychological withdrawal. Robinson Crusoe could live only because society had provided him with equipment, mental as well as physical. After the dawning of consciousness in childhood the individual is never really apart from society, until the moment of his passing out of consciousness. He and society are opposites as long as he pursues anarchic or anti-social self interest, but when he recognises the predominance of the common weal the two become complementary; thus he loses his life in society only to find it more abundantly.

To secure this kind of socialised individual and thus to draw the motivation of life from a more powerful centre than the egoistic self, is the underlying purpose in Party discipline and in Soviet education. In Leningrad immediately after landing, the first labor leader to whom I told the object of my coming replied instantly, *But you must understand that we have a different psychology from your country. You think first of the individual. We think first of society.* This is a most important guidepost in a country whose surface features rapidly become like those of other industrial lands while its underground currents are essentially different. Shortly afterwards, in Moscow, an educational specialist who had studied in Teachers College, New York, remarked in response to the same information, *I was surprised in America to see how much you do for the individual. We expect the individual to do much for society.* So it is not only true, as Radek wrote, that *the new thing in our children's work is the growth of social consciousness. . . . Labor for society is the lever for the education of children,* but every citizen—not only Komsomols and Party members—is expected to do some work for society outside his vocation. In a meeting of a suburban village Soviet, one peasant woman objected to an item in the taxes to provide shoes for needy children. *Why should I give money and get nothing for it?* The chairman replied, *That is socialism, to give and expect nothing in return. That you must learn.* A woman of bourgeois parentage, who in 1924 was far from happy, writes in 1931, *Social consciousness is becoming a reality to me; and since this is a source of joy and energy, I don't regret the heavy price I paid and am paying. It is worth anything you may pay, be it money, or as in our case all kinds of trouble, hardships, and privations.*

It is well known that Communist theory holds that to produce people who are wholeheartedly devoted to the common wellbeing you must first get them to be sacrificially loyal to the interests of the proletariat. The degree to which this doctrine is accepted and practiced, the extent to which solidarity has been achieved in the Soviet Union on the basis of working-class psychology, constitutes an unique historic phenomenon. This has been accomplished first of all by the universal political education. A. Severyanova, in the report previously quoted, proclaims that *we have made supreme for all generations the cause of the class, the interests of the class, the struggle of the proletariat.* The next compelling factor is that every department of life is frankly administered on this class principle. The worker has

by Lenin concerning the larger struggle, *The suppression of the minority of exploiters . . . will cost far less bloodshed than the suppression of the slaves, serfs, or wage laborers, and will cost the human race far less.* So today Communists say, *we are a hard and cruel people, even to ourselves. We keep our eyes on the goal.*

Against the belief that socialist society standardises all the people Soviet writers contend that, by its widespread education and opportunities to participate in affairs, it creates unprecedented opportunities for the flourishing of all the gifts of man which were suppressed in him by capitalist exploitation. They point to the return of the individual in the pictures and news about shock workers and in their characterisation in the new fiction and poetry. The same emphasis appears in calling brigades by the names of their leaders, in assigning machines to the continuous care of the same individual, and in demanding personal responsibility for every job. But in all these cases the individual appears in his social function, not as a supposedly separate entity. The new stories and plays deal with the relations between a man and a woman and with the destiny of persons, as well as with the tasks and problems of socialist construction, but these are interwoven. The person is treated as a living cell in a growing social organism. It is the socialised individual who appears. This is what students mean when they say, *We want people to have their own hobbies, but we don't want them to do things as separate individuals. We want them to follow their tastes and interests in groups.* They have no interest in the problem of personality. They find themselves in collective work.

In the Communist view, the individual is in process of dialectical evolution. The new quality created by the bourgeois revolutions is individualism. The emphasis of bourgeois society is upon the rights of the individual. But these are denied when it is necessary to repress the rising proletariat, who are born within bourgeois society as the capitalist class was born within feudalism. Also the economic failure of capitalism puts increasing limitations upon the development of individuals. Hence capitalist society is deadlocked and static, it can develop further neither the individual nor the community. But in the rising proletarian class the individual who becomes class conscious lives and has his being in subjection to class interests and to the discipline of the Party as the instrument and leader of the working class. This, says Stalin, is *conscious and voluntary submission; for only a conscious discipline can ever become a discipline of iron.* Hence the Communist individual is one who finds freedom in the conscious necessity of co-operating in communal living. It is only the ego that withers as the social world, with which he is consciously united, grows more and more. The real individual, the socialised person, becomes bigger through the enlargement of his sphere of action. The achievement of an organic synthesis between himself and the rest of humanity magnifies his personality by relieving him from the dwarfing effects of being either exploited or exploiter. As he finds increasing security from hunger and from war he becomes increasingly free to give rein to his creative capacities.

Meantime, by challenging the individual to become the creator of this classless society in which his maximum development is to be achieved and by helping him to the means by which it may be realised, the Communists are following with deeds the words with which they attack "biological determinism and technological mechanism." They feel themselves to be creating a new man. Vladimir Ladin outlines his growth in an article on "Soviet Literature":

In place of the old man has appeared a new man. The illiterate peasant of yesterday is now the transmitter of new forms of life. The former idealistic intellectual who never possessed any definite foundation has been replaced by the laboratory intellectual of a new formation. The worker in the plant is not only a man fulfilling his labor discipline but he is also a man who can think politically, a man who declares himself a member of a shock brigade to fulfil the great tasks set before the country. And this is exactly the man whom our literature is bound to depict.

An educational expert who had studied in the United States, in discussing the differences between children in the two countries, said, "Our children are independent and they are socially minded." Here is another controlled interpenetration of opposites. The expectation is that people thus trained will never become slaves, neither to their own appetites, nor to a bureaucratic tyranny, nor to the crowd. It is only when he is an unconscious member of the group that the individual is suppressed by it, never when he is its co-operating creator. An official of the educational workers' union said to me regarding my field of study in the Soviet Union, *You must get acquainted with our Soviet youth; from the kindergarten to the university, he is a new type. He knows where is is going; he knows how; and he knows why.* This consciousness of being a social creator, this certainty of direction, is the core of the dynamic imparted to the individual by the Communist system. This social motivation, he both receives and transmits. If he is an activist, he gives out more than he gets. This is socialist accumulation of creative power, the guarantee of moving forward toward the ideal.

IN THE CHOICE OF VALUES

If the motivation of the Party is to be successfully transferred to the masses, they too must choose the values for which the revolutionary leaders risked everything. For Communists no values can be ultimate in a static sense. They must be developed in historical situations by the dialectical process. Such values as justice, freedom of development for all, solidarity, are accepted as axioms historically demonstrated. These values are also confirmed by present class interests. They therefore become supreme, to be fought and sacrificed for, to be put above immediate needs. They are cultivated in practice and by emotional preference rather than by formal teaching. Ethics as such has no separate place in the educational curriculum. While the younger Communists talk constantly about the new morality, arising on a class base to become universal, the philosophers have not yet gathered up the new experiences into formal generalisations. Some of them are beginning to see that with the disappearance of economic classes, out of whose interests ethical codes have arisen, the base of ethics shifts to the relations between the individual and society as a whole.

The values that are now relied upon to develop harmoniously this relationship are those that led the older revolutionary leaders to revolt and those who were of bourgeois origin to separate themselves from their class. The appearance of leaders of revolt among the class in power is recognized by all students of the history and nature of revolutions as the sign of the disintegration of a social order. Dialectical materialists go further and explain how it leads to the formation of the new order. When they are asked concerning the origin of sacrificial devotion, why it is that one revolting liberal becomes a constructive revolutionist and the other only a cynical critic, they reply that their science is still in its infancy in relation to biology and psychology. Also there remains always the accidental in history for which they, like all philosophers, can find some explanation by tracing chains of causation but which they too have not learned to control. The extension of social self guidance through planning, however, continually reduces the sphere for the appearance and operation of the accidental.

While the founders of Communism were sentimental Utopians in the first stage of their development, being moved by the sufferings of the masses and the universal ferment of a revolutionary epoch, they soon separated themselves from the Utopians and the anarchists and developed what their followers call "scientific socialism," based on the dialectical method. It is expected that the masses will increasingly choose the same values and be led by the same processes that the leaders have followed. With them, it was a combination of emotional choice and intellectual analysis. The former is natural to the masses, according to Communist philosophy, because the highest social values coincide with their class interests. That is why they have such faith in mass initiative and mass creativity. This was one of Lenin's outstanding characteristics. Describing him to the military students of the Kremlin in 1924 soon after his death, Stalin said, *I know of no other revolutionary who believed so passionately in the creative forces of the proletariat and in the revolutionary expediency of its class instinct as did Lenin.* In 1932, on the anniversary of his death, his widow Krupskaya spoke first of this trait before describing his capacity to analyse objective conditions by the dialectical method, *In the ultimate victory of the proletariat, Vladimir Illyich never had the slightest doubt. Even in the darkest moments of defeat, he planned preparations for decisive victory.*

This faith has a twofold reason behind it; first that the masses must see their own highest interests when once the deceptive veil of capitalistic self-interest is torn from their eyes; next, that the natural interests of the masses are identical with, and lead to, the greatest good of the greatest number over the longest period of time. This is why Communists, while denying any abstract categorical imperative either in the starry heavens above or in any moral law within, nevertheless grant supreme authority to mass need. At this point their ethic is not relative but absolute. They assume the same identity of proletarian and general interests that has led the founders of ethical religions to exalt proletarian virtues and to take the side of the people farthest down. So they argue that the norms of proletarian behavior, analysed in the historic situation, provide universal norms because the self-interest of the masses leads to freedom and happiness for all. So they teach their youth that the class-conscious proletariat is destined to emancipate all the toilers and all the oppressed of the world because under capitalism its members cannot get enough reward to become exploiters, because it is in its very nature a constructor and because it has been prepared for fighting leadership by its strikes and uprisings.

But the Communists do not believe in the perfectibility of the masses by way of natural goodness. They decisively reject the idea of automatic progress. The continuing revolution toward the distant and moving goal lies undeveloped in the needs of the masses. In the beginning this course must be seen and shown to them by those, mostly from other classes, who are willing to sacrifice for it. Then, as class distinctions are removed, it becomes a question of the devotion of the individual to the common welfare and of the diffusion of the intellectual capacity to chart the course. This involves also diffusion of the inclination to choose and follow social values, which the Communists call "philosophic partisanship." This is the object of the general training in dialectical materialism. By its method of analysis, as well as by common sense, the Communists are well aware of the deceitfulness and desperate wickedness of the heart of man. But they expect to discipline it effectively, by diffusing both the desire and the power to keep the antisocial factor in the interpenetration of opposites always in the subordinate position.

The extent to which this is actually being done in the Soviet Union constitutes an historic phenomenon of the first importance. The creative desires are being exalted over the possessive appetites by abolishing the possibility of acquisition, limiting ownership to purely personal property, and opening to the initiative of the masses such engrossing tasks that success in achieving social ends becomes more important than personal rewards. The initiative thus created is being guided by a discipline which both represses the ego and enlarges the social self. The urge for unity is being made stronger than the disintegrating tendencies in society by carrying through a cultural revolution that gradually lifts the whole population toward a common level of intelligence and æsthetic appreciation and unites it in pursuit of common ends. Certainty comes to outweigh the uncertainties of existence by the spread of a philosophy for guiding human life which unites the positive qualities of religion with similar aspects of science. For the compensating aspects of religion the Communists have no need, since theirs is a world-conquering faith. In their system the hope of a glorious future and the consciousness of a messianic mission are joined to produce immediate social action. In place of that struggle of the soul for union with the infinite which leads to withdrawal from the world they put a struggle of the person for unity with the social whole in whose creation he thus participates. Their thinking touches the cosmos in its assertion of a unified dialectical law in nature, history, and the mind. This assumes a rational principle in the universe, and an ethical principle in history, with which man must creatively co-operate in order to move toward his social ideal. That the implications of this assumption should in less strenuous times be followed further is inevitable. Already students of philosophy begin to speak of looking for cosmic support for communist endeavor. The proletarian musicians in their resolution on creative principles declare that *there is at present arising the demand for creating monumental musical forms which would embody the sensing of the cosmos by the working class which has entered into the period of socialism.* But it is certain that when the Communist view of man's relation to the cosmos appears it will interpret the universe in social, not personal, terms and will be used to increase, not diminish, man's social creativity.

The movement of socialist society in the direction of the Communist ideal both requires and produces the increasing socialisation of all the incentives as well as all the controls of life. The gain in social motivation in the Soviet Union over capitalist society is at two points. Since motives are anticipated ends, it lies first in the bigness of the end to which the ordinary pursuits of life are devoted. Since ends and means are inseparably united successive series of causation and consequence, the gain lies also in forms of organisation that enable control of immediate need in the direction of long time values. Some of these forms are peculiar to the people and the historic setting. But the general framework is as adaptable to the characteristics of any nation which wants to organise a socialist society as was the framework of parliamentarianism to the different peoples who developed capitalistic industrialism. It is a mixed company of nationalities and races that is building socialism together under the Soviet system. The philosophy behind it is cosmopolitan in origin and development. The end that it seeks has been sought in many lands, in many ages, by a goodly fellowship. The motivation upon which it depends for its realisation subordinates the self seeking tendencies in human nature to its other seeking and self losing capacities. These man, in his quiet moments, has always counted more worthy, and in expressing them has, by common consent, reached his greatest heights. The aristocratic society of the fighters and landowners proclaimed these qualities the glory of the few, proof of their right to rule. The democratic, money-making society of the traders and financiers asserts that these gifts can be generally expressed only in emergencies like war or shipwreck, in ordinary life it expects them to be developed only by those whose profession obligates them to serve their fellows. The creative society of the workers is now democratising the will to serve and extending the spirit of sacrifice to every area of human

SOURCES IN ENGLISH

D. Bokanyi, "Social Insurance in the USSR."
V. Budny, "Absorbing Women in Cultural Work."
L. Kaufmann, "The Collective Agreement in the Fourth, Final Year of the Five-Year Plan."
N. Kaye (translator), "Premiums for Socialist Competition."
P. Kerzhentsev, "Bolshevism for Beginners."
Kolhozniki—"Collective Farmers on Themselves."
V. V. Kuibyshev, "Three Immediate Tasks."
I. Lapidus and K. Ostrovityanov, "An Outline of Political Economy."
V. I. Lenin, "How to Organise Competition."
—— "The State and Revolution."
"Literature of the World Revolution" (Now "International Literature").
Karl Marx and Friedrich Engels, "The Communist Manifesto."
V. Molotov, "Report to Presidium of Executive Committee of Communist International."
—— "The Fulfillment of the First Five Year Plan."
—— "The Struggle for Socialism and the Struggle for Peace; Report to 6th Congress of Soviets."
"Moscow Daily News." Weekly Edition.
P. Nossov, "Results of the Sixth All-Union Congress of Soviets."
Z. Ostrovsky, "The Great Trunk-Line."
A. P. Pinkevitch, "The New Education in the Soviet Republics."
Karl Radek, "Capitalist Slavery versus Socialist Organisation of Labor."
—— "Shock Brigade Workers."
M. Reznik, "The Experiences of a Soviet Efficiency Expert."
"Science at the Cross Roads"—Papers presented by the delegates of the USSR to the International Congress of the History of Science and Technology, 1931.
S. Smidovitch, "Culture and Life in the USSR."
N. Shvernik, "The Trade Unions of the USSR and Their Rôle in Socialist Construction."
"Social Economic Planning in the USSR"—Materials for the

World Social Economic Congress, Amsterdam, August, 1931.
K. Solotov, "Socialist Competition."
J. Stalin, "Leninism."
—— "New Conditions, New Tasks."
—— "Report to 16th Party Congress."
"VOKS" (Now "Soviet Culture Review").
J. A. Yakovlev, "Report to 16th Party Congress."

DATE DUE

GAYLORD PRINTED IN U.S.A.